CW00419397

THE COTSWOLDS

David & Charles Britain

Other titles in this series:

THE BRECON BEACONS NATIONAL PARK, *John Brereton*

THE LAKE DISTRICT, *Michael Dunn*

THE NORTHUMBRIAN UPLANDS, *Geoffrey N. Wright*

THE PEAK DISTRICT, *Lindsey Porter*

THE PEMBROKESHIRE COAST NATIONAL PARK, *Dillwyn Miles*

SNOWDONIA, *William Condry*

THE YORKSHIRE DALES, *Geoffrey N. Wright*

THE COTSWOLDS

Geoffrey N. Wright

DAVID & CHARLES
Newton Abbot London

Title page
On South Hill, above Coberley

British Library Cataloguing in Publication Data

Wright, Geoffrey N. (Geoffrey Norman) 1925–
The Cotswolds.
1. England. Cotswolds
1. Title
942.417

ISBN 0-7153-9318-9

Thomas Bewick's illustrations by courtesy of the Thomas Bewick Birthplace Trust, Cherryburn, Stocksfield, Northumberland

Printed in Great Britain
by Redwood Press Ltd
for David & Charles Publishers plc
Brunel House   Newton Abbot   Devon

CONTENTS

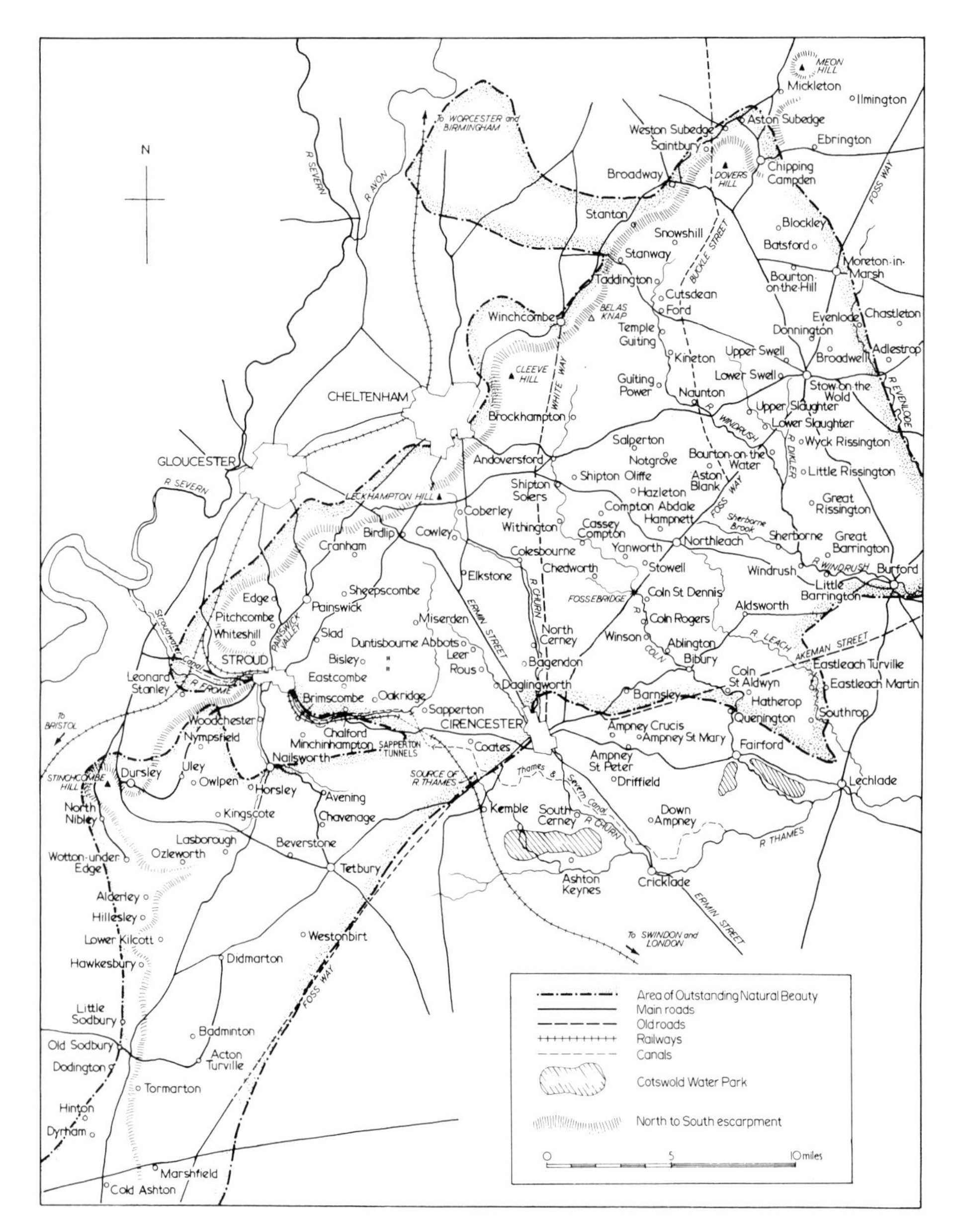

The Cotswolds

INTRODUCTION

What the Romans thought of their frontier road from Corinium (Cirencester) to Venonae (High Cross, Leicestershire) is not recorded. Today the Gloucestershire section of the Foss Way (A429) neatly bisects the Cotswolds, perhaps giving travellers a misleading impression of the area, showing it apparently village-less and unpeopled. Those who travel the busy trunk road, the A40, crossing the Cotswolds from east to west between Burford and Cheltenham or Gloucester – a journey taking little more than a half-hour – might obtain a similar picture of an upland plateau with hedged or walled fields, either corn-growing or sheepy-pastured, with shelter-belts and woodlands but with scarcely a glimpse of a church tower or building other than a wayside inn. Landscapes seem empty.

Earlier travellers have recorded their impressions. When Cobbett rode from Cirencester to Birdlip and Gloucester along Ermin Street – now the A417 – he grumbled (he was given to grumbling), 'Anything so cheerless as this I do not recall to have seen . . . this wold itself is an ugly country . . . having less to please the eye than any other . . . ' Eighty years after the *Rural Rides*, Herbert Evans saw an entirely different scene in 1905, in *Highways and Byways in Oxford and the Cotswolds*, presenting the more romantic, cosy view: 'The long stretches of upland, the winding valleys, the clear trout streams and the grey, venerable hamlets dotted along their banks . . . are all marks of a strange land, marked off by its peculiar genius from the outside everyday world . . .' Today, eighty years later again, both views could be said to be right. On a bleak winter's day, in an icy wind and beneath chill, lowering clouds the Cotswolds are grey and cheerless; but in the warm sunlight of a summer evening the scene becomes almost cloyingly comfortable. We tend to view places subjectively.

I have no personal connection with the Cotswolds, although I did live in a Wiltshire village beyond their southern edge for over twenty-five years and visited them regularly, if infrequently. While working on this book I had expected to look at the area with some detachment, but this soon yielded to affection as the spell and spirit of the Cotswolds worked its special magic and I made my own discoveries. The best of these were not in the obvious places – the guidebook 'musts', the most enchanting villages, the authority-chosen viewpoints, or the proudest churches – but those I found myself: a wooded valley near Brimpsfield in late spring, a flower-filled corner of the White Way above Compton Abdale, quiet churchyards where tall grasses wave gently over lichened, flaking stones; sheep voices in an otherwise silent landscape by lonely Campden Lane, evoking with startling clarity the sounds of medieval times. Shining through all these impressions was the wonderful sense of the past, the realisation that this was for a thousand years and more, a richly peopled countryside full of humanity and life and toil.

Every field, every track, every village, hamlet, farm and small town represents the handiwork of man, and each can be a springboard for the imagination. Perhaps it is this aspect of the Cotswolds as much as the quality of their landscapes and buildings which justified, in 1966, their designation as an Area of Outstanding Natural Beauty, even though the beauty is largely man-made. While such a distinction recognises landscape quality, it carries no guarantee of conservation.

The Cotswolds AONB of nearly 600sq miles (1,554km^2) extends into five counties and affects nine district councils. A Joint Advisory Committee deals with aspects of planning, and the preservation and enhancement of scenic beauty, and seems to have had most success in controlling unsightly development in villages and towns. The tourist potential of the area has been recognised and facilities for visitors have been improved. Certain places have been singled out for 'honeypot' treatment, appropriately the three Bs – Burford, Broadway and Bibury – among others. Incidentally, I have come to the conclusion that what attracts visitors to a place is not necessarily the richness of its local architecture but whether it has a variety of shops selling either souvenirs or food, or displaying antiques. Accessible water is a bonus, which accounts for the enormous popularity of Bourton-on-the-Water, with its additional temptations of a model village, Birdland and a motor museum, none of which is necessarily related to Cotswold history.

On the subject of access to water the Cotswolds fare very badly. Apart from a few miles above Bourton there is no footpath following the valley of the Windrush, and Burford has no riverside access. The Coln has short stretches with footpaths, the Leach very little and the Evenlode even less. Although many miles of footpaths and bridleways do exist throughout the Cotswolds, and the three hundred members of the Cotswold Voluntary Warden Service perform sterling work in promoting them, the provision of stiles, signposts and waymarks is sketchy and inconsistent. As usual, this aspect of recreation and leisure is starved of resources, while motorists are better provided for, even though they are subjected to the Danegeld of excessive parking fees at Broadway and Bourton-on-the-Water.

Change is a fact of life. Landscapes change, though not always for the better, and farms change, as do villages and towns. History is always being made. Two or three generations ago the Cotswolds was an impoverished region. Rural life was harsh and uncomfortable, though not necessarily always unhappy. Now for many people it has become the ideal, but with only 1 per cent of the labour force working on the land most residents in Cotswold villages and towns have probably come from urban areas. Some work locally in small businesses, shops, the service trades, many are retired, some commute, helped by good trunk roads, the M4 and M5, soon the M40, while the Worcester–Oxford–London railway puts Paddington within a 90 minute train journey from Moreton-in-Marsh.

In villages and hamlets newcomers have bought property that was long-neglected or derelict, and restored it. Barns have been converted, usually sympathetically. Large-scale housing developments, mainly based on groups of former farm buildings, have taken place at Elkstone and Hazleton among others. In-filling is commonplace and I hope that the reconstituted stone used, at Naunton, Sheepscombe and many other villages will soon mellow. Exclusive estates of 'executive-style' houses have been added discreetly here and there, and undoubtedly many new jobs have been created for local builders and tradesmen. Large four-wheel-drive vehicles in the drives, ponies in the paddock and burglar alarms on the houses are clues to the new affluence of Cotswold life, and the social balance in villages will have changed markedly, upwards. The voice of the newcomers may proclaim green issues and be strongly conservationist, although it may call, 'Pull up the drawbridge!' But local folk are still there, even if they are an increasing minority. Village activities flourish, many schools thrive, often thanks to the incomers' children, and village pubs continue to give better value for money than the upmarket 'Country House Hotels', or their equivalent in the 'honeypots'. Car-ownership seems to be taken for granted, although some local bus or minibus services do operate from many villages on market days at nearby towns.

Unexpectedly, few poets have praised the Cotswolds, and few painters have portrayed it. It has attracted no powerful regional literature, although John Moore beautifully evoked rural life of its western outlier, Bredon Hill, while Laurie Lee's picture of the Slad valley in the 1920s is superb. Perhaps its charms are too subtle for a broad canvas. But details delight, varying with the seasons and the weather. Visits to the Cotswolds from my home near Ludlow, 60 miles (96km) away, have led me to suspect that the Cotswolds are more frequently clouded than we are here. The high western edge almost certainly experiences more rain than the upland plateau.

Rocks, stones and buildings change colour with the weather and the time of day, but trees, plants and fields change with the seasons. I would suggest a visit in late spring and early summer, for the flowering of the hedgerows and the greening of the beeches sees Cotswold at its most colourful, although the bare brown ploughland of autumn and winter brings fresh contrasts. Similarly, the ripening harvest creates a golden glow across the wolds, often harshly concluded with the burning of the stubble which is still carried out by too many farmers, when clouds of grey, acrid smoke and the scorching of shelter-belts show ugly faces of Cotswold prosperity, mocking the centuries-old co-operation between man and nature on this gentle land of soft outlines, harmonious buildings and a long tradition of excellence. Cobbett was relieved when he descended Birdlip Hill. Today's travellers enjoy an easier gradient: the A417 now bypasses Birdlip village, and the earlier route by Barrow Wake has become a lay-by. The slight detour to reach it is still worthwhile for the stunning view northwards to the Crickley Hill escarpment which, in a way, represents the end, or the beginning, of the Cotswolds.

1
THE MAKING OF THE LANDSCAPE

The importance of geology cannot be over-emphasised. It is fundamental in shaping our lives. Rocks and the topography they create determine what vegetation will grow and hence what livestock this can support. They give the land its basic shape and structure, and, helping to determine the settlement pattern, also influence the routes of communication. They also provide the stone for buildings in villages and towns. In the Cotswolds the oolites have created a landscape of flowing lines, and, except along the western edge, gentle slopes. They have also yielded the most gracious and felicitous building stones, and these Jurassic limestones can be realistically described as the architectural backbone of England.

Subtle variations in colour and texture of the limestones, varying slightly from one quarry to the next, do not disguise their common ancestry of having been laid down in the warm shallow waters of tropical seas far distant in time. What geologists call the Jurassic period happened between 140 and 195 million years ago when the corals, sea-lilies and other plants and organisms flourished in the clear blue seas which then covered the greater part of what was to become England. Falling, when dead, like a suspended powder to the sea-bed, they formed the layers of rock which we now call the Inferior (or lower) and Great (or upper) Oolite, named from the tiny, naturally cemented, spherical specks resembling herring-roe, or even mini frog-spawn. Other material was also deposited: mud, silts, sand, pebbles, shells, and, over millions of years, a complex series of beds of clays, sands and limestones accumulated. As the waters subsequently receded, and the uneven sea-bed became an undulating land surface, these Jurassic limestones dried out, and, smoothed by wind and weather, now form the gracious uplands of central England, with long, sweeping ridges, wide plateaux, gentle valleys, and always with a dramatic escarpment to the west.

Both oolites are soft when quarried, relatively easy to work into fine detail, and harden on exposure to the air. They have another quality, less easy to define, but best described as faithfulness. Although they are used to some extent outside their geological boundaries, especially for major buildings like cathedrals and churches, they do not admit intruders – or did not, until modern times and economics necessitated peculiar hybrids to infiltrate. Thus the oolites invade but are rarely invaded. Because the western edge of the stone forms a very uneven boundary in its north-easterly march across the country, its alien neighbours occasionally intrude its flanks, but the farms, barns, houses and villages on the oolite are true to it because they have come from it. And it came from the sea.

The bed of this Jurassic sea was uneven, in many parts collapsing under the weight of sediments above. At Stowell (*088131*) near Northleach, the lowest beds of the Jurassic series are about 1,000ft (305m) below the surface, while a few miles to the north-east near Bourton-on-the-Water they appear at the surface.

Below the oolites, and therefore older than them, are the liassic series of rocks, thus named early last century by the 'father of British geology', William Smith, who was born at Churchill in the Oxfordshire Cotswolds in 1769. In 1794 he was appointed engineer to the Somerset Coal Canal and, surveying its proposed course south of Bath, began his study of rock strata and their identification by fossils. In 1815 he produced his epoch-making Geological Map of England. Many of the words he introduced into the new science of geology originated in the common vocabulary of quarrymen and builders in his native Cotswolds. The lias limestones occur in their strata among the clays, and as *layers*, or *liers*, were extensively quarried for memorial tablets and flagstones. Stone clapper bridges at Lower Slaughter and Bourton-on-the-Water are blocks of lias, and many local houses had, or still have, lias flags on their floors, particularly the smooth blue lias, which is actually a greyer rock.

Two points need emphasising: first, within the lias rocks the limestones form only thin layers among successive beds of sands and clays which themselves contain fossils, particularly molluscs, ammonites and the bones of small marine creatures and amphibians; secondly, each layer took millions of years to accumulate, the whole Jurassic period lasting about 45 million years.

Looked at as simply as possible, the older rocks are to the north-west, the younger ones to the south-east. The low-lying Vale of Severn is largely of clay, the foothills of the hills are sandy rocks, the Cotswolds themselves are limestone, a neat sequence repeated many times throughout the Jurassic rocks, a rhythmic succession of 'cyclothems', conveniently pointing to different types of sea conditions at the time the strata was laid down. Clays usually denoted rather muddy, deep seas; sands were formed in shallower seas into which rivers deposited sands brought down from surrounding hills, while limestones were formed in clear shallow seas such as may be found today around the Bahamas.

Soils formed from the Lower Lias clays tend to be heavy, cold and difficult to work. Those of the Middle Lias were lighter and more sandy, with loams, quite rich in fossils. Within the main area of the Cotswolds they show their presence on the floor or sides of many valleys by producing soils that support rich meadow pastures. Within the Middle Lias a marlstone forms a terrace or bench along the length and at the foot of the Cotswold escarpment, and can be identified by the thick belt of woodland it often supports. The main Stroud–Painswick road, the A46, follows the marlstone terrace along the western side of a valley while the older route, the B4070, does the same on the eastern side, at a higher level – about 164ft (50m) – the difference in levels having been caused by a fault.

Clays are impermeable, so the sands above the lias clays and marlstone accumulate water seeping through the porous limestones above, forming springs. Along the western edge of the southern part of the scarp a series of towns and villages on the marlstone bench mark this spring-line – Dursley, Stinchcombe, Wotton-under-Edge, Horton and Dodington – with Uley similarly sited in the upper Cam valley. Painswick is on a marlstone spur between two side valleys whose streams meet just below the village. Reservoirs on Robin's Wood Hill (covered), Great Witcombe (open), and Dowdeswell (open), providing water for Gloucester and Cheltenham respectively, are situated on this marlstone terrace. Further to the north-east the same marlstone spring-line has determined the siting of a sequence of villages – Chipping Campden, Ebrington, Ilmington and the Hidcotes, and in the upper Evenlode valley, Bourton-on-the-Hill, Longborough, Broadwell, Oddington and Maugersbury. These and their counterparts around the basin of the Windrush – Upper Slaughter, Naunton, Sherborne, Great Barrington and the Rissingtons – are similarly situated on or a short height above the marlstone terrace, roughly straddling the 500–600ft (152–83m) contours, with the more southerly villages at the lower level, reflecting the general dip of the strata in a south-easterly direction.

Strata are not necessarily continuous across the whole area, nor are they of uniform thickness. However, they are usually consistent in their sequences, and above the lias are the oolites which together form the great mass of the Cotswold uplands, and covering the main plateau above the 800ft (244m) contour. At a few places the Cotswolds reach 1,000ft (305m) – with Cleeve Common the highest at 1,082ft (330m), Broadway Hill 1,026ft (313m), and its ridge running southwards to its 1,046ft (319m) crest above Seven Wells, with the triangulation point on Cutsdean Hill, 3 miles (4.8km) further south at exactly 1,000ft (305m). These highest western hills – Cleeve Cloud, Ham Hill, Charlton Kings Common, Broadway Hill and Belas Knap, as well as the important promontories of Nottingham Hill and Haresfield Beacon – are all capped with the Inferior Oolite, a creamy-buff stone when freshly quarried, but weathering to a harmony of grey and gold, often mottled with yellow or pale grey lichens.

Between this oolite and the Great Oolite above is a thin layer of clay called Fuller's Earth, formerly used in the process of cleansing wool and felting cloth. In the main Cotswold area this layer was not thick enough to justify its being extracted, but in terms of landscape it is more important, in association with an adjoining layer of sands, to form a reservoir from which emerging springs gave settlements in the upper valleys their water supply. Villages on the high plateau were able to tap this water level by sinking wells, as at Brimpsfield, Elkstone and Compton Abdale where the spring near the foot of the path to the church has a decorative stone spout in the form of a crocodile's jaws.

It is probable that the Great Oolite once covered the whole of the Cotswolds, but the tilting of the strata exposed the western edge which was subsequently eroded to the level of the Inferior Oolite. Nevertheless, over a large area of the mid-Cotswolds, this Great Oolite, rarely more than 100ft (30m) thick, is responsible for the wide landscapes and fine buildings in villages and market towns. Typically a hard, white, shelly limestone, often with strongly developed current bedding, it has been used for centuries because of its accessibility and the fact that it can be cut with a saw when fresh, yet hardens on exposure to the air. Quarrying and the use of the oolitic limestones in buildings, are dealt with in a later chapter. Here, we are concerned with the part played by rocks in the landscape.

One aspect of this is the shape of the hill slopes. Generally speaking, there is a fairly even succession of strata, with the limestones dominating, much thicker than the clays and sandstones. Weathering on a steep slope wears away the softer clays more easily than the limestones, while rain falling on limestone usually sinks quickly underground, so that it has little effect on the surface. Reaching the impervious clays, it flows along the junction of the strata, forming a spring-line, and in so doing it carries away some clay, taking it continuously, if slowly, downhill. This results in the lower slopes always being concave, with the clay slightly hollowed below the limestone. As a corollary, upper slopes are left with a convex profile. Thus, from the top of many Cotswold hills you cannot always see the bottom and from the bottom you cannot always see the top. The change in curvature is so subtle that, looking along a slope it is not always apparent, yet from many valley floors the impression is that the hillsides are enfolding you. Further confirmation of the nature of Cotswold slopes is provided by the gradients of roads and lanes where they cross valleys. The steepest sections occur at the lower parts of the hill, well shown with the Foss Way, the A429, where it crosses the Coln at Fossebridge and the Leach a few miles to the north-east. Many minor roads also illustrate this variation in gradient where they cross valleys.

At the western escarpment, continuous weathering, more severe here than anywhere else in the Cotswolds because of its exposure to prevailing winds, has caused the limestones to be so much undermined that huge masses of rock have broken away and fallen down the slope, gradually to be further eroded, while at the same time leaving new surfaces to be attacked, with more concavities resulting. Thus, any position of the Cotswold edge is but a temporary one, and, though the process of denudation is slow, it is relentless, and over millions of years it must have receded a considerable distance south-eastwards. Two particular sites on the western escarpment illustrate many features of Cotswold geology.

Crickley Hill

The Barrow Wake viewpoint already referred to shows the characteristic western scarp face of the Cotswolds. A more detailed look reveals other features. The deep valley between Barrow Wake and Crickley Hill is partly the result of a geological fault, one of many relatively small ones which occurred at various places in the Cotswolds, mainly orientated roughly east-west, and usually with a throw of about 65ft (20m) downwards on their northern side. Across this steep-sided valley the prominent cliffs form the finest British exposure of the Pea Grit limestone within the Inferior Oolite. This is richly fossiliferous and takes its name from the rounded pea-sized growths in a shelly matrix, cemented by a fine-grained lime deposit; they are similar to,

The view north from Barrow Wake to Crickley Hill, near Birdlip, showing old quarry outcrops along the escarpment

but larger than, the usual ooliths, and were formed by the action of algae.

Crickley Hill Country Park, covering 62 acres (25ha) of beautiful countryside, jointly managed by Gloucestershire County Council and the National Trust, with good car parking and visitor facilities, provides an almost ideal introduction to the rocks of the Cotswolds. A 'Scarp Trail', followed with the aid of an informative leaflet, is an outdoor lesson in simple geology. An easy 40 minute walk passes many rock-faces exposed by quarrying and illustrates how the hill is made up of a number of different layers of limestone, each reflecting the different marine conditions when they were formed millions of years ago. The Pea Grit, sometimes as much as 30ft (9m) thick, has yellowed with weathering. Above it, surface weathering has produced a thin brown soil; below, the oolite is much whiter. Ironically, the limestones of Crickley Hill were found to be unsuitable for building as they weathered too readily. Until the quarries closed in 1963 their products were crushed and used mainly for roadstone and constructional fill.

Below the quarry faces and continuing below the Scarp Trail, hummocky ground illustrates how the scarp is gradually retreating. The process of quarrying has itself exposed extensive jointing in the limestones. Some of these have been further weathered, especially by water action dissolving away the limestone, resulting in a loose rubble known as 'gulls'. Rock slippage over these causes bigger cracks, and further slippage over the thin clay layers below the oolites, with more slumping and cracking, has gradually resulted in more and more debris accumulating on the lower slopes, and continuing, so slowly, to move downhill.

Leckhampton Hill

Even more impressive than Crickley is Leckhampton Hill, 2 miles (3.2km) south of Cheltenham, and now owned by Cheltenham Council who acquired Leckhampton Hill as an open space area in 1928. Leckhampton Quarry itself was officially opened in 1793, and over the next thirty years was the main source of the stone used in the building of Regency Cheltenham – a time when blocks of dressed stone cost 1d per ton delivered.

The B4070 runs north-eastwards from the Air Balloon roundabout, and in little more than a mile (1.6km) curves down the escarpment to run due north below Leckhampton Hill. A minor road swings off to the east by Salterley Grange and soon reveals the abandoned cirque of Salterley Grange Quarry, beyond which the Cotswold Way footpath leaves the road on the left. After an initial steep rise the path levels out as a rewarding grassy track along the edge of the plateau, giving easy access to the famous landmark of the Devil's Chimney, and beyond it, to Leckhampton Quarry face, both signposted.

However, from a geological point of view, although a more strenuous approach, it is better to continue along the Cheltenham road for almost ¾ mile (1.2m) and turn off right along Daisy Bank Road, where, almost

An old quarry face at Leckhampton

immediately, a car parking area appears on the right (949188). Nearby, the straight course of the old quarry railway runs steeply up the wooded slopes, the cottage at the foot of the slope being called significantly Tramway House.

Paths wind steeply up the slopes of the lower sandy beds of the Upper Lias strata, planted here with larches to try to stabilise the soil-creep. Hummocky ground is the result of similar slippage to that of Crickley Hill, but the slope levels out at the top of the lower limestone strata, coinciding with the tramway's upper limit near the ruins of old lime kilns which were in use until 1927. Towering above the kilns to a height of almost 170ft (52m) are the strata of limestones quarried between 1793 and 1850, colour-graded from cream to russet, from top to bottom, indicating the more ferruginous nature of the lower rocks.

The character of the various strata is very evident. The lowest 30ft (9m) shows the Pea Grit, familiar from Crickley Hill, with about 70ft (21m) of freestone above. This is part of the Inferior Oolite and is so-called because, being devoid of any large fossils, and remarkably fine-grained throughout, it can be worked freely with saws and other hand tools in any direction. Another striking feature of it here at Leckhampton is the regular spacing of its horizontal bedding planes and the right-angled joints between them, making it appear almost as if it had been hand-made. Bedding-planes are caused by pauses in the process of deposition on a sea-bed, and also by a slight change in the nature of sediment being laid down. Obviously the thicker the sections between bedding planes the more continuous the process of sedimentation. If the bedding planes are close together, occurring as wedges or little more than thin sections, they are called Ragstones, a name also given to well-bedded hard limestones that are so fossiliferous that they cannot be regularly worked, but break into irregular pieces. They were usually quarried for rubble, road metal and constructional in-fill. Some of the better ones may have been used for walling. 20–30ft (6–9m) of Ragstones cap the Leckhampton quarry.

Valleys of the Western Scarp

Cotswold streams and rivers flowing south-eastwards down the gentle dip-slope have long broad valleys, but those flowing northwards and westwards from the escarpment, choosing initially a much steeper route to the sea in the Bristol Channel have, as a result, carved deeper and narrower channels. This has caused them to cut down through their beds far more rapidly, with their headwaters carving back into the plateau. As a result the upland surface along the edge of the plateau, especially in the Stroud area and to the south, has been serrated into a series of combes, mostly clothed with rich woodland, and having much shorter, narrower floors than the spacious ones of the dip-slope rivers. The plateau itself has been broken, or dissected into narrow, irregular strips, some sections being entirely cut off from the main upland mass.

Cam Long Down, well seen from Uley Bury or the hill above Dursley, is a clear example of such a separated portion of the upland plateau, while Stinchcombe Hill to the west remains linked to the rest of the high ground only by a narrow ridge between the Dursley valley and Waterley Bottom. Robin's Wood Hill, Churchdown, Bredon Hill and Dumbleton Hill are all similar, detached outliers.

Most prominent of all the valleys intersecting the Stroudwater Hills is that of the River Frome, which, rising near Brimpsfield, flows southwards in a steep-sided valley below Miserden and Edgeworth, gradually swinging westwards at Sapperton, to create the dramatically beautiful, partially industrialised Golden Valley through Chalford, to Stroud and beyond. Its tributary valleys – Slad, Toadsmoor and Nailsworth – have similar physical characteristics, while to the north, the little rivers Chelt and Isborne, with the By Brook at the Cotswold's southern edge, have carved landscapes very different in character from that of the main area of Cotswold.

The Ice Age and its Effects

During the past two million years a vast arctic ice-sheet advanced southwards and retreated at least twenty times. The southernmost limit of these movements varied, but at its furthest extent the ice reached a line running

Spring on the River Windrush at Swinbrook

roughly from Chelmsford to Bristol, then south-westwards to the coasts of North Devon and Cornwall as far as the northern part of the Scilly Isles. Thus, at some time or another the Cotswolds were ice-covered, probably on a number of occasions. The region would have been thickly covered with snow, and the severe climate would have supported a tundra vegetation similar to that in parts of northern Canada and Siberia today. Lichens, a few grasses and sedges, together with some dwarf birches, and frost-tolerant shrubs like juniper would have been the only greening in a harsh, frozen landscape that stretched eastwards to the heart of Europe.

During those times when the ice retreated, known as inter-glacials, various plant species and animals migrated northwards from milder lands of southern Europe. Fossil remains found in valley clays and gravels, where they had been swept and deposited by meltwaters of the subsequent thaws, prove that mammoth and rhinoceros, wolf and wild horse, roamed over the land we now call Cotswold. But when ice-sheets blanketed the land, permafrost gripped its subsoil, and after each cold phase ended this melted, deeper and deeper over the years, until eventually it froze no more. But so long as permafrost existed, surface meltwaters could not soak through it, so that their only escape was by flowing downhill, often taking the saturated surface as well, creating smooth-sided hollows and valleys.

All the main Cotswold rivers, and most of their tributary streams, are obvious misfits in the spacious valleys through which they flow. None of these valleys ever saw glaciers, but were created by the meltwaters of the thawing ice-sheets. The Evenlode and upper Windrush valleys in particular are out of all proportion to the modest, though beautiful rivers that drain them. Above many such valleys hang small intimate dry valleys also scoured by melting ice and snow, and a journey along almost any of the upland roads reveals examples of these (a number can be identified from the A429 between Northleach and Bourton-on-the-Water) while a study of the OS 1:50,000 Map 163 (Cheltenham and Cirencester) shows by its contour shapes many more examples.

The hanging valleys are so called because they 'hang' above the stream and river valleys to which they were once tributaries. Main valleys, watered by springs and rainfall run-off, have continued to flow, slowly and imperceptibly deepening themselves, leaving the dry valleys suspended. Their life was a temporary if dramatic one; now they give to the Cotswold plateau much of its secret, intimate charm. Lacking regular water-supply they have never been settled; often too steep-sided they have not always been ploughed but now provide quiet permanent pasture for grazing stock. Fortunate is the walker or rider who identifies and finds a footpath or bridleway penetrating such rewarding places.

One major episode during the Ice Age was the formation of a huge lake in the southern Midlands almost 40 miles (64km) long and 20 miles (32km) wide, extending from Coventry and Rugby in the north to near

Moreton-in-Marsh. Ice hemmed it in on the north and west, while the Cotswold scarp formed its margin north-eastwards from Moreton. Given the name Lake Harrison, it was formed twice over, once when the ice advanced and later as it retreated. The lake was large enough for the creation of forceful wind-waves, which cut a bench along the shoreline at a height of about 410ft (125m). For this level to have been maintained over a long period of time, one or more outlets at this height must have existed, and as ice blocked any western exit, these were most likely to have been through gaps in the Cotswold scarp, the most likely one being probably at Fenny Compton, to the north-east of the main Cotswold area, with subsequent drainage into the Cherwell valley.

Another aspect of Lake Harrison, which was caused by the advance of an ice-sheet from the north halting near Moreton-in-Marsh, was the deposition of a huge terminal moraine of boulder-clay, now represented by the broken landscape east and west of the A429 1 mile (1.6km) north of Moreton. Deciduous woodland, mainly oak, clothes large areas of the resultant heavy clay soils, and the rather featureless landscape of the area immediately around Moreton, drained by the headwater streams of the River Evenlode, was formed by the outwashing spread of sands and gravels left by the meltwater streams from the moraine-dammed ice. East-bound motorists using the A44 from Moreton see very flat landscapes on both sides of the road. Surviving place and farm names include the word 'heath', indicating the sandy, gravelly nature of the local soils, most of which have now been reclaimed and are good farmland.

2
FIGURES IN THE LANDSCAPE

Early humans, the hunter-gatherers, who lived on game and wild fruits, are thought to have slowly infiltrated the Cotswold area before about 4000BC. By then, oak, elm, lime and alder had replaced the earlier birch and pine, and the men of the Middle Stone Age, using flint axes and tools made from animal bones, started to clear the woodland. Almost certainly they used fire to speed the process, thus creating glades attractive to deer and wild cattle. Archaeologists have found traces of their activities in some south Cotswold valleys, while the Cotswold plateau has yielded quantities of tiny arrowheads that were used, probably, by these Mesolithic tribes, thought to have been of Nordic stock.

About 3500BC, in a warmer, drier climate, a new wave of settlers, this time of Mediterranean origin, entered the area probably via the Severn estuary. Finding the damp, thickly wooded clayland of the vale unattractive, they moved eastwards to the Cotswold edge, and, discovering beyond it the well-drained and reasonably fertile limestone soil, they probably settled in small groups, pioneers of the herdsmen and farmers who have tended stock and tilled the land ever since.

About a hundred long barrows in the Cotswolds are a memorial of these early settlers. Many of the barrows have been plundered through unscientific digging and the plough has flattened others, but a few survive, their construction revealed by archaeologists. Large cairns of stones, having internal passages, roofed chambers and walled with drystone, were, in effect, man-made caves on the surface of the ground, initially bare but now covered with earth and turf. A few human remains were found in each cairn, usually piled up in the burial chambers. Presumably these mini-mausoleums were

The Rollright stones

for tribal chiefs and their families. Three are worth visiting: Belas Knap, above Winchcombe, Hetty Pegler's Tump and Nympsfield Long Barrow, both in the southern Cotswolds above Wotton-under-Edge. This last-named is uncovered, so that its internal layout is revealed.

Two factors seem common to these funerary monuments. Their burial chambers are approached through a portal, often protected by a huge boulder, and recessed between two protruding horns of dry-walled masonry at the mound's wider end. When constructed they must have been impressive features in those prehistoric landscapes, for their siting seems always to have been on cleared land and at a high place. They were obviously built to be seen, and it seems likely that they were territorial symbols of local, tribal importance.

Also built to be seen, at the opposite corner of our area, the Rollright Stones pose the usual question: 'Who built and used them, and for what purposes?' Dating the stones is perhaps easier than explaining them, and it seems that the stone circle tradition began in the Neolithic period but continued into that of the Bronze Age; the Rollright Stones are thought to date from 2000–1500BC. On this high stretch of northern Cotswold (about 700ft (213m) the minor road from Great Rollright to Little Compton splits three separate Bronze Age sites, of which the King's Men, by a shady grove, consists of a 100ft (30m) circle of about seventy weather-worn stones of various shapes and sizes, although most stand less than 4ft (1.2m) high. ½ mile

(880m) to their east the Whispering Knights of five much larger stones represent the remains of a Neolithic burial-chamber, while across the road, in Warwickshire, the King's Stone is a huge monolith of contorted shape. Folklore has ascribed strange legends to the Rollright Stones, which, though imaginative and fascinating, are useless archaeologically. Impressive though these ritual monuments may be, they are relatively insignificant compared with the centuries of relentless toiling on the land by peasant farmers. The apparent paradox, the unanswerable questions, are, how, why and by what organisational powers were resources of manpower and time devoted to the building of these, and the great long barrows, ventures which yielded no material gain whatsoever? Other Bronze Age monoliths in the Cotswolds include the Longstone near Minchinhampton (886999) and the Hangman's Stone where Hampnett, Stowell and Yanworth parishes meet (087152).

Less spectacular but far more numerous are the round barrows, usually marked 'tumulus' on the map. Between 350 and 400 have been identified, many revealed by aerial photography. Survivors are low, circular, usually grass-covered mounds, much smaller than the Neolithic long barrows, and often found in clusters, for example near Bisley, Bourton-on-the-Water, Coln St Dennis, Hawling, Longborough, Sezincote, Snowshill, Upper Swell, Upper Slaughter, Temple Guiting and Wyck Rissington. Broadly contemporary with the Rollright Stones, these barrows seem to represent pit burials

The annual summer archaeological dig at Crickley Hill

after the cremation of prominent people and were probably used repeatedly over generations. But where their occupants lived is still a mystery, and we know more about the deaths of Bronze Age dwellers on the Cotswolds than we do about their lives.

Archaeology yields slices through time and we are left to suppose a degree of continuity of life. By jumping a thousand years we come to the most impressive aspect of Cotswold prehistory. Celtic people from the European mainland probably introduced iron tools and weapons to England from about the sixth century BC, with successive waves of settlers bringing increasingly advanced technology. Perhaps the presence of iron ores in the wold country of Oxfordshire encouraged their favouring the Cotswolds; the ditched and embanked enclosures of their hillforts, built by later arrivals, often replacing earlier and simpler structures, provide acceptable proof of settlement as distinct from burial sites. Seventeen such Iron Age forts spaced out along the edge of the Cotswold escarpment, invariably in strongly defensible sites and enclosing areas from 2½ to 120 acres (1 to 48ha), imply social reorganisation and concentrated communities living in or near them. Today the areas within their ramparts are featureless, but their earthen banks are marvellous viewpoints.

Continuing excavation at Crickley Hill over twenty summers has proved human occupation spanning 4,000 years up until a post-Roman phase of small round houses about AD500. In early Iron Age times (600BC) there was a large settlement of rectangular houses that were soon sacked and replaced by a settlement of small round houses that itself was destroyed a hundred years later. The untrained eye, however, sees little but a few grass-covered banks. The 'Hill Fort Trail' leaflet, supplemented by vivid imagination, may help to clothe the wind-swept grass.

Although the 9 acre (4ha) site at Crickley Hill has been extensively excavated, it is, visually, one of the least interesting. Nottingham Hill, a Cotswold outlier 3 miles (4.8km) west of Winchcombe, covers 100 acres (40ha), Shenbarrow above Stanton (on the Cotswold Way) is only 3 acres (1.2ha), which is slightly larger than the defensive structure on Cleeve Common, but only half the size of Leckhampton's hillfort above the quarries. However, it is Uleybury Hill Fort (785990) in the south-western Cotswolds which evokes for me the clearest picture of Iron Age times. Covering 30 acres (12ha), it is the biggest on the route of the Cotswold Way, a massive site on the edge of the scarp, with 300ft (91m) drops on all sides except the north, where additional defences to the huge ditch and rampart must have ensured impregnability. As no large-scale excavation has taken place, it retains a sense of inviolability. However, it did yield a gold coin of the Dobunni, now in Gloucester City Museum.

Tiers of ramparts surrounding the hill at Painswick Beacon probably originated much later as tribal tension increased and smaller groups became absorbed into larger, more powerful tribes during the century before the

Roman conquest. Hillforts and other systems of earthwork defences such as Minchinhampton Bulwarks are only part of the pre-Roman story. Little is known of the lives and houses of most Iron Age inhabitants who lived in unfortified settlements, farmsteads and fenced enclosures that have been revealed by aerial photography but that are scarcely noticeable at ground level.

However, a new window on the Cotswolds' past opened in the 1950s. Until then it was thought that Cirencester was a tribal capital that was subsequently taken over by the Romans, but a 1951 excavation proved that there had been no previous settlement on the site, and a local archaeologist, Mrs E. M. Clifford of Witcombe, deduced that nearby Bagendon was a more likely place for such a capital of the Dobunni, a Belgic tribe which had spread northwards from Wessex. They did, indeed, found their *oppidum*, or capital, at Bagendon, a low-lying site in the Churn valley, and built earthworks enclosing a 200 acre (80ha) settlement.

One length of earthwork, now partially hidden by a shelter-belt, runs along the south side of the Welsh Way west of the inn at Perrott's Brook, with a slightly longer stretch by Cutham Lane, the upper way to North Cerney. Within their walls the Dobunni built circular huts, with walls of timber or wattle, thatched roofs and often with stone floors. Metal-working was carried out, using iron from the Forest of Dean, and lead and silver from the Mendips. Bagendon town issued coins of silver and bronze, presumably using Cornish copper and tin for the latter. The Dobunni traded extensively, importing glass, pottery, jewellery and wine from France and the Mediterranean countries during the early Christian years of the first century AD. Herds and flocks grazed peacefully within the protection of the earthen defences, but huge numbers of discovered bones indicate a pastoral farming based on cattle, sheep and pigs that was carried on in the surrounding countryside, while large storage jars and querns prove the plentiful supply of corn. It seems likely that oxen were used for drawing ploughs, and small native ponies served as pack animals as well as pulling the Belgic people's war-chariots. Inter-tribal strife there may have been, but the picture of Cotswold life in the immediate pre-Roman years shows a degree of sophistication and skill within an agricultural and trading framework, which included a system of road communications adequate for its purposes. Throughout Britain a population of two to three million people lived in farmsteads, hamlets and fortified settlements, organised into tribes and kingdoms. The Dobunni in the southern Cotswolds formed just one part of a civilised productive country, but by the time of the Roman conquest, the evidence of coins indicates that the tribe had split into two factions, each under a separate king, with the eastern Dobunni still centred on Bagendon. It seems probable that, under King Bodroc, they surrendered to Plautius, commander of the Roman army which landed in Kent in the late summer of AD43.

The Roman Legacy

Within their political, economic and ideological aims the Romans pursued a policy of absorbing an existing society into their empire, protecting it from external enemies and promoting a framework of law and order. In so doing they enjoyed the advantages of a successful bureaucracy, an efficient military machine, and a high level of technology, agriculture and architecture, and with these skills they brought to the landscape three features new to Britain – planned towns, country estates, and, most importantly, a new system of communications to link the towns and the new military forts necessary to an invading power. Much of the road system, which lasted throughout the Roman occupation, and in many instances for centuries afterwards, is, in a modified way, still in use. Yet, considering the length of their stay, the Romans left remarkably few visible traces in the landscape. In the Cotswolds these are the roads and relics of country estates.

The roads that were built during the early years of the Roman occupation formed part of the process of conquest. Later roads were built for more economic purposes associated with the general civilising of Britain, while a localised network evolved serving rural estates. Of an estimated total of 10,000 miles (16,093km) of Roman roads and tracks it is the early military ones which had the most dramatic impact, a fact probably recognised by motorists travelling along the A417 between Cirencester and Gloucester, and on the A429 between Cirencester and Moreton-in-Marsh, and illustrated graphically on the 1:50,000 OS Sheet 163.

By AD47 the line from Exeter to Leicester and Lincoln represented a frontier between the newly conquered south-east of Britain and the defiant Iron Age kingdoms beyond. Along it the Foss Way was engineered as a frontier road used for military purposes and communications, crossing Ermin Street coming up from the south-east, at what is now Cirencester. A Roman camp was set up at Chesterton, in the southern angle of this crossing, but was soon moved to Gloucester (Glevum) in anticipation of further advance. Cirencester's importance as a road junction made it a suitable place for the tribal capital of the Romanised Dobunni, and by about AD70 it seems that the older site at Bagendon had become deserted.

Archaeological excavation, especially over the past thirty years, has revealed much of Cirencester's early history. Called by the Romans Corinium Dobunnorum it was a *civitas*, or cantonal capital, established as an adminstrative and marketing centre for the pre-Roman tribal area of the Dobunni. Once the troops, housed in the early fort at Chesterton, were no longer needed to deal with the natives in Wales and had been moved northwards, a new settlement was planned on a large scale. By the end of the

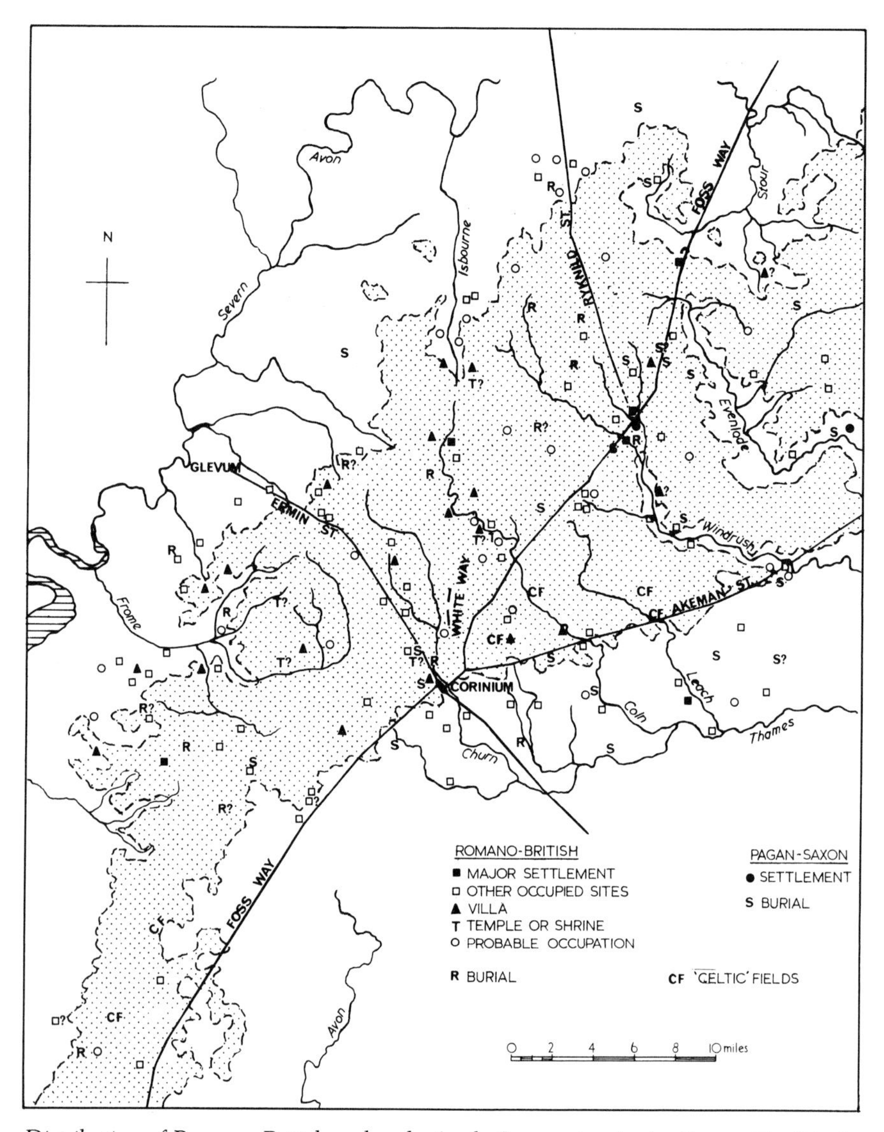

Distribution of Romano-British and early Anglo-Saxon sites in the Cotswolds. Stipple indicates land above 400ft. Monuments situated west of the Cotswold escarpment are not included

first century a grid of streets had been laid out, dividing an area of about 240 acres (96ha) into fifteen blocks. Although by modern standards this is small (little more than 1,000yd (1km) square), for those days it was second in size to London, rivalling any other large city in north-west Europe. Great public buildings – the forum and basilica, for example – were at the centre (some distance south of the present market place). Now beneath The Avenue, the basilica was a huge aisled hall 325ft (99m) long, while the Forum next to it served as a large open market place.

Most buildings within the town were houses and shops. For the first time Britain was introduced to a new concept for a house – a rectangular building of timber, stone or brick, roofed with tiles, and structurally divided into compartments, each having a different use. Porticos, wall-paintings, heating, to British eyes, must have had enormous impact. Town houses in Corinium were usually long, narrow structures on strips of land at right-angles to the street and entered from it. The front probably was a shop or workshop, with living accommodation above. Many houses, even by Roman standards, were luxurious, suggesting a high proportion of wealthy people, presumably local nobility and the upper echelon of bureaucrats. Distinctive tessellated pavements decorated the floors of many houses and by the early fourth century Corinium was the centre of a school of mosaic artists.

Before then, probably in the late second century, and continuing to the end of the Roman occupation, defences were added to the town. Initially ramparts and ditches, these were supplemented by stone turrets, gateways, some masonry walling, and eventually polygonal bastions. Beyond the defences, and now outside the modern southern ring road, was the amphitheatre, preserved today as a grass-grown elliptical hollow, with stone-faced terraces, now turf-covered, forming an auditorium rising 27ft (8m) above the level of the arena.

Of the Roman town and its buildings nothing of significance survives above ground, but in the splendid Corinium Museum in Park Street outstanding finds are imaginatively displayed. These include beautiful mosaics, full-scale reproductions of rooms and workshops inside Roman houses, personal possessions, jewellery, pottery and coins, as well as funeral monuments, statues to distant deities, and the unique acrostic preserved on a piece of plaster discovered beneath New Road in 1868, the only Christian find from Cirencester. It is known that Christianity arrived in Britain in the second century, and, although remaining a minority religion for a long time, had become well established by the fourth century. The acrostic, which reads the same in any direction,

ROTAS
OPERA
TENET
AREPO
SATOR

has been translated as 'The sower Arepo holds the wheel carefully'. The constituent letters can be rearranged as 'PATERNOSTER', or 'Our Father', which, with A and O added at the beginning and end, the ALPHA and OMEGA of the Greek alphabet, suggests a secret, symbolic device used in private Christian worship.

Beyond Corinium and its urban population, the land of the Dobunni,

The Roman mosaic floor at Chedworth villa

our Cotswolds, provided stone for its buildings and food for its people. No matter who ruled and governed, agriculture, both arable and pastoral, had to continue. The nearby military colony at Gloucester (Glevum) and the more distant but thriving Roman resort of Bath (Aqua Sulis) also required food, and only a prosperous neighbourhood could have supplied this. Good soils and improved farming techniques would have helped. Most ancient forests would have been cleared, and it is likely that areas of woodland that had been carefully managed for centuries, satisfied the considerable pre-Roman needs for construction, fencing and food. During Roman times these demands intensified, especially the provision of wood for fuel to feed the burgeoning smelters which were producing iron, copper, tin and lead.

Roman Villas

At least twenty sites of known Roman villas have been found in the Cotswolds, a dozen within a 10 mile (16km) radius of Cirencester. In Roman times the term *villa* denoted a farm and its outbuildings; now it implies any domestic building on stone foundations, in a rural setting and containing one or more proven Roman features such as a mosaic floor or baths. Many more villas probably await discovery. Some, like the few which have been responsibly excavated and investigated, were luxurious country houses; others, doubtless, were more modest structures.

Most Roman villas were the centres of great country estates, occupied by the top people of the day, not dissimilar in idea to the mansions and estates of Tudor times. Current thinking suggests that many of the villa estates represented a Romanisation of existing ones, with stone structures, mosaic floors, tiled roofs, central heating and baths replacing earlier timber buildings on the same site. Two Cotswold sites, at Chedworth (NT) and Great Witcombe (EH), have been excavated and are open to visitors, but they are disappointing. Perhaps one goes with high hopes, but, as is the case with almost all Roman remains in Britain, what survives is very meagre. Imagination is needed to flesh out the bones of a few feet of masonry footings, to picture the life that went on in those homes of luxury. One over-riding impression I always come away with is that their cultured occupants must have spent a lot of time in their baths. A huge peasant labour force would have been necessary to supply the fuel for heating both the houses and the water, and high organisational skills ensured the smooth, efficient running of these large-scale enterprises.

Buildings excavated at Chedworth and exposed to view, albeit partly in roofed sheds or in a marquee, occupy three sides of a courtyard, and their construction spanned two centuries. Of thirty-two identified rooms, obviously at ground-level, about one-third were concerned with bathing. Mosaic floors were found in at least fifteen rooms, and parts of the best of these can be seen. What cannot be seen, but what almost certainly existed, were the outbuildings – storage barns, stables, workshops, perhaps wool-sheds and labourers' housing. Gardens and orchards and the fields beyond probably ensured that villa-estates were self-supporting.

The Great Witcombe Roman villa, reached along a farm road from near the foot of Birdlip Hill, has masonry walls over 5ft (1.5m) high in places, and there is one tessellated pavement on view (under cover). By far the most superb mosaic pavement of all, however, lies beneath the churchyard of St Mary's old church (840030) at Woodchester, near Nailsworth. Uncovered for public viewing every ten years, the art of Corinium paviors has been poured into a scene depicting the Orpheus myth, with vibrant beautifully drawn animals arranged in two circles. Since the room this decorates was almost 50ft (15m) square, the villa itself must have been the most sumptuous in the Cotswolds. It is known that it was built around two courtyards, one for the house and the other for the farm, and there was a domed gatehouse, a granary and possibly a brewery.

Wool is known to have been produced in substantial quantities during the Roman occupation, and it seems likely that many villas were centres of sheep-rearing enterprises. Villa sites in the upper Coln valley, in addition to Chedworth, would have been very suitable – Withington, Whittington, Compton Abdale, Listercombe Bottom and Bibury – as well as others in the upper Windrush valley, near the Slaughters, and above Sudeley may have been forerunners of the great industry which flowered almost ten centuries later. But of life in the Roman-British countryside, and of its continuation after the Roman occupation, little is known.

We do not know what happened when Roman military and political rule vanished, around AD410. No historical or documentary evidence exists; there is no topographical writing on Roman Britain, no detailed references to agricultural methods, administration or land-ownership; boundaries are not defined, and even the names of places do not merit a mention. This vacuum of historical fact and documentation continues until at least AD650. Only archaeology can offer pointers to an apparent steady disintegration of a Roman way of life.

Recent estimates put the population of Roman Britain at between four and five million, a much higher figure than previously thought and considerably higher than it was to become in early medieval times. The Cotswolds, being a favoured area, would have been relatively well peopled; its land was in good heart, cultivated through its flourishing estates, although some were probably starting to decay before the end of Roman rule. In the uneasy times that followed it is likely that Roman-British people reverted to their tribal territorial way of life. Crickley Hill shows evidence of a short-lived repopulation, and other hillforts, their interiors not yet excavated, may have similarly been reused. Corinium, its function as an administrative centre for Romanised civilisation in the area having ceased, simply withered away; scarcely anything is known of what happened to rural settlement, yet it certainly persisted. A form of peasant farming continued, the land had to be tilled, crops sown and harvested, livestock tended. Life for thousands pursued its uneventful, routine course, but it is not known whether this was in communities or dispersed settlements and is a subject for archaeologists and historians to discover. In a classic study thirty years ago Professor Finberg suggested that the parish boundaries of Chedworth, Withington and Compton Abdale, in each of which there was a Roman villa, represent the demarcation boundaries of Roman estates. While it would be satisfying to accept continuity of estates as units of land use, neither archaeology nor history can confirm this, largely on the grounds that the vital point of ownership is not possible to prove. No immediate post-Roman farm and no sixth-century Cotswold village have been identified.

The Anglo-Saxon Chronicles, written by clerics three centuries after many of the recorded events took place, refer to many battles during the so-called Dark Ages. Kingdoms rose and fell, but it is likely that for much of the time there was an uneasy peace. No matter who were kings or overlords the great mass of a peasant population remained where they were, for no retreat was possible. If trouble threatened they would take to the woods; when danger passed they returned to the fields. In 577, according to the Chronicle, 'Cuthwine and Ceawlin [of Wessex] fought against the Britons and killed three kings . . . at a place which is called Dyrham [near Bath]; and they captured three of their cities, Gloucester, Cirencester, and Bath'. Fifty years later a Mercian Anglo-Saxon leader recaptured Cirencester, assisted by Northumbrian Christian princes, and subsequently the Mercian kingdom included Gloucestershire, Worcestershire and south-west Warwickshire, whose people were known collectively as the Hwicce, a name surviving in modern form as Wychwood. The population of this territory, which embraced all the Cotswolds, was a mixed Anglian, Saxon, Northumbrian and British stock.

British forms of speech persisted so far as names of natural landscape features were concerned – Avon, Churn, Coln, Severn, Thames and Windrush – while 'dun' may refer to hill-pasture. 'Crue', a hill, survives in part at Churchdown, a Cotswold outlier near Gloucester, and almost certainly at Crickley.

Saxon settlement was well under way in the south Cotswolds by the early seventh century by settlers using the valley of the Thames and its tributaries, the Windrush and Evenlode, and making use of the surviving Roman arteries – the Foss Way, Akeman Street, Ermin Street and Ryknild Street. Later in the century, Anglian colonisers moved into the north Cotswolds, if the evidence of place-names (which is not always reliable) is to be accepted. Although Anglians and Saxons were heathen, no Cotswold place-name suggests a heathen shrine.

Numbers of incomers are impossible to assess, but they were probably far fewer than has earlier been thought. For reasons not yet fully understood, the existing population had fallen by the seventh century to between two and three million, far outnumbering the Saxon and Anglian settlers. As Christopher Taylor suggests, this new settlement resembled 'the political, tenurial and administrative takeover of a going concern rather than a new beginning'. What is probably more significant is the recognition that the early Saxon and Anglian settlers did not create villages, as has been thought. These came several hundred years later.

Aerial photography and archaeological excavation at many sites, though not in the Cotswolds, indicates that settlement was very dispersed – similar to that of Roman and prehistoric times. Large Saxon villages did not exist during the sixth and seventh centuries. The landscape in favoured areas probably had small occupation sites almost every ½ mile (800m), usually with no plan, no greens or streets; just a small cluster of timber houses or farmsteads that did not bear any resemblance to village forms as we know them today. The evidence is that most present village sites are on or near those inhabited in Saxon times, but there is not necessarily a proven continuous occupation. Although settlements are quite evenly distributed, it is probable that the thinner, drier soils of the upland plateau attracted settlement before the damper, more wooded valleys, although the well-drained gravels near Bourton-on-the-Water and Moreton-in-Marsh were quickly favoured. Little or no enthusiasm was shown for the more heavily wooded region along the crest of the western escarpment.

Firm evidence proving the existence of ecclesiastical estates shows that upland areas in the Cotswolds were extensively used as sheep-pastures. The Mercian King Coenwulf founded a monastery at Winchcombe about 798, and in time this acquired vast estates in the northern Cotswolds. Earlier in the century the Abbess of St Peter's, Gloucester, obtained Pinswell, between Coberley and Withington, as a sheep-walk, and at the same time the Abbess of Withington added to her existing land-holdings in the upper Coln valley 800 acres (324ha) of upland pasture where the Shipton villages are now grouped (Shipton = sheep-farm).

Withington, on the headwaters of the Coln, has two distinct parts. Anglo-Saxon charters indicate that the first settlement, Upper Withington, in the area now centred on the church, was probably settled in the last quarter of the seventh century. A century later another document shows the existence of a separate group at Brockhole End, above the east bank of the river. The open-field system of farming which continued at Withington until the enclosures of 1819 confirm the duality of its settlement, for Withington had four fields, not the two or three usually found in medieval villages. Upper Withington had its two fields extending north from the church, including valley-floor land west of the river, and the higher land now bisected by the straight enclosure road running northwards. Brockhole End's two fields lay to

Harvest bales above Compton Abdale: the view from the A40, looking south-west towards Withington Woods

the east of the river's loop, south of the road to Cassey Compton, with some former arable strips faintly visible to the north, on the steep scrubby slopes below Ravenswell Farm, crossed by a footpath leading to Shipton. Since this path ignores field boundaries, it was obviously a pre-enclosure track, so the question arises whether it was a route between the two monastic estates of St Peter's Abbey.

Between them, monasteries and the church owned large areas of land throughout the Cotswolds. In addition to Winchcombe Abbey's possessions, the Bishop of Worcester acquired estates in the northern Cotswolds around Blockley and Upton, Evesham Abbey had land around Stow-on-the-Wold, while the lesser foundations of Tetbury and Bibury had smaller estates. These may have been based only on minster churches; they have vanished, together with the greatness that once was Winchcombe's abbey. However, Saxon sculpture survives at Bibury as well as at Coln Rogers, Daglingworth, Duntisbourne Rouse, Edgeworth, Miserden and Winstone. Such Anglo-Saxon fragments in churches do not necessarily indicate a particular pattern of settlement. We need to wait for Domesday's great survey for a fuller picture of life at the close of the Saxon period.

3
THE MEDIEVAL LANDSCAPE

'The new men took over as landlords but farming still had to go on.' Professor Hoskins' dictum should be engraved on the hearts of all who have an interest in landscape history. Those same new men, under William the Conqueror, sought to know the resources, in the land and buildings, farms, fisheries, mills, woods, ploughs and people, that this country then possessed – hence the Domesday survey. All the evidence revealed through recent research suggests that, as with much of the English landscape, the Cotswolds were fairly evenly settled, well managed and farmed carefully. Most of today's villages were in existence, although probably they were smaller and more fragmented than we see them. Indeed, almost all of medieval, pre-Conquest England operated in communal 'building-blocks' of territorial packages known as vills, which were neither estates nor parishes, but each of which represented a self-supporting peasant community. Some probably had Roman, some possibly prehistoric, pedigrees, and were apparently very durable.

Winchcombe was the only Domesday borough, with under 1,000 people; elsewhere the population of the Cotswolds as a whole was probably 5,000–6,000, that is, less than half of present-day Cirencester. It was highest in the south-eastern Cotswolds, most thinly scattered on the high plateau. The number of mills mentioned in Domesday is an indirect pointer to population, and although these are naturally related to their river and stream sites, there was a greater concentration in the western valleys, particularly that of the Frome. The extent of monastic land-ownership was confirmed, and religious bodies as a whole are calculated to have held about 400 hides of land (1 hide was equivalent to an average 120 acres/48ha), representing almost 50,000 acres (20,000ha), or 75sq miles (194km²), about an eighth of the present AONB area.

Domesday records show a new market at Cirencester, an obvious choice for such an enterprise, with two Roman roads and the medieval White Way meeting there. Within a century Cirencester had become commercially more important than Winchcombe, with burgesses appearing in 1133, and the town paying ten times as much tax by 1171. Merchants and artisans in Cirencester during the twelfth century were steadily gaining more control over the town's affairs at the expense of the abbey's influence.

The twelfth and thirteenth centuries saw the founding of more markets, not only in the Cotswolds, but throughout the country as a whole. Market charters were granted for Stow in 1107, for Chipping Campden in 1180, for Moreton-in-Marsh in 1226, for Northleach in 1230, for Minchinhampton in 1269 and for Painswick in 1321. By then, Tetbury was described as having an 'ancient' market, while others had been, or were soon to be, established at Brimpsfield, Blockley, Burford, Fairford, Guiting Power and Lechlade. A good riverside site was an advantage but did not necessarily guarantee success. Far more significant was a site on a busy road, or at an important junction, hence the flourishing markets on the Foss Way, at Campden and at Tetbury, usefully placed on the Cirencester to Bristol road. Blockley and Fairford probably failed because they were too close to Campden and Cirencester respectively, while Brimpsfield and Guiting Power lacked the advantage of an important road. In the far south of the area Wotton-under-Edge had an established market by the end of the twelfth century, but apparently the town was badly affected by a fire, and did not regain market status until 1253.

A grant of an annual fair often accompanied the market charter, and while the latter would be normally a largely local weekly event attracting people from up to about 7 miles (11km) away, a fair was intended to attract traders from much farther afield. Fair day was usually chosen to coincide with the local patronal feast or some other great Christian festival, preferably between May and October, since travelling conditions were likely to be better then than during the winter months. If a market town prospered it might be granted additional market and fair days, one of these usually being in the autumn, when, in later years, workers in a district, standing in the market place with the tools of their trade, sought employment contracts for the following year. These hiring fairs, frequently known as 'mop fairs', presumably because a majority of women attended them, still retain this name in the October fairs at Cirencester and Chipping Norton.

Within the market towns, particularly those with borough status, burgage plots clustered around the market place or along the main road. These were freehold tenements, carrying special privileges for their owners. Houses occupied a narrow street frontage with a long strip behind, for workshops, yard, stables or small warehouse, together with a small garden. Beyond the burgage strips ran a back lane, and a number of towns retain this feature.

The ruins of the Banqueting Hall and Presence Chamber at Sudeley Castle

In Chipping Campden it is known as Back Ends, and at Stow, which was never a borough, the lane behind Sheep Street is Back Walls, with narrow walled passages which I have paced out at about 100yd (91m) along the sides of former plots. The relevant OS 1:25,000 'Pathfinder' map is a useful guide to the existence of burgage layout, as its scale is large enough to show plot boundaries. Plot frontages appear, as at Winchcombe and Northleach, to be 5–6yd (4.5–5.4m), or a multiple of this amount. Of the dwellings themselves virtually nothing is known. Even in the stone-rich Cotswolds, early medieval buildings were of timber, mostly roofed with thatch. It is known that in the early twelfth century the Abbot of Winchcombe allowed some poor townsmen to build such cottages around the abbey precinct, presumably to help keep away marauders. In the following century two houses in Winchcombe are known to have had stone tiles, but this was both unusual and costly.

Castles are particularly thin on the Cotswold ground. Substantial earthworks near the church at Upper Slaughter, in the park above Castle Combe, in woodland at Miserden, and more prominently at Brimpsfield, are all of eleventh- to early thirteenth-century date, while Ascot-under-Wychwood claims earthworks of two castles. At Cirencester Castle Street recalls the existence of a castle, but scarcely anything survives of fortified structures known to have stood at Tetbury and Chipping Norton.

Beverstone Castle (*861939*), south of Nailsworth, has much more to offer, with substantial masonry remains of a probable quadrangular structure, built about 1225 and having large drum towers at the angles. In 1330 Lord Berkeley bought the manor of Beverstone and modernised the castle's domestic accommodation by adding a gatehouse, and a south-western tower which included a chapel with Berkeley's own chamber and small oratory above. Later alterations have not markedly changed the appearance of Lord Berkeley's castle. The present house to the south of the castle was probably built by Sir Michael Hicks, who owned Beverstone in 1612, but the windows and roof date from the end of the seventeenth century. Although not open to the public, there is a reasonable view of Beverstone's ruined towers from the church porch to its north-east.

Sudeley Castle near Winchcombe is much later than Beverstone and much grander, its oldest parts dating from the early fifteenth century, when it was owned by the Botelers between 1398 and 1469. Forfeited to the Crown during the Wars of the Roses, it was granted by Edward IV to his brother Richard, Duke of Gloucester, who had it until 1478 and then regained it in 1483 when he became king. Sudeley Castle remained Crown property until 1547 when it was given to Lord Seymour, who married Katherine Parr, Henry VIII's widow, in the same year; the couple lived at Sudeley for eight years. Katherine died at Sudeley and is buried in the small church in the castle grounds. Subsequently passing into the ownership of Lord Chandos, in whose family it remained until the Civil War slighting made it largely uninhabitable, Sudeley was sold in 1810 to the Duke of Buckingham and

Minster Lovell. The church is framed in the ruins of the fifteenth-century hall

Chandos. He sold it in 1837 to the Dent family, and it is now the family home of Lord and Lady Ashcombe.

Relatively little survives of Boteler's building: the north gateway into the outer court, the roofless ruins of the great barn, the church and two towers. The beautiful ruins of the great banqueting hall, with its royal suite of accommodation, evoke the years of Richard, Duke of Gloucester, while much also survives of Lord Chandos's day, 1572. Internally, the various Victorian restorations that took place between 1840 and 1890, and more recent ones of the 1930s are disappointingly prosaic after the first impressions of Tudor power generated by the outside view. In a beautiful parkland setting, towers and battlements of golden stone fretting a noble skyline raise hopes of more than melancholy memories. Here history and commercialism seem to have made an uneasy alliance.

The ruins of Minster Lovell on the banks of the Windrush a few miles east of Burford have had no such Victorian gutting and restoration. In spite of the characteristic over-tidiness associated with what is now English Heritage, they are picturesque in setting and reflective in decay. Built by William, 7th Lord Lovell, in 1431–2, it passed eventually to Francis, a prominent Yorkist whose support for Richard III cost him the estates in 1485. In 1602 Sir Edward Coke bought the manor from the Crown, and in 1747 the hall was dismantled by Thomas Coke, Earl of Leicester. Ruinous, it served as farm buildings until the Ministry of Works bought the ruins and made them safe in the 1930s. Their layout shows the hall was built around three sides of a courtyard, the fourth side being open to the river. High roofless walls of the former hall, with more modest survivals elsewhere, are all that remain of one of Oxfordshire's most aristocratic houses. Its life spanned three centuries, its death almost two and a half, yet it still tugs at the heart.

Monasteries

Nine centuries have passed since Domesday, and for four of those the monasteries exerted a powerful, far-reaching, if not always benign influence on lives and landscapes. Even from pre-Conquest times monastic estates were growing, but subsequent grants of land and manors extended this monastic ownership, to which should be added land within the ecclesiastical estates such as that held by the Bishop of Worcester at Bibury and Withington in the Coln valley, and the manors of Blockley and Upton in the northern Cotswolds.

Gloucester Abbey's estates lay mainly in the central part of the plateau, including the manors of Coln Rogers, Aldsworth and Eastleach, as well as Buckland, while the Abbot of Evesham's holdings were mainly centred on Stow-on-the-Wold, although there was a grange at Broadway. Winchcombe Abbey's estates were initially concentrated around the south-east of the town, but subsequently spread to take in a chain of manors that ran across the uplands, including Bledington, Snowshill, Stanton, Hawling and Sherborne, the centre of the abbot's sheep-farming enterprises. Llanthony Priory (Gloucester) had sheep-pastures at Barrington, as well as a centre for shearing and wool collection.

Pershore Abbey's sheep-walks were at Buckland, Cowley and Hawkesbury, while the Abbot of Tewkesbury owned land at Taddington, near the western escarpment, and Stanway just below it, where he built the great barn in the fourteenth century, presumably to store the wool-clip as well as corn from his arable land.

Abbeys from far beyond the Cotswolds, absentee landlords in modern parlance, also held significant estates. Westminster Abbey owned the manor of Bourton-on-the-Hill, while the nuns of Caen, who were given land at Avening and Minchinhampton, are known to have had huge sheep-flocks grazing on Minchinhampton Common in the early twelfth century. The French abbey of St Denis owned the manor of Coln St Dennis up to 1415 when Henry V gave it to Tewkesbury.

Cistercian monks arrived at Kingswood, near Wotton-under-Edge, as early as 1139 and immediately acquired some of its manors, including Hazleton near Northleach, but more than a century elapsed before the only major Cistercian monastery was established in the Cotswolds. In 1246 Richard, Earl of Cornwall, younger brother of Henry III, founded the abbey of Hailes, near Winchcombe, endowed it with great riches and completed the building of church, cloister, dormitory and refectory during the next five years; the abbey was quickly colonised by Cistercian monks from Beaulieu Abbey in Hampshire. Richard gave an immediate 1,000 marks (£666) to buy land and houses.

Within thirty years a more characteristic Cistercian austerity prevailed. Although much of the best land was already in monastic or ecclesiastic hands, Hailes gradually acquired holdings on the hills above the abbey, with a grange at Farmcote, land above Stanton and Croscombe, and further property at Swell and Longborough. Scarp woodlands yielded valuable timber, and it is likely that the abbey's swine contributed to its economy.

Within the Cotswold area Hailes is the only monastic site worth visiting, even though, by the standards of northern Cistercian ruins, its remains are meagre. The despoilers at its Dissolution on Christmas Eve 1539 were particularly savage, perhaps because in 1270 it had been given a relic by Richard's son, Edmund, Earl of Cornwall, consisting of a phial of Christ's blood, apparently guaranteed by the Patriarch of Jerusalem. A special shrine was built for it at the new east end of the abbey church; pilgrims were expected but did not materialise until the fifteenth century. The fame of Hailes spread throughout England and Europe, and Hailes grew even richer, so that it became a more tempting prize for Henry VIII. The proud relic was later found to have been a fake.

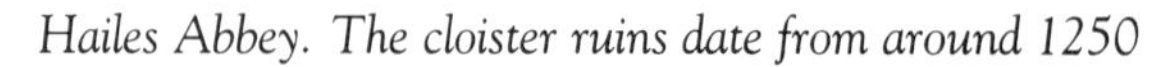

Hailes Abbey. The cloister ruins date from around 1250

A few cloister arcades of mellowed stone frame in their masonry stately chestnuts, yews and cypress in a parkland setting beneath the hills. Footings of walls identify what was a substantial east range. Trees mark the positions of nave and chancel piers, and the site of the high altar, together with that of the four-bayed chancel, ending in an apse with five radiating chapels, give only a hint of the glory that once was. A modern museum contains many pieces of richly sculptured masonry, roof-bosses from the chapter house and vault of the cloister, glazed armorial tiles, an impression of the abbey's seal, together with life-sized models of a Cistercian monk and a lay-brother.

In 1543 the site and its ruins were given to Katherine Parr, Henry VIII's last wife. After her death in 1548 it passed to her second husband, Thomas, Lord Seymour, and subsequently through the hands of various families. The National Trust acquired it in 1937 and the ruins are in the guardianship of English Heritage.

The nearby small parish church, which was there long before Hailes Abbey, possesses a small amount of stained glass from the abbey, while the church at Teddington (964329), a few miles to the north-west, claims its tower arch and west window from Hailes. At Wormington (038364), another tiny church is said to have been built by the Abbot of Hailes in 1475. Some barns at Farmcote, above Hailes, are believed to date from the time that the monks occupied a medieval grange there, which can now be reached by the narrow, stony, sunken lane that climbs the escarpment.

Farming

While it may be pleasantly cosy to think that the Cotswold villages we see today suggest a degree of permanence in the landscape, and that they have always been there, the reality is very different. There is not a Cotswold village that remotely resembles now what it looked like in the high Middle Ages. Nor, except in a few cases, do we know how life in the medieval village was organised. Certainly in the century following the Norman Conquest more woodland was cleared and more arable land was brought into cultivation. New settlements appeared, often as hamlets towards the edge of existing parishes, and some new parishes were created during the twelfth century, including Chalford, Nailsworth and Southrop. Open-field farming was practised, probably with some regional variation both in the numbers of open fields and their rotation, although the two-field system prevailed. Throughout medieval times the Cotswold landscape was one of great spaciousness, with vast sheep-walks alternating with common arable fields of up to several hundred acres. Most manorial tenants owed a specific labour to their lord of the manor, and the lord's demesne was largely farmed through this service. With so many ecclesiastical and monastic estates across the Cotswolds absentee landlords were common, and the lord's appointed bailiff was in charge, usually of a number of manors, but centred on a main one.

Thus, the Bishop of Worcester's Cotswold manors at Bibury, Blockley, Bredon, Cleeve and Withington seem to have been organised from Blockley. Christopher Dyer's patient research into the manorial accounts illuminates some interesting aspects of fourteenth-century farming. Only about one-third to one-half of the potential arable land was actually under the plough, and during the fourteenth century this gradually diminished, either through letting extra parcels of land to tenants, converting arable to pasture for the increasing size of demesne flocks of sheep, or simply because it had become derelict.

Barley was the commonest crop, particularly on the Bibury manor, probably at the expense of livestock, as the following table for 1389 shows:

	Horses	*Oxen*	*Cows*	*Pigs*	*All Sheep*
Bibury	4	5	–	–	190
Blockley	6	20	1	78	910
Bredon	3	11	3	9	637
Withington	4	19	31	119	278

As for the numbers of tenants on the bishop's estates, another table covering the period 1290–1544 is very revealing:

	1299	*1349*	*15c*	*1544*
Bibury	31	7	12	12
Blockley	98	45	–	–
Bredon	101	40	–	–
Cleeve	94	61	53	52
Withington	57	23	–	–

The marked fall during the first half of the fourteenth century, averaging almost 50 per cent needs an explanation. Before this is discussed, however, it is well to consider Cotswold farming in medieval times.

The two-field system which seems to have been practised was obviously intended to keep the soil fertile. Medieval land fertility did not come in sacks but from livestock, and the key to good crops lay in achieving a balance between corn – barley, wheat and oats, together with peas and beans – and sheep, whose dung, trodden into the soil through folded grazing, maintained its fertility. Manorial documents relating to Temple Guiting in the thirteenth and fourteenth centuries estimated that a ploughland of about 100 acres (40ha) would be accompanied by 300–400 sheep. Probably three or four peasant families tenanted the arable area, each holding being known as a yardland, which in the Cotswolds varied between 30 and 40 acres (12–16ha). At Temple Guiting this would apparently imply peasant sheep flocks of well over 100 sheep. Flocks of this size were highly unusual, and although the peasant farmer left practically no records at all, available evidence suggests that individual flocks averaged about twenty sheep, with ones of thirty being unusual over much of England, although more likely in the Cotswolds.

Peasants' well-being depended on their farming. Money required to pay the manorial landlord would come from the sale of produce at market, or earnings on the labour market, perhaps for help given to a local trader or craftsman. On the whole, life continued at little more than subsistence level. Archaeological investigation of deserted village sites indicates that peasant families lived in small 'long houses' of timber, on stone footings, whose outlines in the grass, delineated by the low-angle sunlight of winter, reveals their presence. Tax lists of 1327 give a good idea of village sizes as well as showing how populations had steadily risen since Domesday: in the valley of the upper Windrush, the Guitings, Bourton and Naunton probably had ten to twenty taxpayers each, representing populations of between one and two hundred, with Notgrove, Aston Blank and Lower Slaughter only slightly less; Aylworth, Harford and Upper Slaughter were very much smaller. All could be regarded as nucleated, though not necessarily in the form they have now. Within their scatter-pattern, not more than 2 or 3 miles (3.2–4.8km) apart, each village looked across its open fields of arable, its small paddocks and meadows, to its open sheep-pastures and the woods beyond.

Deserted and Shrunken Villages

The OS 1:25,000 maps of the Cotswolds mark in many places, in the Gothic script reserved for antiquities, 'Medieval village of . . . (site of)', with a settlement name in the space. Pathfinder sheet 1067 (Stow-on-the-Wold) identifies seven such sites: Pinnock (*076281*), Castlett (*089258*), Hawling (*067234*), Lower Harford (*130225*), Aylworth (*109217*), Sennington (*024219*), and Whittington (*015206*). The 1972 list gives another five: Aston (*147214*), Eyford (*146246*), Postlip (*000270*), Roel (*074249*) and Sudeley (*032276*), making a total of twelve within an area of 77sq miles (200sq km). Over the whole Cotswolds over fifty known former village sites have been identified. At most of them there is little to be seen on the ground save a few bumps, ridges and hollows. At some – Pinnock, Aston, Lower Harford, Castlett – a single farm stands on or near the site; at Sudeley the castle and its park cover everything, while at Hawling and Whittington the village has moved a few hundred yards.

No single common denominator explains the loss of these medieval settlements. Conversion of arable into pasture for sheep farming has been blamed for much of the depopulation and was certainly a factor in many cases. Of possibly greater significance were the effects of the various plague infestations from about 1340 onwards, together with deterioration in the climate. Population had grown since Norman times and it has been reckoned that in Gloucestershire, including the Cotswolds, it peaked during the first

Medieval ridge-and-furrow, with sheep grazing, by the Cotswold Way above Wood Stanway

part of the fourteenth century. Settlements established in the later part of the period tended to be on land of poorer quality, usually the more exposed uplands as at Eyford, Harford and Aylworth, all west of Stow-on-the-Wold. On such marginal land even slight climatic changes would be keenly felt: a bad harvest meant not only less food in the winter but less seed-corn for the following year. If there was an early snowfall, trouble would be compounded as farm stock was deprived of fodder, and community starvation would not be far away. Disastrous harvests occurred in 1315–17, following heavy royal tax demands of two decades previously, and these events drove vulnerably small populations into poverty, debt and retreat.

Thus, well before the Black Death, as the Great Pestilence of 1348–50 was called, the agrarian economy was declining. Over England as a whole the population fell by at least a third, and although few, if any, Cotswold villages were wholly depopulated as a result, those which had been already weakened were made even more vulnerable.

At Little Aston (*147214*), seven out of ten householders are known to have left their homes shortly before 1340. What happened to those who remained, or to their holdings, is not known. Harford and Aylworth, in Naunton parish, had gone out of cultivation by 1341. In the thirteenth century Roel had its own parish church, but within another two centuries the settlement had been absorbed into Hawling parish. At Upton, in the

Bishop of Worcester's manor at Blockley, the land supported seventeen peasant families and there was a good balance between arable and pasture. Accounts of 1383 suggest that by then depopulation was almost complete, accelerated by the plague of 1349, together with additional pasture for the bishop's increasing flocks.

Population decline and the post-plague surplus of arable land becoming available for grazing, which in itself resulted in a substantial reduction in the labour force, almost certainly caused some changes in settlement pattern. Many villages shrank in size. Some manors sought to consolidate holdings and there were the beginnings of piecemeal enclosure. The swing from corn to pasture was almost irreversible, and fields near many Cotswold villages show evidence of this today in the corrugations of their 'ridge-and-furrow' grass-lands. Low-angle sunlight of winter or of summer evenings or early mornings, picks out this landscape feature. Although recognised throughout the area, particularly on the wolds, I recall most vividly a series of 'ridge-and-furrow' fields along the Cotswold Way near Stanway and Wood Stanway, and above Chipping Campden.

Ridge-and-furrow was produced only by the action of a heavy plough capable of turning over a sod. An asymmetrical mould-board plough is drawn by a team of oxen along a ½ acre (0.2ha) strip perhaps 220yd (201m) (a furrow) long – about as far as an ox can pull before needing a rest. The long unwieldy nature of the outfit makes straight-line ploughing awkward and necessitates for turning purposes a slight curving of the furrow, producing a shallow 'reversed S' curve on the land. The ploughman continues round and round this 'selion' always in the same direction, shifting one plough's width of soil inwards each 'up-and-down' journey, thus creating a small ridge in the selion. By ploughing a series of narrow strips a set of slightly raised ridges, separated by furrows, will result; and repeated ploughing along the original strips, over a long period of time, results in higher ridges and deeper furrows. It is probable that some correlation existed between an individual peasant's holding of strips of land and the ridge and furrow, with a number of strips on the one ridge, or adjoining ridges, held by one person while another two or three ridges held the strips of his neighbour. Research shows that peasant holdings were scattered about the arable fields and not usually held in large single units.

When depopulation occurred, with the conversion of arable to pasture, there was no more ploughing. Grass soon covered the former ridge-and-furrow, thus fossilising its profile. Since it takes many years of concentrated cross-ploughing to eradicate ridge-and-furrow and over the Cotswolds as a whole pastoral farming continued over the centuries, ridge-and-furrow remains the most extensive form of surviving medieval archaeology. To see sheep grazing ridged fields below the Cotswold edge is to catch a hint of the farmed landscape of five or six hundred years ago.

In the late fourteenth century grain prices fell, but wool remained profitable, so that pastoral farming was not only maintained at a higher level than grain, but tended to increase. It was less labour-intensive with a single shepherd able to manage manorial flocks of 200–300 sheep, whereas three men were needed for even the smallest demesne where arable farming was dominant. Evidence from the Bishop of Worcester's manors throws more light on the sheep farming, and shows that younger stock were kept on lowland pastures, while full-grown ewes were concentrated on the upland manors of Blockley, Bredon, Cleeve and Withington. A form of transhumance was practised, with lowland flocks – ewes and lambs – being taken with their shepherds in June to upland pastures on other manors perhaps 30 or 40 miles (48–64km) away, and brought back in September. Most manorial flocks were driven to Blockley for shearing in June, but where some manors sheared locally the wool clip was taken to Blockley.

Proof of animal husbandry and care is shown in the building of sheepcotes, large barns for storing fodder, and in which part of any flock could shelter in bad weather. Records of 1383–4 reveal that at Blockley an eight-bay sheepcote, 120ft (36m) long was built, with stone tiles for its roof costing £11 7s 7d, and ten years later Bibury had a smaller sheepcote, about half the size of Blockley's, roofed at a cost of £6. It is thought that one of the stone barns at Farmcote (*062292*) may have been a fifteenth-century sheepcote attached to the grange of nearby Hailes Abbey. Indeed, a mid-fifteenth-century charter shows that the monks of Hailes had little compunction in depopulating an occasional village. At Longborough, north of Stow-on-the-Wold, the Abbot of Hailes

> hath (900 sheep) and dayly exacteth and requireth and oppressith with divers exaction to the intent to dryve them oute of the said lyvingys because he woolde have the said manor holy decayed and converted into pasture contrary to the kyngs lawes and statutys.

Earlier, a statute of 1402 declared that monks and other subjects of the king should not be called 'depopulators of the fields'; in 1489 an act made it an offence to convert open fields to pasture if it necessitated removing smallholdings of over 20 acres (8ha). If that did happen, overlords were expected to try to see that such arable holdings were reinstated. One reason for the Crown's worry about deliberate depopulation was that it could so often bring about an increase in numbers of landless peasants. Nevertheless, sufficient numbers remained in the existing villages to till the arable land which was necessary to provide life-sustaining crops. Beyond lay the open pastures grazed by thousands of sheep manorial, monastic, ecclesiastical, and

Opposite *Wyck Rissington*

Overleaf *Autumn in Cranham beechwoods*

Cleeve Cloud

Spring at Eastleach Martin

peasant flocks, on whose backs grew the wool that ensured the present and future prosperity of the Cotswolds.

Churches

Churches stood at the heart of village communities and most Cotswold churches are of pre-Reformation date. In an age when life for most people was 'nasty, brutish and short', they were the largest and oldest buildings, sanctuaries in a world where fear stalked the wildwood, evil was in the storm and Hell was terrifyingly real. Churches offered colour and ritual in a peasant world of toil and dirt, and in good times they were places of rejoicing, regularly the focus of communal life. Our modern minds can scarcely conceive the verities of good and evil which faced our medieval forebears, when, in John Betjeman's words, 'All thought, all sight, every breath of the body, was under God.' Men's fears were expressed in grotesque carvings, particularly on exterior north walls (the devil's side), their hopes in images of our Lord, the Virgin, angels and saints. Compared with the hovels which were medieval homes, churches were spacious; they may even have provided a degree of warmth and light, even if this never penetrated to the darkest corners. What dangers might the medieval mind have imagined

Duntisbourne Rouse dates from Saxon and early Norman times. The tower was built later

Above *The chancel and east window of Elkstone Church, c1160–70*

Opposite *Fairford Church, c1490–1500, one of the great 'wool' churches*

lurking there, what hopes were offered by the tortured Latin of services taken by poorly educated priests? Five centuries have passed since most of the great 'wool' churches were built, and it is eight centuries since many of the small village churches were erected. Although between us and the worshippers of past centuries there is an unbridgeable gulf of mystery, we can at least appreciate Cotswold churches as buildings, which were important in the lives of unnumbered generations.

We can be thankful today that it is possible to visit almost all of the Cotswold churches and find them unlocked. During the past three years I have visited over a hundred, and been denied entry to less than a handful, and with two of those I arrived too late in the evening. Even more encouraging is that an increasing number positively welcome visitors, and not necessarily as worshippers. The Churches and Visitors Group of the Diocese of Gloucester publishes a number of leaflets about churches that are closely grouped geographically, outlining briefly their architectural history: 'Churches off Ermine Street', 'Churn Valley Churches', 'Hill and Valley Churches', 'Churches around Bourton-on-the-Water', and the 'Nailsworth Ring of Churches'.

There is no typical Cotswold church and all periods of architecture are represented. At Cirencester the Saxons built one of the longest churches in England, although nothing of this survives above ground. What there is of Saxon origin can be seen at Bibury, Coln Rogers, Daglingworth, Duntisbourne Rouse, Edgeworth, Miserden and Winstone, with the sculptures at Daglingworth most significant and rewarding. Many of the churches in villages on the upland plateau retain the simple Norman character of early 'field' churches – chapels that were built by local manorial landowners where none previously existed and consisting merely of a small hall-like nave separated from a tiny chancel by a low arch, or, as at Brimpsfield and Ozleworth, by a tower. Indeed, Ozleworth's rare hexagonal tower, dating from before 1311, may have been the original nave. Brimpsfield, together with Aston Blank, Baunton, Notgrove and Winstone, has no east window, possibly representing the survivals of an early Celtic church plan.

Avening, Elkstone and Hampnett retain that rare Norman feature, a stone-vaulted chancel, and the small windows there as well as at Clapton, Edgeworth and Tarlton are also suggestive of early Norman work. Perhaps the most outstanding feature of many Norman Cotswold churches is the elaborately carved doorway, usually with geometric ornamentation, chevron or stylised beak-heads, as vigorously illustrated at Windrush, while Burford and Elkstone have both designs. Many of these Norman doorways incorporate sculptured tympana, with Christ in Majesty and the Harrowing of Hell common subjects among a variety of themes, vividly portrayed at Elkstone, Quenington and Eastleach Turville, while Ampney St Mary has, above its north doorway, a carving supposedly showing the Lion of Righteousness triumphing over the agents of evil represented by faces with snake-like bodies.

At Condicote, Farmington, Southrop and Winstone, tympana have diapered designs of stars, fish-scales or lozenges, while that at Great Washbourne's small but enchanting early Norman church shows a Maltese cross within an elaborately decorated frame which includes the branching tree of life with a dove plucking an olive branch.

Still within the Norman theme, the font at Southrop is unique in Gloucestershire, with sculpture far ahead of anything else of the mid-twelfth century. The figures include those of armoured women, representing the Virtues, whose names are inscribed on arches, trampling on the Vices, with names given backwards on the panels. Rendcomb has a memorable font, similar to that in Hereford Cathedral with figures in relief within an arcade beneath a rare Greek-patterned frieze above and a honeysuckle design around the base.

Most Cotswold village churches are modest buildings, the majority showing some Norman work, often of outstanding quality. Sheep and wool formed the basis of the local economy then and for the following seven centuries, but this experienced bad times from the late thirteenth to the mid-fourteenth centuries. Architecturally, this coincided with the Decorated style which, as a result, is poorly represented throughout the area, although the church at Eastleach St Martin was almost wholly rebuilt then, and the fine south transepts and windows at Longborough and Minchinhampton show the graceful Decorated tracery.

The Perpendicular style, originating in Gloucester Cathedral as early as 1331–7, continued with little change for two hundred years, a period of increasing prosperity and wealth, particularly for the Cotswold woolmen. Few Cotswold churches do not show some traces of this period, when those in many villages were enriched by an additional aisle, a fine south porch, larger windows, a clerestory, or a higher Perpendicular tower as at Chedworth, Coberley, Compton Abdale, Elkstone and Withington. It is the 'wool' churches at Burford, Chipping Campden, Cirencester, Fairford, Lechlade, Northleach, Rendcomb and Winchcombe which command attention, but to claim that one is superior to another is pointless. We know many of the names of their benefactors, the woolmen and merchants commemorated in the glinting, superbly carved brasses on walls and floors. More anonymous are the master masons who worked the golden Cotswold stone and created the buildings of beauty and dignity that grace so many towns and villages.

4
COTSWOLD WOOL AND CLOTH

In Europe the best wool is English,
In England the best wool is Cotswold.

Thus ran a popular saying of medieval times, but it is still something of a mystery why English wool was so prized throughout medieval Europe and which led merchants of Italy and Flanders to come to England to buy it in such huge quantities. Doubts exist as to the actual quality of the wool, whether it was fine or coarse, long or short, and we do not even know what medieval sheep were like, or how their wool compares with present products. Selective breeding from the eighteenth century has been directed towards improving meat yields from sheep, with a consequent coarsening of the wool, so it is probable that medieval and Tudor wool was as fine as, if not finer than, any present-day English wool.

Medieval sheep were bred for their wool, for making into cloth both at home and abroad. There was always a strong home market, but until about the middle of the fifteenth century most English wool went to the Continent, mainly to Italy and the Low Countries, where Florence and Antwerp were the main cloth-making centres. For the European clothiers to have favoured Cotswold wool implies that the product must have been short and fine. Primitive sheep breeds had two coats – a short fine inner one and a long coarse outer one – and, while historians disagree about the nature of medieval Cotswold wool, one writer (Kenneth Ponting), who has spent all his working life in the West Country woollen industry, suggests that medieval sheep breeders may have succeeded in breeding away the coarse coat, leaving the finer wool predominating on the fleece. What *is* certain is that the large-bodied 'Cotswold Lions', with their heavy fleeces of long curly wool, seen at the Cotswold Farm Park today are unlikely to have been the type of animal yielding the fine wool of medieval times.

Wool is not a simple commodity but varies with the breed of sheep, its environment and diet, even the part of the body from which it comes. Generally, small active sheep, free-ranging over hilly, exposed land with short grass such as occurs on downs and wolds, produce short fine wool suitable for carding and for making into woollen cloth – the medieval and Tudor 'broadcloth' – while larger sheep favour rich valley and lowland pasture, their heavier fleeces yielding longer-stapled, coarser wools which could not be carded but required combing before they were manufactured into worsteds. Although the 'Ryeland' breed of Herefordshire and south Shropshire produced the most valuable wool in medieval times, it was the Cotswold sheep, whatever it may have looked like, that produced the enormous amount of wool, the 'Golden Fleece' of medieval England.

While much of the Cotswold wool came from monastic and ecclesiastical estates, most was probably produced by peasant flocks. Dr Hoskins has estimated that a numerous peasantry, with each farmer owning no more than twenty sheep, would account for between four and seven times as many sheep as those owned by the abbots and bishops. But it was the large landowners who contracted with the buyers or their agents to supply wool not only from

Winter pastures near Hawling. Cotswold prosperity grew on the backs of sheep

their own demesne but also from their manorial tenants. Estimates for the numbers of sheep grazing the Cotswolds around the early thirteenth century suggest a figure of half a million, and Italians as well as Flemish buyers were visiting the area regularly to purchase wool 'clips' for years ahead, and pay cash in advance for them.

Before the wool could be collected came the high-spot of the shepherd's year, the clipping or shearing, then as now usually done in June. Compared to the rest of his lonely life tending the flocks, this was a communal, social, convivial occasion, although the shepherd himself rarely did any actual clipping. Most villages had their washpools, usually on valley streams or rivers, into which sheep were driven and washed. Near Painswick the name of the Washbrook valley doubtless indicates such usage, while below the northern slopes of Cleeve Hill, in the narrow valley above Postlip, 'Washpool' is named on the OS map (997264), and near the small pool today a small keyhole-shaped, brick-built sheep dip is of more recent origin.

Winchcombe Abbey accounts for 1485 record that the abbot rode 13 miles (21km) across the high wolds to his manor at Sherborne where flocks for clipping had been collected from his estates at Snowshill, Roel, Hawling, Charlton Abbots, as well as at Sherborne itself, to be washed in the Sherborne Brook. From there the flocks went for clipping, where teams of men supervised by the flockmaster took four days to shear the 2,900 sheep. The total cost was £6 12s 3d, or just over 9s a sack.

Merchants or their agents would come to inspect the wool, by now stored in great barns, and arrange the collection of that already contracted for. But not all dealing was in the hands of agents or even landowners. Up-country wool-brokers, usually burgesses of market towns, were entering the scene as dealers or middlemen, especially concerned with peasant flocks. By the end of the fourteenth century a new class of rich local merchants had emerged. William Grevel is the best-known example, and his beautiful house at Chipping Campden (see p129), built shortly before his death in 1401, is evidence of the prosperity he achieved. His descendants became the Earls of Warwick.

By then Gloucester, Cirencester, Northleach, Winchcombe and Campden were flourishing wool-market towns, and the Woolstaplers' Hall at Campden, contemporary with Grevel's house, was built for a merchant, Robert Calf. As early as the thirteenth century certain English towns were designated as 'staple towns', where wool was brought for taxation. These staple towns varied according to local or international needs, the main ones being London, York, Lincoln, Newcastle, Norwich, Winchester, Exeter, Bristol and Shrewsbury.

Taxation on wool exports was an important means of raising revenue for the king; the more profligate the monarch, the more revenue he needed. During Edward II's reign, 1307–27, 30,000 sacks of Cotswold wool were sent annually to the king's household. Regular levies on wool exports continued, and successive monarchs exploited this source of revenue to such an extent that by the late fifteenth century taxation was one cause of the decline in exports of wool.

Cranham Church tower dates from the fifteenth century and features two pairs of sheep shears carved on its west face

Influential merchants increasingly preferred a single staple town abroad through which English wool exports were directed; smaller woolmen preferred the existing arrangement which enabled them to obtain better prices, while the king did not mind so long as he received his revenues. Eventually, in 1399, the staple for English wool was fixed at Calais, then still an English town, although special licences were issued allowing English wool to be shipped directly to Italy and Flanders mainly through London, Southampton and Boston, then the main wool ports.

The Staple gradually became an English monopoly and as a corporate company it involved, at most, about four hundred merchants, dealers and woolmen of the late fourteenth and fifteenth centuries. Membership of the Company of the Staple was obtained by apprenticeship or purchase, with members having to follow strict rules of conduct. We know much about the business transactions of the merchants of the Staple from the letters of various members of the Celys, an Essex family, which present a detailed view of the running of a medieval business between 1472 and 1488, from their London headquarters. During that time the family was concerned with the buying, selling, trading and shipping of wool, mainly from the Cotswolds.

Frequent references are made to trade with the woolmen of Northleach, particularly William Midwinter and John Bushe. In one transaction Richard Cely contracted to buy 'of Will Midwinter, 40 sacks . . . at a great price . . . 13s 4d a tod'. A tod was 28lb (13kg), and there were 13 tods to a sack of 364lb (165kg). Thus, that transaction alone involved the payment of over £330. On another occasion Richard Cely paid about £750 to Will Midwinter for a large quantity of wool. These figures may sound trifling by today's standards, but a conservative multiplier to convert them, very roughly, is 300, so those two deals between Cely and Midwinter involved about £100,000 and £225,000 respectively, at 1990 prices. These were by no means exceptional. In 1452 John Townsend, a Lechlade merchant, contracted to supply wool to two foreign agents for £1,078 – well over £300,000 today.

Financing these wool transactions was based on a long chain of credit which, by the fifteenth century, operated from seller to buyer. Cotswold woolmen bought on credit from the sheep farmers, paying probably one-third down on the agreed price. Merchants such as the Celys bought on credit from the woolmen, and the European customers bought on credit from the Celys. When, some months later, the Celys presented their bills the stream of money would start to flow, from Italy or Flanders to London, from the Celys to the Cotswold woolmen and from them to the sheep farmers, bringing prosperity to the Cotswold woolmen and dealers. Now knowing something of their lives, their businesses, and the people they met we can better appreciate their memorial brasses in the proud churches they largely paid for – the Midwinters, Forteys, Taylours and Bushes at Northleach, Grevel at Campden, Tames at Fairford, and many others at Cirencester and Lechlade – where they are depicted in cold, gleaming metal, their feet resting on the humble sheep, or on a woolsack, or, with John Fortey and William Midwinter at Northleach, on both. Inscriptions, as in the case of the elaborate brass commemorating Thomas and Joan Bushe at Northleach, 1525, 'Offe your charite pray for the soule of Thomas Bushe sumtyme M'chant of the Staple of Caleys . . .' gain an extra meaning.

Most of the brasses include the woolman's individual trademark or merchant's mark, usually a monogram, used to identify ownership of goods – a necessary safeguard when such vast quantities of wool were packhorsed to London or Southampton for shipment abroad. After initial sorting and grading at its Cotswold source wool was made up into bales or 'sarplers' of stout canvas, sewn with strong thread. A sarpler contained 2½ sacks (just over 8cwt (about 412kg). Total wool exports declined, from an annual average of 32,000 sacks (5,200 tons) before 1360, to about 12,000 a century later, but this still represented a huge amount of movement of raw wool. The decade of 1431–40 seemed to mark the turning-point, when the amount of cloth exported exceeded for the first time the equivalent quantity of raw wool exported (reckoning one sack of wool equivalent to 4⅓ cloths).

English wool was exported and made into cloth abroad, but the high duties on raw wool (33⅓ per cent in the mid-fourteenth century) burdened foreign manufacturers with heavy costs, thus giving protection to England's home clothing industry. Export duties on English cloth were only 2 per cent, thus making it very competitive. At the same time the formation of the quasi-monopoly of the Company of the Staple, restricting the channels of export of raw wool, had no such influence on cloth exports, with the result that English cloth, made from English wool, could be sold much more cheaply both at home and abroad than could foreign cloth. By the end of the fourteenth century exports averaged 43,000 cloths annually, almost ten times the figure for fifty years earlier, and for most of the fifteenth century and throughout the sixteenth, woollen cloth was England's major export.

Cloth-making is a complex process and, under the medieval guild system, involved numbers of urban craftsmen, each responsible for one part only of the manufacture, with the product changing ownership as it moved from original fleece to finished cloth. Present-day surnames still commemorate the old processes: Weaver, Fuller, Walker, Tucker, Dyer. During the later Middle Ages the English cloth industry became much more widely distributed, and with the general adoption of the fulling-mill by the thirteenth century, became increasingly a rural industry which eventually was concentrated in three main areas – the West Country (Devon, Somerset, Gloucestershire and Wiltshire), East Anglia and the West Riding, with the West Country predominating, where it prospered along river valleys, with their water supplies suitable for cleansing the cloth and operating the fulling-mills.

Fulling or tucking is the process whereby wool, after being woven, scoured and washed, is shrunk, felted and thickened into cloth. Originally done by treading or 'walking' (hence, walk-mills), it became mechanised.

Arlington Row, Bibury, is owned by the National Trust. The seventeenth-century weavers' cottages were probably converted from a medieval wool store or barn

Heavy wooden mallets or hammers, controlled by cams on an axle driven by a waterwheel, fall alternately on to soaped and folded cloth in a trough of warm water. After further washing and drying, by being stretched on racks between oak tenter-posts, large quantities were exported as undyed broadcloths. From the sixteenth century these tended more and more to be 'roughed', a post-fulling process involving raising a 'nap' by stroking with teasel-heads in a handle, later on a rotary frame. The raised woolly surface was then shorn with large hand-shears, and the resultant cloth was dyed in the piece before tentering.

The location of the cloth industry was not necessarily related directly to wool supplies, although the nature of the latter obviously influenced the type of cloth produced. Good supplies of running water were far more important in cloth-making than readily available local wool, which could always be easily transported.

Domesday Book records many water-mills in the Cotswolds, and although most were undoubtedly corn-mills, it is possible that some, especially in the steep-sided, cornless valleys near Stroud, were fulling-mills. The first documentary reference to a fulling-mill is in 1185, which was owned by the Knights Templar at Barton in Temple Guiting parish. A fulling-mill was recorded at Winchcombe a few years later, and by the end of the thirteenth century others are mentioned at Bourton, Cerney, Fairford, Chedworth, Hawkesbury, Sherborne and near Minchinhampton, while the Abbot of Cirencester owned fulling-mills to which local people brought their cloth for fulling – at a fee, of course.

By the late fifteenth century cloth-making was a well-established rural industry over much of the Cotswolds, organised by capitalist clothiers who bought and owned the wool but arranged for all the work, except fulling, to be done in the workers' own homes, usually with their own tools and looms. Women and girls did the spinning, and the men did the weaving and other finishing processes. Occasionally, clothiers themselves owned the implements used, and in any case marketed the finished product, primarily the undyed broadcloths which dominated the export trade throughout the sixteenth century. Coloured cloths included the 'Stroudwaters' and scarlet 'Castle Combes' which were as well known in Europe as in this country. Although it lies in Wiltshire just beyond the southern boundary of our area, Castle Combe merits mention, not only since, visually at least, it is the apparently perfect Cotswold-type village with stream, bridge, cottages, market cross and church grouped in glorious harmony, but could be regarded as an early industrial rural community. In 1409 Sir John Fastolf acquired the manor through marriage, and for the next thirty years he recruited men for the French wars and clothed them in the red and white cloths made by his tenants. In 1454 the village was inhabited by seventy cloth-workers with their servants and apprentices.

After the Dissolution of the Monasteries, some buildings at Cirencester

Abbey were used as loom-shops, having the space and light suitable for broadcloth looms, which is more than can be said for most of the hovel-like cottages in the villages. It seems possible that the need for space and light within the domestic-weaving ethos may have led to the evolution of certain aspects of traditional vernacular building in the Cotswolds. Indeed, the Dissolution, with its consequent release of vast amounts of monastic land and buildings, coincided with increasing prosperity in the cloth industry.

Around the middle of the sixteenth century English wool became longer and coarser, possibly as a result of improved pasturage arising from early enclosures, or possibly through selective breeding. In any event, heavier fleeces with a longer staple, and hence a different wool quality, brought changes in the textile industry. This coarser wool was more suitable for making worsteds (light fabrics) than for the familiar broadcloths, although these continued to dominate the export trade of cloth. Cotswold clothiers continued to produce their traditional broadcloths during the Tudor period. All evidence suggests there was little or no dyeing of the wool or yarn before making up into cloth. Yarn was spun in the white, dyed in the piece, a standard broadcloth measuring over 60in (1.5m) wide and 26–8yd (23–5m) long. But by the turn of the sixteenth century the cloth trade was moving away from woollens to worsteds, partly as the result of technical improvements in spinning. The clothing industry shifted, geographically, towards Somerset and Devon, East Anglia, and later on to the West Riding. Within the Cotswolds themselves the industry had largely died out in the north and east but was expanding around Stroud and Painswick, Dursley and Wotton-under-Edge.

This increasing importance of the south Cotswold area is revealed by John Smith's list of able-bodied men for 'His Majesty's Services in the wars within the County of Gloucester', compiled in 1608 (see table on p66), which showed that at least 40 per cent of all male workers were engaged in the clothing industry. Most of these were employed as weavers and fullers or tuckers. Only about 5 per cent of the available men were described as clothiers, but it is their houses, and sometimes those of a few broadloom weavers, which offer the most tangible evidence of the seventeenth-century prosperity. Elsewhere in the Cotswolds 28 villages had only 1 weaver each, 5 villages had 2 weavers, and over the main wolds area only about 60 weavers were recorded in Smith's survey.

The clothing industry of the southern Cotswolds was organised on an essentially capitalist basis from Tudor times to its decline early last century. As Josiah Tucker wrote in 1757, 'one person with a great stock and a large credit buys the wool, pays for the spinning, weaving, milling, dyeing, shearing, dressing etc. That is, he is master of the whole manufacture from first to last and probably employs a thousand persons under him.' Larger clothiers, such as the Halydays and Spillmans of Rodborough, the Sheppards at Horsley and the Playners at Woodchester, owned mills at which their cloth was fulled. Others, like Witchell of Wotton-under-Edge, were large-scale manufacturers,

Workers in Woollen Manufacture 1608 (extracts)

	Clothiers	*Weavers*	*Broadloom Weavers*	*Fullers, Tuckers*	*Dyers*	*Total*	*Total of all workers*
Minchinhampton	4	33	-	23	1	61	169
Woodchester	7	16	-	6	3	32	50
Rodborough	6	43	-	11	1	61	118
Horsley	1	36	1	12	1	51	124
Avening	-	16	1	-	-	17	90
Nailsworth	2	8	2	13	-	25	30
Painswick	4	33	-	10	-	47	161
Bisley	1	36	-	16	1	54	164
Uley	3	10	19	-	-	32	56
Owlpen	-	13	-	1	-	14	17
Wotton	15	34	-	6	1	56	152

although they neither owned nor rented a mill. Lesser clothiers were lessees of fulling-mills who worked on a much smaller scale, but still owned the cloth at all stages of its manufacture. Employees of all clothiers had few possessions themselves, but managed to remain semi-independent and often worked for several clothiers.

The super-fine broadcloths were prescribed by statute to be 26–8yd (23–5m) long and to weigh not less than 44lb (20kg). Weaving looms, which varied in width and detail according to the cloth being produced, would be housed in larger-than-average rooms in the weavers' cottages, either on the first or ground floor. No early cottages survive, although many small seventeenth-century houses in places like Painswick, Wotton-under-Edge and Bisley would have been weavers' houses, where, with the help of his family a weaver could produce 10–12ft (3–4m) of cloth a day, so that a single broadcloth would take two to three weeks to make, and a good weaver might make twenty such cloths a year. Woven into each cloth was the clothier's mark by which he could be identified, usually an angular design sometimes incorporating a cross or a sign representing a shepherd's crook, and often including the clothier's initials.

Although in Tudor times Cotswold cloth was sold white, or undyed, and most was intended for the overseas market, the seventeenth century saw coloured cloths coming more into prominence, when it was realised that the pure, clear water from springs and streams in the southern part of the area produced the finest dyes. Writing around the middle of the century Thomas Fuller commented that '. . . the best of Reds are dyed Stroud Water. Hence it is that this district hath afforded many wealthy clothiers.' Water had always been necessary to wash wool, to full and rinse cloth, and once mechanisation had been introduced, to turn waterwheels. Now it became even more important.

Deep, steep-sided valleys around Stroud, and from Dursley down to Kilcott, spring-fed and dissected down to the impermeable lias clays, were admirably suited to the building of small reservoirs needed to conserve water to supply large fulling-mills and dye-sheds of the coloured broadcloth industry. The climate was suitable, and an average rainfall of 34in (86cm) helped to maintain sufficient air humidity to make for the easier working-up of wool into cloth.

Not a great deal is known about the dyes used, although some were obtained from local plants. Dyer's Greenwood (*Genista tinctoria*), sometimes known as Dyer's Broom, was used for making a yellow dye. Mixed with woad or indigo it could produce various shades of green. Dyer's Rocket (*Reseda luteola*) also yielded a yellow dye, while Woad (*Isatis tinctoria*), now very rare, was commonly used as a mordant or base for black dye. Celia Fiennes, visiting a relative near Moreton-in-Marsh in 1694, wrote that on her ride from Toddington, over the 'high hills' to Moreton she saw 'some of this land improved in the produce of woads which the dyers use . . . a plantation of about 12 acres [4.8ha] would employ 2 or 3 familyes men women and children, and so they generally come and make little hutts for themselves for the season to tend it.' She noted the process: 'In the mill with a horse they grind the leaves into a paste, so make it up in balls and drye them in a Penthouse to secure it from the raine, only the wind dryes it.' There was a woad-mill on the Ey Brook near Moreton which was apparently working in 1656. Madder (*Sherardia arvensis*) was also in demand for the red dye extracted from its roots, but once a good overseas trade in cloth was established imported dyes became more popular, particularly cochineal and indigo, and many shades and colours could be obtained from the crushed wood fibre of exotic trees that were shipped into Bristol. Synthetic dyes were not available until the second half of last century.

Throughout the seventeenth century clothiers gradually extended their range of colours. Merino wool, imported from Spain by 1570, was being brought to the area already dyed to make a material known as Spanish cloth, or Medleys, and proved very successful, although it naturally aroused local jealousies, upset the wool market, and produced yet another breed of middlemen, the yarn-broggers. However, after unsettled decades around the middle of the century a more settled period followed the Restoration, and between about 1670 and 1720 many Cotswold towns, especially in the south, took on the appearance we admire today.

The few early mills that survive do so because they changed from cloth to corn-milling before the 1820s when many older mills were rebuilt. Four streams water the Painswick valley, all of them now so insignificant that it seems hard to realise how many mills they once powered. The most important one served at least a dozen mills, most of them named on the 1:25,000 map

Loveday's Mill at Painswick. The mill house (right) dates from 1670–80; the 'new' factory behind is early nineteenth century

(Pathfinders 1089 and 1113), and an exploration of the Painswick stream from Cranham to Pitchcombe, much of it by footpaths, shows many of these mills and the mill houses. Most mills have been converted, either into houses or flats, but without greatly disguising their former uses. All date from the seventeenth century, confirmed by date-stones: Damsell's Mill, 1674; Cap Mill, 1678, but known to have existed in 1622; Painswick Mill, 1634; Loveday's Mill and King's Mill, architecturally the most interesting, were probably built *c*1670–80, the latter having a wing showing impressive loom-shop windows on two floors. These were used as a pin factory in 1863, when Painswick Mill had turned to silk manufacture.

The story of Painswick's mills, their fluctuating fortunes and the adaptation to other uses, is repeated elsewhere in the southern Cotswolds. It may be difficult to imagine Painswick as the busy centre of a thriving industry, yet it was that clothing trade which was responsible for its late seventeenth- and eighteenth-century prosperity whose houses delight us today. More importantly, its clothiers stayed put, most of them for five or six generations. This was not the case everywhere. At Wotton-under-Edge, easily the most charming of the other clothing towns of the south Cotswolds, Hugh Perry, a local mercer, who subsequently became an alderman in London and died in 1634, left £300 for an 'Almshouse, to be laid with gardens etc, as the trustees should think fit, for six poor men and six poor women'. Another local benefactor, Thomas Dawes, was similarly generous. Today, the Hugh Perry Hospital Buildings and the Dawes Hospital form a beautiful group in the heart of the town, modernised to provide ten flats of varying sizes for old people. An inscription above the entrance appropriately includes the representation of a woolsack. At Cirencester and Campden, Northleach and Tetbury, at Stroud, Horsley and Bisley as well as many other places, seventeenth-century clothiers bestowed their charity, no longer on the already improved churches, but on endowing almshouses and schools.

Eighteenth-century writers and historians describe the rise and fall of the fortunes of Cotswold villages and towns. Around 1720 Defoe had found Cirencester 'a very good Town, Populous and Rich and full of Clothiers and driving a great Trade in wool', yet less than sixty years later Rudder could only report 'formerly the clothing business flourished here, but at present little is done in that manufacture . . . the business of wool-combing is on the decline'. In 1757 Bishop Pococke described Stroud as 'a sort of capital to the clothing villages', and with increasing prosperity was approaching the status of a small town.

In that year Gloucestershire's sheep population was 400,000, but the cloth industry in and around Stroud required 2–3 million fleeces annually. Dealers bought wool from all over the country – from the Midland counties, Kent, Ireland. They regularly visited the markets of Hereford, Leominster and Ross-on-Wye for the still unrivalled Ryeland fleeces, and waggonloads of wool poured into Cirencester and Tetbury, the two great wool-staples of the area.

Finished cloth was still exported to Europe, but most of the West of England's products, which included Cotswold cloth, seems to have been directed to the growing New World colonies and to the East India Company's trade with the Levant. But a great deal was for the home market. Uley Blues clothed elegant country squires, Stroudwater Scarlets clothed the army on the battlefields of Europe, and the less conspicuous dun or olive-coloured cloths, heavily felted to produce almost waterproof capes, protected coachmen and carriers on their hazardous journeys along the new turnpike roads. Children in the Charity Red Coat and Blue Coat Schools wore cloaks made in the south Cotswolds. It was Edward Sheppard, maker of the Uley Blues, of the great Horsley and Minchinhampton family of clothiers which had set up business early in Jacobean times, who built Gatcombe Park in 1770. Yet Edward's son Philip fled to Dunkirk early in the following century to escape his creditors, having spent £100,000 in thirteen years.

While these rich clothiers could generally survive fluctuations in trade, the vastly overmanned workforce was the first to suffer in the lean years, and many weavers were reduced to cheating, stealing and sometimes rioting. Punishment was severe; theft of even a small amount of wool would invoke imprisonment, while the stealing of cloth from the tenters on which it was drying might result in the death penalty. A weaver's wage towards the end of the eighteenth century, for an average working day of fourteen hours, was

10s a week. Employment was by no means continuous, and usually one day every two or three weeks was in any case an unpaid one, when a weaver would have to walk up to 6 miles (9.6km) to fetch wool from a wool-store and to take back the woven cloth. It is not surprising that the earnings of women and children from their carding, spinning and winding were necessary supplements to a weaver's income.

Clothing prosperity, which peaked around the end of the eighteenth century, almost inevitably brought in its wake some complacency, some new clothiers and a degree of competition. Small mills were built wherever available space occurred along the banks of streams and rivers, some little more than cottages with a couple of rooms above a small mill-leat channelled beneath, turning an internal waterwheel. Many of these have vanished and others have been so converted as to be unrecognisable as mills. Reeds and rushes with overhanging willows mark the sites of old mill pools and small reservoirs and it is hard to realise that between 1790 and 1825 about two hundred new mills or associated buildings were added to the south Cotswold scene, and dozens of new settlements sprang up to house the spinners and weavers. Almost all of these were on common land unsuitable for farming, and the hillsides above Chalford, Nailsworth and Stroud show cottages and

Dunkirk Mill, near Nailsworth. Today it is being converted into flats

terraces of this period, linked by narrow, tortuous lanes among the garden plots. Some such groups represented speculative building, with terraced cottages each housing two looms let at an annual rent of £6–£9, about the same as agricultural labourers would have to pay for their rented cottages. Wages were around 10s a week, supplemented by the meagre earnings of wife and children, to a total of 12–13s a week. A weekly food budget for a family of six at the beginning of the 1800s would have been about 8s. With the cost of fuel, candles and soap there was little to spare, and poverty was widespread.

Yet great mills were built, none finer than that at King's Stanley, which was begun in 1813. No wood was used in its construction. Walls are of brick, with stone quoins, and its five floors are supported on a cast-iron frame whose decorative arcades survive. Window-frames and glazing-bars are also of iron, and the whole structure was designed to reduce fire risk. Marling & Evans now occupy the mill, manufacturing clothes for their 'County Collection'. It was Samuel Marling who built the great mill at Ebley in 1818, in fine, coursed freestone, with stone-mullioned windows, to which was added a split-level wing in 1862. The whole building has been recently cleaned and adapted for use as the Stroud District Council offices.

Dunkirk Mill, near Nailsworth, is probably the largest mill in the Stroud area, the result of accretive growth over at least sixty years. In 1767 it was a corn-mill but was repeatedly enlarged through to the 1820s as indicated by a series of date-stones; the last stone (1820) bears the initials of Peter Playne, its most successful owner. Although only a few of the many early and later nineteenth-century mills in the Stroud and Nailsworth valleys continue to produce cloth, a number of the buildings survive and are best seen by exploring the Stroud Valleys Pedestrian and Cycle Trail which follows the tracks of the old Midland Railway branch line from Stonehouse to Nailsworth.

But these great buildings reflect only the past glories. As early as 1830 the clothing industry of the south Cotswolds was approaching a crisis, facing strong competition from Yorkshire and Europe. By 1840 the power-loom had replaced the old hand-looms, and younger workers were overcoming their hatred of factories, realising that they could earn better wages there than at home. By 1861 the number of Gloucestershire workers in the woollen industry had fallen to about 6,700; thirty years later the figure was 3,900, but diversification and the introduction of new industries have helped to keep many of the nineteenth-century mill buildings still occupied, and the well-known, so-called teasel tower at Woodchester has been converted into a private house.

5
COTSWOLD BUILDINGS

Social changes which gradually evolved during Tudor times accelerated following the Dissolution of the Monasteries, 1537–40, and continued into the early seventeenth century. The wool merchants and clothiers who had prospered particularly during the fifteenth century built fine churches, enlarged others, founded and endowed schools and almshouses. For such people the Dissolution opened up new opportunities since the resultant availability of monastic land, coinciding with the new prosperity, made it possible for them to join the ranks of the gentry and build new houses. Where available, stone quarried from monastic ruins was used, as in the case of Newark ('new work') Park near Ozleworth, where Sir Nicholas Poyntz, former steward of Kingswood Abbey, built his house soon after the Dissolution. It could be claimed that the first flowering of the Cotswold style of domestic building, with its distinctive medieval mannerisms such as gables, dripmoulds, four-centred arched doorways, mullions and decorative finials, originated in the rich clothier district of the south Cotswolds.

The relative remoteness of the Cotswolds allied to a long tradition of building by skilled masons helped to maintain a style that was suited to the locality. Expressed simply, the Cotswold style was the result of three things – money, masons and materials – and these continued to be available, creating an awesome continuity which extended even into the early nineteenth century. The style reached its full flowering, however, between the last quarter of the sixteenth century and the first quarter of the eighteenth, but continued to flourish, happily absorbing Renaissance and Georgian influences, as well as the early Victorian and later Gothic revivals. Details and proportions changed but the noble unity imposed by stone obtained from local quarries and used by local masons survived intact – all of which sometimes creates dating problems.

David Verey has estimated there are over a hundred manor-type houses surviving in the Cotswolds, varying from the modest to the sizeable, and dating from c1550 to 1650, all of which are very similar in style. Most are predominantly domestic and rural rather than urban, and most are vernacular rather than 'polite', a distinction mooted by Dr R. W. Brunskill, which requires some explanation.

Vernacular buildings are those which are permanent rather than temporary, traditional in design and inspiration rather than academic and formal, made from local materials by local craftsmen, to serve the everyday needs of local people in their homes, farms and simple industries. They are, nevertheless, designed and built with some thought given to their appearance. 'Polite' architecture is more likely to be produced by professional architects, following stylistic rules and often using materials to suit these rather than simply making use of what is available nearby.

The real difference is one of degree and this varies with social status and time. Broadly speaking, houses of the 'first Cotswold rebuilding' of c1540–1640 would have been the homes of people of local importance – the lord of the manor, wealthy merchants, woolmen, clothiers, yeomen farmers

The east side of High Street, Burford, features some good examples of fifteenth- and sixteenth-century frontages

or lesser gentry. From 1660, after the Civil War interregnum, perhaps until about 1720 or 1730, as wealth spread down the social scale, more and more clothiers, farmers and professional people, such as merchants, attorneys, doctors and clergy, built themselves new houses. From later in the eighteenth century until about 1850–60 cottages were built in villages to house the increasing numbers of workers in the clothing trade, quarrymen and other artisans. Although many of these were in small terraces they continued the vernacular tradition.

No pre-Reformation houses built by the great medieval wool merchants of Northleach, Cirencester and Fairford remain. William Grevel's house at Chipping Campden, completed before his death in 1401, is a rare survival, a hall-house which is still occupied, with its most distinguished feature a two-storey Perpendicular bay-window, gabled and surmounted by gargoyles. Burford, which prospered from the wool trade from the fourteenth to sixteenth centuries and then declined, has a number of houses dating from that period, many having timber-framed upper parts on stone lower storeys, and some still showing original wooden-framed windows on their upper floors. Other known fifteenth-century houses were altered in Georgian times, sometimes to accommodate shops on the ground floor. Fourteenth-century stone doorways are incorporated into a number of houses of later rebuilding, and identifying these is just one of the many pleasures of strolling through Burford's streets.

Two houses in Broadway have associations with Evesham Abbey, which owned the manor. Both the Abbot's Grange, off The Green, but not overtly visible, and Prior's Manse in High Street, date from about 1320. Both have been extensively altered but retain recognisable medieval features, but far more satisfying is the priest's house at Buckland, nearby. Buckland Rectory is the most complete medieval parsonage in the Cotswolds, stone-built and dating from the fifteenth century, with an impressive hall complete with open timbered roof. Occasionally open, the rectory presents a virtually unaltered front to the west, and is easily seen from an adjoining lane. Elkstone's priest's house, south of the church, though older, was extensively altered in the sixteenth and seventeenth centuries.

At Shipton-under-Wychwood the Shaven Crown Inn, traditionally a guest-house of Bruern Abbey, was more likely to have been built as an inn catering for visitors to the abbey, and dates from the fifteenth century. Somewhat later, although mutilated by subsequent alterations, the George Hotel at Winchcombe, built for pilgrims to the abbey, and possibly to Hailes Abbey nearby, has carved in the spandrels of its doorway the initials of Richard Kidderminster, abbot immediately before 1525. There is a timbered courtyard with an open gallery on one side and an arched stone doorway.

Although many timber-framed houses were refronted in stone in Georgian times, exposed timbering, probably dating from the sixteenth century, is seen at Chipping Campden, Cirencester, Northleach and at other Cotswold towns as well as in many villages. Cruck-framing is less common, although

Owlpen Manor, near Uley, has parts which date from the sixteenth, seventeenth and early eighteenth centuries

Friday Street in Painswick shows an example. By far the best known is a cottage at Didbrook, below the scarp near Stanway, whose crucks are exposed almost in text-book perfection at one end of the building, and may be of fifteenth-century date, although the cottage was later encased in stone. Of the many houses built during the century after the Reformation, most remain in private ownership and are not normally open to the public. Edward Silvester, a Burford clothier, built in 1558 Falkland Hall, in High Street at the corner of Priory Lane, a magnificent three-storey house with a tiny first-floor oriel window. Why its important façade is now visually wrecked by a huge, untidy notice-board, which could be well placed elsewhere, baffles me. Simon Wisdom, who had founded Burford's grammar school in 1571, lived in a handsome courtyard house in High Street, probably built about 1555 and now occupied by an antique shop. Wisdom's initials, SW, appear on 'The House of Simon' a little way up the street, dating from the 1580s, and he also built the three-gabled cottages at the bottom of High Street in 1576.

The southern Cotswolds are particularly rich in sixteenth- and early seventeenth-century houses. Owlpen Manor, arguably the most picturesque of all Cotswold manor houses, retains medieval timber framing in its east wing which had Georgian sash windows inserted in 1720. The central hall and great chamber above were added in 1540 and the three-storey bayed west wing in 1616. Chavenage House, near Tetbury, has a date-stone of 1576 and is a typical E-shaped Elizabethan house, not unlike Ablington Manor near Bibury, built by John Coxwell in 1590. Unfortunately, this latter hides behind a high wall in the village, and in the view from the south side of the river it is largely obscured by trees.

Prinknash Abbey originated as a fourteenth-century grange and hunting lodge belonging to the Abbot of Gloucester, but was enlarged about 1514 by the last abbot. It was given in 1928 to the Benedictines of Caldey and formed the first abbey building. It can be visited today, on foot only, by a short walk from the modern building, and is revealed largely as an early sixteenth-century house, albeit with Victorian alterations. Whittington Court east of Cheltenham and visible from both the A40 and the minor road to the village, dates from the 1550s. Although part of the house has been destroyed, the surviving three-gabled structure, with Renaissance details, is convincingly Cotswold Tudor. So, too, is Chastleton House, just over the Oxfordshire border near Stow-on-the-Wold. Built by Walter Jones, a Witney wool-merchant, shortly after he obtained the estate in 1602, this is one of the least-altered houses in the Cotswolds. Its memorable south front, which is three-storeyed with five narrow gables and massive staircase towers at each end, suggests a Robert Smythson influence, but there is no documentary proof of such a connection.

The Jacobean lodges and gateway of Sir Baptist Hicks' manor house at Chipping Campden only lightly hint at the grandeur of the house itself, which was built in 1613 and destroyed either deliberately or accidentally during the

Chastleton House was built around 1600 by Walter Jones, a Witney wool merchant

Lodge Park, built in 1655 as a deer-coursing pavilion. It is now owned by the National Trust (Sherborne Estate)

Civil War in 1645. An eighteenth-century drawing, presumably a copy of a contemporary illustration, shows a five-bay house of three full storeys plus gables, rich in Renaissance detail, with a cupola above the centre, all ornately Italian. The curtain-wall between the two lodges contains chimneys in its two finials. In the grounds and visible over the wall, the former almonry and two pavilions also survive, while in Church Street nearby the Hicks Almshouses of 1612 of eight gabled bays with some Renaissance features were built as an elongated 'I' (for King James) to house twelve pensioners from Campden. They continue to do so.

Bibury Court, now an hotel, was built largely in 1633 by Sir Thomas Sackville, and shows Renaissance enrichments, although it is not so dramatically and gloriously ostentatious as the gatehouse to Stanway House, which was possibly the work of the Cotswold master-mason, Timothy Strong, who used one of the best of all local stones, that from Temple Guiting quarry, an orange-yellow which positively glows in the sunlight of an autumn afternoon. The house itself, 1580–1640 but extensively modified since, presents a rather bleak appearance by comparison.

Forming an interesting contrast with Stanway's gatehouse but probably contemporary with it are a number of early seventeenth-century houses in the large parish of Bisley. Many were built and ornamented by lesser clothiers who also farmed and reared sheep in the intricate and remote side valleys north-east of Stroud. Apart from some careful alterations and additions by

Norman Jewson, c1930, they have survived remarkably little changed, but to find them good navigation along a web of minor roads and very narrow lanes is needed. Lower Througham (*921078*) typifies them, a little gem of a gabled courtyard house with dovecotes in two gables, mullioned casement windows with continuous dripmoulds, decorative quatrefoils, stone rainwater gutters and chutes, and a magnificent stone-slate, moss-mottled roof.

Two miles (3.2km) south of Sherborne is one of the Cotswolds' most unusual and distinguished buildings. Lodge Park forms part of the Sherborne estate acquired in 1987 by the National Trust, and was designed as a lodge at the centre of John Dutton's new deer park, with a great banqueting hall on its first floor, and a broad balcony and the roof leads above from which ladies and gentlemen could watch the coursing of deer by greyhounds. Valentine Strong is said to have been the master mason for Dutton, who was a friend of Cromwell's and was thus able to build Lodge Park probably in the mid 1650s, an unusual time for new building.

More settled conditions following the Restoration allied to a revival of the wool trade and an expanding cloth industry encouraged an upsurge in new building throughout the area. Many towns and villages acquired their characteristic appearance during the second half of the seventeenth century. Classical ideas slowly infiltrated; steep gables were maintained but houses

Bisley Street, Painswick. This is 'The Chur', which is late fourteenth century with a doorway of that period and walls of large, rough masonry

Medford House at Mickleton was built in 1694

became more symmetrical, often square with two parapeted gables on the front, with a one- or two-light window in each gable, and increasingly larger windows beneath, all stone-mullioned with dripmoulds. Chimneys tended to be moved from gable-ends to inner walls, and stacks were given individual treatment in the clean, moulded ashlar, while restrained classical ornament was applied. But it is the secondary gables with their dormer windows lighting rooms in the roof space that are the most characteristic feature of the Cotswold scene. Cutting into the pitch of the roof, with resultant valleys in the angles, they provide not only a varied skyline in a row of cottages or even a single house but also introduce a fresh interplay of sunlight and shadow in roof texture changing throughout the day.

As Alec Clifton-Taylor has pointed out, the Cotswold style avoids monotony because, 'with no structural features other than gables, chimney-stacks and windows it was possible to play a large number of variations on the theme'. The stone allowed the introduction of the occasional extravagance as finial, date-stone, doorway or fine bay-window.

Painswick, more than any other Cotswold town, suggests that no clothier of the late seventeenth century would dream of living in a house that was mean or ugly. Few places have such a concentration of superb houses both of that period but also of the early part of the following century. The silver-grey, light-holding limestone shows to perfection the exuberant expertise of masons, with gables, porches, pillars and mouldings creating a succession of surfaces, shadows and textures, so that each corner reveals a fresh delight.

By the turn of the century a new middle class was emerging, some members rising from the ranks of labourers. Recognising the need to equip itself with the appropriate signs of wealth, if only modestly at first, the newly affluent would introduce elements of more elaboration, especially to house façades, through improved doorways, canopies or hoods above them, larger windows, or decorative roundels. Thus were the former Tudor-style fronts given a new look. Again, almost any village or small town provides examples. At Mickleton below the escarpment's northern foot Medford House is a text-book illustration of the transition from Cotswold vernacular Tudor to the calmly classical Queen Anne. Mullioned and transomed windows persist, small dormers in a hipped roof have replaced the former tall gables, the doorway and the pediment above the central window show Renaissance decoration, and the ovals on each side would earlier have been in the front gables. In the quiet heart of the wolds north of Withington the surviving half of Cassey Compton, contemporary with Medford House, has very similar details, while Nether Lypiatt Manor near Bisley, built in 1702–5, illustrates how the Queen Anne style has absorbed the Cotswold idiom. This miniature 'grand house', only 46ft (14m) square, apparently influenced by the far grander Coleshill in Berkshire, has perfect symmetry, and although some windows retain mullions and transoms, those of the important entrance front (west) show full height sashes within restrained architraves, and the whole building is elegantly set some distance behind a screen of stone piers linked by wrought-iron grilles with a pair of very fine wrought-iron gates. On a more modest scale, the Vicarage, formerly Loveday's House, and Dover House, both in Painswick, show Cotswold early Georgian at its best, and date from around 1720.

Throughout the Cotswolds neat, modest houses grace town streets or occupy prominent positions in village after village. Too numerous to mention, they illustrate the elegance and charm characteristic of the period, almost always handled with a degree of restraint. Because local stone continued to be used for walls, dressings, details and roofs, the harmony of an urban street or a village group was rarely disturbed. Ground-floor bay-windows such as those in the High Streets at Chipping Campden, Burford and Broadway often combined with the front door beneath a single hood, probably represent early nineteenth-century additions, sometimes to accommodate shop fronts.

By then increasing numbers of terrace cottages were being built and these smaller houses departed from tradition only in often having wooden lintels above doors and windows. Some were wholly plain, others retained small dormers. One result of these nineteenth-century additions, which at the time probably represented in-filling, is that streets in places such as Chipping Campden, Blockley, Burford, parts of Painswick, Wotton-under-Edge, Tetbury and particularly Cirencester, acquired the continuous frontages that may be seen today, creating a satisfying architectural harmony. Admittedly, many of the larger houses, especially in Cirencester, have new uses, but their frontages remain little changed, so the image of eighteenth-century prosperity persists. The later artisans' cottages have become highly sought-after 'desirable residences' commanding high prices, although their present appearance and condition bears little resemblance to those of the original structures. If these humbler cottages continued the vernacular tradition into the nineteenth century, 'polite' architecture was introducing to an increasing extent the more formal and elegant houses gracing the streets of many Cotswold towns, especially in the south. These, and the few large country houses, have nothing to do with 'Cotswold style'; only the use of local stone in the skilled hands of masons continued the vernacular thread. Finely cut ashlared stone, crisp details in columns, capitals, pediments, door-hoods and window surrounds mark the work of these Georgian craftsmen, as a walk around Cirencester, Tetbury, Burford, Painswick and Chipping Campden will illustrate. Many older houses show clearly their new, imposing, higher frontages added in the eighteenth century, with individual examples too numerous to mention, while in the country the modest houses of Cotswold's gentry had their Georgian changes and additions, with Snowshill Manor (NT) being a good example.

Romantic ideas infiltrated quite early. Adlestrop Park, east of Stow-on-the-Wold, shows Sanderson Miller's pioneering exercise in Gothic Revival, 1750–62. On the opposite side of the A436, and even less visible in its parkland, is Daylesford House, designed by Samuel Pepys Cockerell for Warren Hastings in 1787. Cockerell, who was architect to the East India Company, was obviously inspired by Indian-Muslim architecture and later designed for his brother Charles one of the most famous and distinctive houses in the country. Begun in 1805, Sezincote was basically a Georgian house encased in an exotic oriental skin, faced with orange-coloured stone said to have been artificially stained to produce an Indian tone. A viridian-green copper onion dome dominates, balanced by dainty, small-domed minarets at the corners, linked by a very deep cornice at eaves level. The whole concept, set in parkland and gardens for which Repton's advice was sought, is, in Alec Clifton-Taylor's words, 'a most original and unusual house . . . a building of true delight'.

The Industrial Revolution did not bring widespread wealth to the Cotswolds, and even in the few towns there was no large-scale factory development requiring a big influx of workers who needed housing in the concentrated numbers which happened in the north. However, the huge increase in demand for food provided golden opportunities for the Cotswold farmers, whose individual prosperity peaked about the middle of the nineteenth century, albeit against an overall background of rural poverty arising from the decline in the wool and cloth industry. In addition to reorganising and developing their farms, many landowners started to build new cottages in villages for their labourers, from materials quarried locally, probably on their own estates, and following the traditional style, so that Victorian estate cottages are almost indistinguishable from those of earlier centuries, except that they tended to be in terraces and invariably had gardens. Upper Slaughter, Windrush, Sherborne, Great Barrington, Hatherop and Beverstone are a few examples that show estate-building.

By the end of the nineteenth century the Cotswolds was suffering from the agricultural depression that had affected most of rural England, brought about by increasing competition from the farms of the New World. Without work rural labourers drifted away from villages and farms became untenanted. Arthur Gibbs graphically described the wolds just before the century's end in his classic *A Cotswold Village*:

> 'Tis a wild deserted tract of country that stretches from Cirencester right away to the north of Warwickshire. For fifty miles you might gallop across undulating fields and meet no human being on your way. We have ridden forty miles on end along the Fosse Way and, save in those curious half-forsaken old towns of Moreton-in-Marsh and Stow-on-the-Wold, we scarcely met a soul on the journey.

He could have written similarly about Burford, Campden, Fairford, Lechlade

Opposite *Sezincote House (1805–7), showing the south front*

Below *Nineteenth-century estate cottages in Great Barrington*

and Northleach, though not about Winchcombe which had Adlard's paper-mill at Postlip, or the places around Stroud which had increasingly become the centre of the cloth industry in the south Cotswolds and is the most Victorian in appearance of all Cotswold towns.

Arthur Gibbs was pessimistic about the future of Cotswold villages, but unknown to him the seeds of a revival had already been sown, largely through the influence of the Arts and Crafts movement. Although its ancestors were the great Victorian architects Butterfield, Scott, Burges, Street and particularly Pugin, all of whom designed churches, public buildings, country houses and vicarages, they rarely designed for the common man. It was William Morris, who had studied architecture under Street, painting under Rossetti, and was greatly influenced by Ruskin, who became the innovative inspiration behind the Arts and Crafts movement. What interested him most about architecture was that every aspect of it involved co-operation and should involve craftsmanship, a philosophy arising from his veneration for all things medieval, when 'buildings were the work of associated labour and the thought of the people'.

As a reaction against the mass-production methods of the Industrial Revolution he founded in 1861 the firm of Morris, Marshall, Faulkner & Company (in 1875, just Morris & Company) to design and make decorative work of all kinds for houses and churches. In 1871 he acquired the lease of Kelmscott Manor, by the Thames east of Lechlade. This Tudor-style Cotswold house remained a lasting joy to him for the rest of his life, representing his ideal if confused world in which reality and romanticism reigned together, with the latter usually dominant.

Morris found constant delight in the traditional buildings of the Cotswolds where he travelled extensively. Passing through Burford on one occasion on a visit to Broadway he was so angered by Street's proposed restoration of the church, which in his view would destroy its medieval character, he wrote a letter, from Broadway Tower where he stayed, which subsequently led to the formation in 1877 of the Society for the Protection of Ancient Buildings.

As exemplified by Morris, the Arts and Crafts philosophy, which peaked roughly between 1880 and 1914, combined a belief in the importance of arts and crafts with a belief in social reform. He lectured widely on these themes, on the need to abolish ugliness in towns, advocating a return to medievalism, and exerted an enormous influence on younger architects of different religious and political persuasions – Norman Shaw, Detmar Blow, J. D. Sedding, W. R. Lethaby, Edward Prior, C. R. Ashbee, C. F. A. Voysey, Edwin Lutyens, Ernest Gimson, Ernest Barnsley and his brother Sidney, who was articled to Shaw. Gimson, the Barnsleys, Ashbee and Blow all came subsequently to live and work in the Cotswolds.

In 1894 Gimson (the 'G' is soft) leased Pinbury, a handsome seventeenth-century stone house in the Frome valley above Sapperton, from Earl Bathurst. Formerly the home of the great Gloucestershire historian Sir Robert Atkyns, it had a good range of outbuildings. Joined there by the Barnsleys, Gimson quickly set about restoring the dilapidated house and gardens, made cottages and workshops from the outbuildings, to which he brought four skilled cabinet-makers from London, including Peter Waals, his Dutch foreman. He also set about training local men and boys, and in Alfred Bicknell, a Sapperton wheelwright, he found an ideal craftsman in metalwork. Although trained as architects, Gimson and the Barnsleys worked in other crafts, particularly furniture-making, but it was inevitably expensive and within reach only of the richer people of the Cotswolds.

About 1900 the trio added a new wing to Pinbury, with a beautiful ceiling and chimney-piece in plaster by Gimson, and in 1904 Earl Bathurst, delighted with what they had accomplished at Pinbury, offered them in exchange for the house a choice of sites on his land at Sapperton where they could build cottages for themselves at his expense. Ernest Barnsley was given the challenge of restoring nearby Daneway House for use as a showroom for their furniture, and to use the outbuildings for new workshops. Three years later Norman Jewson, a young architect working in London, stepped out of a train at Cirencester to begin a walking holiday in the Cotswolds. He visited the Daneway House workshops, called on Gimson in Sapperton, almost immediately fell under the spell of honest craftsmanship, and decided to stay. He later married one of Ernest Barnsley's daughters and moved into Batchelors Court, an early eighteenth-century farmhouse and cottage which he altered.

Jewson worked principally with Ernest Barnsley, largely on alterations and restorations for the SPAB on properties in the area. Barnsley's most important work was Rodmarton Manor (1902–26), near Tetbury, probably the last 'great' house in the Cotswolds, where the Arts and Crafts principles were given full rein. He also designed some cottages in the village. Sapperton itself shows much of the partnership's own housing: in 1901, Gimson built The Leasowes, Sidney Barnsley built Beechanger, Ernest Barnsley built Upper Dorvel House and, in 1912, the Village Hall. Two cottages on The Green were also built by Barnsley. Gimson's last design was for the war memorial cross at Fairford, which was built under Jewson's supervision after Gimson had died in 1919. Jewson himself bought and restored Owlpen Manor in 1926, and around 1930 was responsible for altering and restoring a number of houses around Bisley, including Lower Througham, Througham Slad and Sydenhams.

Contemporary with the activities at Sapperton around the turn of the century a parallel development was taking place in the northern Cotswolds. C. R. Ashbee, who had been training people in various crafts in London's East End, decided to move 150 men, women and children to Chipping Campden, housing them in semi-derelict cottages in High Street. The Woolstaplers' Hall and a derelict silk-mill became workshop premises, where Ashbee's craftsmen made furniture and metalwork, with weaving and other crafts also going on. Board of Education grants made possible the setting up in a disused barn of a school for arts and crafts; guild members taught arts and crafts to local schoolchildren, who were also given swimming lessons in a pool made behind an old mill-dam. A social club was opened, Morris dancing was revived and for Ashbee's guild, Campden seemed an ideal place in which to continue craftsmanship and the decorative arts. But it eventually proved to be the death of the Guild of Handicrafts. This was partly the result of an economic slump but also because Ashbee had removed himself from his markets, and the guild went into liquidation within a few years and many members returned to London. However, an Indian admirer, Dr A. K. Coomeraswamy, bought the guild's printing presses and moved them to the derelict Norman chapel at Broad Campden in 1907, and Ashbee himself had obtained American financial backing which enabled him to acquire a farm, with the aim of running it as part of a dual-economy system in which guild members also continued their crafts in the Sheep Street workshops. The idea failed to take on, World War I intervened and the guild eventually closed down in 1920.

In the few years of its existence the guild had started to revitalise the rather moribund town as well as to repopulate it, with the result that Campden became a modest centre for arts and crafts. Some of the guild's aims had been achieved and sufficient numbers of its craftsmen had remained, attracting others of similar sympathies. In 1924 the Campden Trust was formed by Jewson, F. L. Griggs and others, 'to promote the reputation of the town as an art centre and to continue as far as possible the work of the guild formed by Mr Ashbee'. He died in 1942, but his influence continued. Campden's present appearance undoubtedly owes much to him and those like-minded people who have followed his philosophy. Skilled craftsmen, particularly in silver, continue to work in Campden, and what happened in Campden had a spin-off effect on other Cotswold towns and villages.

George Russell bought and restored the Lygon Arms at Broadway and turned it into a famous hotel. His son, now Sir Gordon Russell, established workshops to repair antique furniture and initiated attempts to adapt Gimson's ideas on furniture-making on to a more commercial basis. Both Broadway and Painswick, once in as depressed a state as Chipping Campden, enjoyed an influx of artists, craftsmen and literary people who, recognising the potential of their adoptive communities, determined to support and protect them, and a guild founded at Painswick in 1933 still flourishes. But it is probably due to Jewson, Gimson, the Barnsleys, Ashbee and Guy Dawber, a young architect who was clerk-of-works to Sir Ernest George at Batsford Park, for Lord Redesdale's new mansion in 1882–92, that the 'Cotswold style' was revived, continuing to influence local building styles between the wars.

Although Morris's romantic dreams of medieval simplicity – some may call it prettifying poverty – exerted a profound influence on buildings and design, the inevitable flaw in the ideals of Arts and Crafts architecture was that, being craftsmen-built, such houses were expensive, far beyond the means of the ordinary working man for whom such homes were conceived. However, the Cotswolds can offer one example of labourers' cottages that were specially

An eighteenth-century barn at Daglingworth, which has been converted into a modern house

commissioned. Clough Williams-Ellis designed and rebuilt much of Cornwell village near Chipping Norton in the late 1930s. Although the whole is rather contrived, the situation and constituent parts charming, with everything in Cotswold stone, the Art-Deco effect is now distinctly dated and not really a patch on a genuine Cotswold village that has evolved organically.

Barns

Apart from monasteries and churches, barns were, and many still are, the largest buildings in the Cotswold landscape. A few originated as monastic or ecclesiastic tithe barns, built to store the tenth part of the land's produce that was paid to an abbot or to the clergy to help the relief of the poor and the upkeep of the monastery or church.

An outstanding medieval barn survives at Stanway, built for the Abbot of Tewkesbury in the fourteenth century. Its massive stone roof, with two finials, is supported on massive cruck frames bedded in the walls, with curved braces and two-tiered wind-braces. The fifteenth-century barn at Postlip, with cruck-trusses rising from the stone plinth, has a weather-worn figure carved above a gable, while a contemporary one at Ablington, bigger than most Cotswold churches, has five bays, with finials above the gables. Together with its 1727 extension, also with a porch, it forms part of one of Cotswold's most memorable groups. Arlington Row at nearby Bibury probably originated in the fourteenth century as a wool-store before being adapted into weavers' cottages in the early seventeenth century. At the foot of Bourton-on-the-Hill is Richard Palmer's splendid barn of 1570, with seven bays and gabled porches on its two long sides.

Neither this nor many of the other large barns in the Cotswolds were necessarily tithe barns. Throughout the area, until the time of the late eighteenth-century enclosures corn grown on Cotswold farms was mainly for consumption by the farmer, his family and his workers, so one season's harvest had to last through the year as well as provide seed for next year's crop. In addition oats were a vital source of food for livestock, straw was needed for bedding and a base for animal manure with which to fertilise the fields. When in the eighteenth century more root crops and green animal feed were introduced, yet more storage space was wanted, and at the century's end William Marshall commented:

> The size of the barns in this country is above par. On height above anything I have observed, 52 × 20 feet to the plate [eaves] is esteemed a good barn. This size admits of four bays of 10 feet each with a floor in the middle. And of threshing floors 12 by 14 to 18 by 20 feet. The best of oak but some of stone.

Farms within villages had such barns and after the enclosures brought a migration of village farms to the centre of their newly enclosed fields, new barns of similar size continued to be built up to the beginning of this century. Now, the produce of endless acres of corn goes into vast grain stores. Barns which remain in use store farm machinery and fertiliser; many barns in field situations are disused and derelict, but those within villages are being transformed into luxury homes at luxury prices. Planning permission for these seems readily available, particularly if such buildings are in key positions. A well-converted barn with its shape and character retained is far better than a roofless ruin. Generally, such conversions are most successful where, in the case of very large barns, most of the rooms are concentrated at one end, with the largest amount of space left for storage. Ideally, there should not be too many windows in the long sides, and if integral features such as a dovecote within the gables of a porch can be retained, even if the pigeon-holes have to be blocked up, so much the better.

During the late 1980s several million pounds' worth of redundant barns and other farm buildings such as the gabled dovecote at Coln St Aldwyns have been granted planning consent for conversion into houses, and it is likely that the late twentieth century's contribution to Cotswold buildings will be the large barn conversions at Northleach, Taynton, Southrop, Broadwell, Great Rissington, Hazleton, Avening, Elkstone and a host of other villages.

In addition to dovecotes built into gables of many barns and farmhouses like those at Lower Througham and Turkdean, a number of free-standing dovecotes survive. Documentary evidence about their dates is rare, but generally the circular ones are earlier than c1600, square ones later. Good circular dovecotes exist at Bibury, Farmington, Little Comberton, Daglingworth and Minster Lovell, with square, gabled examples at Lower Slaughter, Naunton and Chastleton, this latter probably being the most unusual and elegant, and the only eighteenth-century representative. By then, the need for encouraging manorial pigeons to nest, and subsequently provide fresh meat for the winter months, was passing. Farming was changing, with ideas for new crops, cropping techniques, animal husbandry and advances in machinery slowly introduced, as though to prepare for large-scale agricultural changes from the late eighteenth century.

Stone and Quarries

Stone for all Cotswold buildings has always been readily available, an apparently limitless supply lying just beneath the surface of the ground throughout the area. Varying considerably in colour, quality and texture from one quarry to another, the best came from the Great Oolite series and was found mainly along an arc running from north of Bath, through Minchinhampton and Northleach to just north of Burford. Good stone came also from certain strata within the Inferior Oolite, in a broader band running across the higher wolds to the north of this. Not all layers yielded stone that was suitable for domestic buildings, and material from the poorer beds was used for lime-burning, road-metal and aggregate, with some for field boundary walls. Nevertheless,

Seventeenth-century cottages at Little Barrington

freestone, the quarryman's name for stone which is closely bedded, free from shell fragments, comparatively soft when first quarried, and which can be cut freely in any direction either with a saw, or with chisel and mallet, can be dressed to produce smooth ashlar or the beautiful and decorative refinements associated with the Cotswold building style.

Generally, the stone is warmer-toned in the north of the region, and is revealed in the rich golden-coloured houses of Broadway, Blockley, Chipping Campden and the nearby villages. To the south, in the Painswick area and down to Wotton-under-Edge, the tone is greyer, sometimes quite pearly. From whatever quarry the stone originates, it is responsive to light and the moods of the day, having the elusive quality of seeming to retain and glow with sunlight. It can also grow lichens, support a range of flowers in its wall crevices, and is always in visual accord with the landscape from whence it came. Atmospheric pollution has not adversely affected the Cotswolds, so its buildings have not been disfigured by dark deposits.

Every town, and probably most villages, had quarries supplying stone that was suitable for buildings. Some quarries are known to have been worked in Saxon times. Taynton is one of these and is also recorded in Domesday. Stone for every Cotswold church probably came from a nearby quarry. A medieval quarry site known to have existed near the Foss Way crossroads was the likely source for stone for Northleach church, while the early clothiers' houses at Burford were of stone from nearby Burford quarries. These, with others at Taynton, Little Barrington and Upton all lying beneath the hills that enfold the lower Windrush, are known to have been worked in the fourteenth century, and were owned by the Strongs and Kempsters during the seventeenth century, when their stone was used for rebuilding in the City of London. The gentle hollow at Little Barrington around whose perimeter are grouped the honey-gold cottages and houses of this lovely village, is believed to have been the quarry from which their stones came.

Medieval and later quarries never became too large, for big quarries were difficult to work. When more stone was needed a fresh quarry would be opened near the previous one, which would soon grass over. Parish and township quarries were usually on common land and even after eighteenth-century enclosures, although villagers lost some common rights, they did retain the right to dig stone from the parish quarry. Estates and large farms had their own quarries which were worked only when stone was needed for new building or repair and a few of these are still used, though only occasionally. Most, however, have long been abandoned, are now grassed over, and have elder and blackberry growing from them, so that they are absorbed into the landscape.

Because good stone was near the surface it was rarely necessary to gouge deep holes, so that, until the advent of huge excavating machines to extract stone for crushing into aggregate, or to make artificial stone bricks, quarrs, the old name for them, were always modest in size. Started by clearing away a rough semi-circle of top-soil, workings gradually bit back into hillsides producing, after many years, rounded cliffs that were rarely more than a dozen feet in height, with a cartway leading away from the base. A broad, flat dressing-floor evolved, with working space for crane and windlass, and for trolleys or sleds to be moved close to the base of the rock-face.

On many hillsides stone was mined rather than quarried, so that the base of the best beds could be reached more easily by tunnels than by having to remove a large overburden of brash. The pillar-and-stall method of extraction was used, and one such mine was at Westington Quarry above Chipping Campden, which yielded most of the stone for the town's buildings. It was entered by a 250yd (229m) tunnel from the quarry-face, but has not been used since early this century when demand for good building stone had slumped to such an extent that mining there became unprofitable. Good examples of once-prolific but now disused quarries can be seen at many places, particularly at Scottsquar above Painswick, above Broadway where the Fish Hill picnic site occupies old workings, above Snowshill and Stanton, and near the Coaley Peak picnic site, where the Cotswold Way threads its route past old quarries just below the scarp edge. Minchinhampton and Rodborough Commons are pitted and pockmarked with old quarries, particularly at their edges. These and most small deserted quarries throughout the Cotswolds have none of the depressing aspects of other forms of industrial wasteland because grass, shrubs and a wide range of plant species have gradually taken over and softened with colour and vegetation the earlier bareness of stone litter and hewn rock.

Some strata within the oolites yield stone sufficiently fissile for use as roofing material. Although it is, geologically, neither slate nor tile, when used for roofing it is usually referred to as Cotswold slate. Formerly quarried near Bisley, Naunton and Stonesfield in the lower Evenlode valley below Charlbury, where slate mines had shafts descending 60ft (18m) below the surface, Cotswold slates of rough, uneven stone attractive to lichen and moss adorn the roofs of countless Cotswold churches, barns, houses and cottages. New slates are not obtainable now, artificially produced substitutes being cheaper. It seems ironic, even though it may make economic sense, that in an area which for centuries produced some of the most felicitous building materials in the world, with enormous quantities still available only four small quarries do produce stone on a regular basis for building or walling. Six larger and deeper workings where stone is extracted mechanically yield a variety of products from beds of different quality. This is used in aggregates, as a basis for reconstituted stone and other concrete products, and for use as agricultural lime. These quarries tend to be shallow (under 40ft (12m) deep), with a large lateral spread, and leave a considerable waste of unusable stone. Extracted material is transported by heavy lorries, as motorists know to their cost. Present planning policy aims to permit present quarries to expand rather than allowing new ones to open, and reserves are estimated to amount to 20 million tonnes, sufficient for many years of extraction at the present rate.

6
COTSWOLD COUNTRYSIDE

Enclosure of Fields

In 1788 William Marshall wrote that the Cotwolds formerly 'lay almost entirely in an open state, namely in arable common field, sheep-walk and cow down. At present it may be said to be in a state of enclosure though some townships remain open.' Enclosures of some open fields, usually by private agreement, had been occurring on a small scale since before the Dissolution, for a commission appointed in 1517 to enquire into agrarian distress had found that 3,843 acres (1,555ha) in Gloucestershire, mainly in the Cotswolds, had recently been enclosed, a process that continued sporadically until well into the eighteenth century.

Ampney Crucis parish, near Cirencester, was enclosed in 1628, its peasants having to accept allotments as compensation for losing their arable strips in the former common fields. In Condicote every individual furlong seems to have been enclosed by 1711, while at Broadwell and Oddington hedges were held in common to provide timber for implements and buildings, although enclosures there were not completed until the late eighteenth century. Peasants at Stowell and Sezincote suffered the complete loss of their villages which were depopulated through emparkment rather than enclosure in the seventeenth century.

Starting as a trickle in the 1720s and 1730s, the scale and pace of enclosure, brought about through parliamentary acts, grew to an irresistible tide that swept village communities into the new world of commercial farming. One factor that contributed to this was the successful introduction to the Cotswolds during the 1670s of the new forage plant sainfoin, a member of the pea family. By the early eighteenth century this, with clover and rye grass, was transforming the gentle slopes of the southern Cotswolds, 'formerly styled the barren part', as a Gloucester farmer wrote. Resultant improved pasturage and the fertilising by animal dung, followed by ploughing and the sowing of corn made it possible for wheat to outstrip barley. In 1712 the manorial lord at Salperton allowed eleven tenant farmers to plough up 18 acres (7.2ha) of common arable land, grow corn for four or five years, then lay down a sainfoin-clover-rye grass for a short time before ploughing again.

As a result of this, Cotswold farms could support more cattle than earlier, without necessarily causing a decline in the numbers of sheep. The additional fodder crops could support both, and inventories show larger flocks than ever before. A substantial farm running 400–500 sheep in the 1660s was able to double this by 1720. Over much of the Cotswolds wheat, barley, oats and peas were the main arable crops, with clover and sainfoin continuing to increase after 1740, together with turnips. Improved fodder crops made it possible for larger farmers to overwinter livestock on their own farms instead of sending them down to better land in the vales.

Enclosures made control of cropping and grazing more efficient. Taking a few parishes at random, their enclosure dates span over a century, with the earliest, 1713, at Farmington, followed by Sherborne, Little and Wyck Rissington in the 1720s. Parliamentary commissioners were parcelling out land at Hawling in 1756, Little Barrington in 1759 and Snowshill in 1761, while the 1770s saw a flurry of acts which changed the landscapes at Adlestrop, Bibury, Bledington, Clapton, Condicote, Hazleton and Naunton. Chipping Campden's arable fields were enclosed in 1799, Great Rissington delayed until 1813, but it was not until 1819 that Withington's four great open fields were enclosed. Attempts to enclose those at Bisley in 1733 were resisted by the hand-loom weavers who were living in small hamlets on the edge of the waste and who kept a horse or donkey to carry yarn or cloth to the local mill. Enclosures were not completed here until 1847, by when almost all of the open arable fields of Cotswold parishes had been enclosed, with most of the wastes and upland commons.

Both Marshall (1788) and Arthur Young, who visited the Oxfordshire Cotswolds in 1809, considered that enclosure had beneficial effects on farming, although they regarded the social cost as a separate problem. Enclosure certainly benefited the larger landowner through increased production. At Aldsworth, enclosed in 1793, cattle on one large farm increased from 10 to 20, sheep from 200 to 1,800, and grain production trebled. But small farmers suffered and cottage smallholders suffered more, losing not only their grazing rights on village commons, but often being left with the worst parcels of land; they then had to pay the cost of fencing this and meet their share of the cost of the Enclosure Award as well. Some landless labourers gave up altogether and moved to the towns, but although some depopulation occurred this was not as large-scale as Cobbett had criticised in the 1820s. Aston Subedge, for example, declined after its enclosure in 1751–73 from a population of 104 to 63, but by the 1801 census it had recovered to 101. Cowley shows a different picture following its first enclosures in 1739. Before then there was 1 large farmer with 143 acres (58ha), 10 medium-size holdings and 14 cottage smallholdings. By its last enclosure, 1828, 4 men farmed 1,500 acres (607ha), there were 4 smallholders and 24 landless cottagers. By the middle of last century there was dire poverty among Cotswold labourers but relative prosperity among bigger farmers and landowners.

Although he was writing of Surrey, George Bourne's comments could well apply to much of the Cotswolds. 'To the enclosure of the common more than to any other cause may be traced all the changes that have subsequently passed over the village.' The face of the landscape was changed and, in many instances, so was that of the village. Instead of farmers, cottagers and tradesmen all living in the village street, farmers with consolidated and increased holdings moved out and built themselves new Georgian-style farmhouses at the heart of their blocks of land, leaving their own farmhouses to be subdivided into labourers' dwellings, often identifiable but much-desired cottages today. At Aston Blank, now Cold Aston near Bourton-on-the-Water, names of new farms and the pattern of their fields of 1794 shows clearly on the 1:25,000 map: Windrush Farm, Camp Farm, Elmbank Farm, Bangup Barn (formerly a farm), leaving Manor Farm surviving in the village. In Eastleach parish,

Macaroni Farm, an eighteenth-century enclosure farm, near Eastleach Turville

enclosed in 1773, Macaroni Farm (*185054*), a mile (1.6km) west of Eastleach Turville, typifies the enclosure farmhouse, four-square Georgian within its shelter-belts. Almost every Cotswold village has examples, more likely to be seen by walkers and travellers venturing along the minor roads, lanes and tracks of the area. Some villages do not show this 'farm migration', but retain farmhouses, barns and associated buildings within the village street. Ebrington, in the north, with Winson and Coln Rogers in the Coln valley, are good examples.

The building of 'enclosure' farms away from villages necessitated new roads linking them to the existing network. Indeed, the opportunities presented by the enclosures resulted in many new by-roads coming into existence, often recognisable on the 1:50,000 map, even better on those of larger scale, by the direct way in which they run across country, sometimes from village to village, frequently from village to main road. Aldsworth parish shows good examples in its roads to Sherborne and Northleach, while at Withington the most dramatic change in the landscape was the creation of a new road running in a straight line for 2 miles (3.2km) northwards to meet the main Gloucester–Stow road, the A436, near the significantly named New Farm. Thus, in one year, 1819, Withington's communications with the outside world were changed, and the old 'market way from Cheltenham' running westwards from the village as a ridge route described in an Anglo-Saxon document as 'the old stone way' is now a quiet country lane.

Commenting on the 'field fences' Marshall observed that 'Walls are far more frequent than live hedges. Where good stones are not to be found in plenty near the surface, whitethorn (common hawthorn) is planted and thrives well. But live hedges are expensive to raise. Ditches cannot be sunk, but walls are raised at small expense . . .' Ideally, he felt, a wall and a live hedge together provided the best form of barrier and shelter. This 'belt-and-braces' type of field boundary, a common feature of many upland landscapes, may be the result of walling having been attempted in winter conditions that were so severe that work was brought to a standstill, so hedges were planted. These were not grubbed out when walling was resumed. But walls always had one attraction for landowners in that they could not be broken and burned for fuel by the poor labourers.

Dimensions specified by the parliamentary commissioners were for walls to be 26in (66cm) wide at the base, 18in (46cm) at the top, and 4½ft (137cm) high excluding the coping. Sometimes a comb of stones set in edgeways would provide a finish for the top. Such a wall in 1798 on Guiting Hill would cost 4s 6d per perch (16½ft – 5m) to build, including the cost of stone, digging and hauling. A hedge would cost 6d or 7d, or 1s 6d with a ditch.

Although many field boundaries have been removed during the past two decades the pattern of Cotswold landscape seen from any of the ridge roads is still one that is aesthetically pleasing. The view eastwards, say, from Buckle Street, or from any of the upland roads radiating from Stow, shows walls

The mature landscape of enclosure: the ripening harvest above Guiting Power

and hedges of the late eighteenth-century enclosures softened by maturing hedgerow trees and shelter-belts planted since then. In Marshall's time there was very little woodland, except on the western escarpment. Not only were farms 'in general destitute of wood', there was, 'not a pole upon the farm for a temporary fence or even a handle of brushwood to kindle a fire'. Faggot wood had to be brought from 8–10 miles (13–16km) away, and 'coals fetched 20–30 miles by land carriage', presumably from the Forest of Dean.

Recognising how, 'in winter, the poor, on these shelterless hills, must be in a wretched state, as to fuel', Marshall, who was essentially a practical man, made a suggestion which would not be out of place today in these times of agricultural 'set-aside' and grants for amenity tree-planting. 'It strikes me, forcibly, that the corners and asperities of every estate ought to be cut off, and the angles filled up with coppices; sufficiently extensive to admit of a plot being felled every year, for the use of the farm, and the cottages of the township it lies in.' Whether any notice was taken of this advice is doubtful, for at the turn of the century Cotswold tree-planting took the form of windbreaks, shelter-belts, game coverts and ornamental woodlands, all on a modest scale, around the seats of the gentry and the new isolated farmhouses, and alongside roads, particularly the ever-widening droves. A long strip of beeches and larches was planted early last century to enhance the borders of Stowell Park by the Foss Way, and adjoining the minor road running north-westwards to Puesdown Inn. In recent years restocking with the same species, together with Thuja, has maintained this important landscape feature west of Northleach. Travellers on the A40 here will also see a 2 mile (3.2km) strip of beeches north of the road between the new roundabout and Puesdown, which sheltered the earlier London to Gloucester coaches which preferred this upland route to avoid the stony and marshy way in the valley through Northleach and Hampnett. A few miles east Sherborne Park's shelter-belts still border the A40.

Estate maps and the early Ordnance Survey maps suggest that, by about 1820 or 1830, the Cotswolds were more wooded than they are now, a situation that continued until World War I. Many hillsides were covered with rough woodland and scrub while beeches favoured the thin soils. Much of this marginal land came under cultivation then, and there has been extensive afforestation, private and public, ever since. Today, in the Gloucestershire Cotswolds alone there are over 20,000 acres (8,000ha) of private woodlands, mainly broad-leaved, and the Forestry Commission leases and manages about 2,000 acres (800ha) of mixed broad-leaf and coniferous woodland, including the ancient Guiting woods at the heart of the area, and much of the Stanway estate. Recent conservation policies, with grant-aid available for amenity planting, have encouraged an increasing number of landowners and farmers to enter into dedication agreements with the Forestry Commission to ensure long-term maintenance of the landscape.

Where areas of poor-quality land existed and was of little interest to farmers, stretches of manorial waste tended to remain as unenclosed common land, and in the Cotswolds about 3,500 acres (1,400ha) of commons survive. Most of these are on or near the western scarp, grouped into three main areas. Cleeve Common, 1,000 acres (400ha) dominates the north, controlled by the Cleeve Hill Commoners since 1890, while nearby the 75 acres (30ha) of Charlton Kings Common was bought by Cheltenham Corporation for the benefit of local people in 1927.

Numerous commons in the Painswick area, totalling about 1,050 acres (420ha) include the Beacon, Rudge Hill, Buckholt Wood, Cranham Common, Barrow Wake, Coopers Hill and other woodlands, while in the Stroud area Minchinhampton and Rodborough Commons are fine areas of limestone grassland totalling 820 acres (328ha), which is now in the care of the National Trust, and on the opposite side of the Nailsworth valley Stroud District Council regulates the 150 acres (60ha) of Selsley Common's grassland. To the west Stinchcombe Hill and Stinchcombe Hill Common, covering together about 320 acres (128ha), are magnificent viewpoints near the crest of the scarp, with rough grazing. It is, perhaps, the commons and woodlands that show the greatest concentrations of wildlife interest, and this aspect may be considered now.

Woods, Fields and Commons

Woodland The thin soils which had been left by the Ice Age on the highest parts of the Cotswold plateau supported initially only scrub and light woodland, but as milder conditions gradually returned, predominantly deciduous forest established itself. Peat-bed deposits near Cheltenham, dating from around 6000BC, have revealed pollen grains of hazel, pine and elm in large quantities, with lesser amounts of oak, birch, willow and alder, trees which are still the commonest at the foot of the scarp valleys. Charcoal deposits from the long barrow at Notgrove have been analysed and found to contain ash, cherry, hazel and elm, while the Nympsfield long barrow of c1800BC has yielded charcoal deposits with hazel, beech, ash, oak, alder, yew, cherry, hawthorn, elder and horse-chestnut, all characteristic trees of today's Cotswolds.

As almost any journey across the area will show, ash trees are particularly common, often growing to a considerable height in hedgerows. However, pure ashwood exists only as thin shelter-belts or coppice on the thin valley-edge soils. Mixed ash-oak woodland tends now to be found on the clays of the Upper Lias, as at Guiting and Withington. On the western scarps and in the combes an upward succession tends to occur, with pure oak or oak-ash woodland at the bottom of the slopes, through oak-ash-sycamore to oak-ash-beech near the top, climaxing with pure beechwoods bordering agricultural land on the crest of the scarp. In earlier times beechwoods probably clothed all these areas which are now the Rodborough, Minchinhampton, Selsley and Stinchcombe Commons near Stroud, but woodland clearance for pasture has produced the landscapes seen here today.

Travellers on the M5 south of Gloucester, if they are able occasionally to glance eastwards to the Cotswolds' western scarp, will see the dense, darker woodland that marks the edge. A closer view shows the preserved 'hanger' nature of semi-natural beechwoods clothing the scarp face. Too steep for grazing, and not always easily accessible for convenient exploitation by man, although some felling and coppicing has been practised, there is still an element of wildwood about it. Undoubtedly the best scarp-edge beechwoods occur between Birdlip in the north and Wotton-under-Edge in the south, lying almost wholly on the Inferior oolite. Most are named – Buckholt and Cranham Woods, Pope's Wood, Maitland Wood and Stockend Wood near Painswick, Randwick, Standish and Pitchcombe Woods nearer Stroud, and the almost continuous beechen screen embracing Dursley in a wide arc following the sinuous contours from Stinchcombe Hill to Selsley Common. Westridge Wood sheltering Wotton-under-Edge and Midger Wood east of Hillesley continue the theme southwards. It is significant that the natural history and scenic importance of these beechwoods are safeguarded either through their ownership by conservation bodies or by their designation as nature reserves. The National Trust owns Standish, Stockend and Maitland Woods, Westridge Woods, and a small area of woodland at Coaley Peak. The Woodland Trust owns some beech woodland at Coaley, Laycombe (Wotton-under-Edge) and Stanley, while the Nature Conservancy Council protects 675 acres (273ha) of Cotswold commons and beechwoods above Cranham, collectively the best-known and finest of the beech woodlands of the scarp crest.

Waymarked footpaths and bridleways give good access to most parts of Buckholt Wood (*894131*), where tall mature beeches stand throughout above younger specimens. Common whitebeam, oak, ash and wych elm are also present, with some willow and alder where damper soils occur. Although the tall grey beech trunks support a canopy often so dense that the shrub layer and ground flora are occasionally scanty, an understorey does show a flourishing variety of sapling species such as ash, hazel, hawthorn, holly, wayfaring tree, willow and yew, with an inevitable invasion of sycamore. Brambles and wild roses form a thick ground-cover in many places, and, provided the light intensity is not too low, dog's mercury seems to dominate, with sanicle and enchanter's nightshade on well-drained ground. In shady areas ivy forms gleaming carpets without necessarily showing a desire to climb tree-trunks. The occasional presence in spring of the strange, rare green hellebore, accurately described as a green buttercup, but growing to a height of well over 1ft (30cm) confirms the lime-rich soil. Wood anemones, wood violets, wood sorrel and primroses add to the spring enchantment of this and other woodlands.

Part of Buckholt Wood was formerly coppiced. Present management involves thinning out some timber trees, thus opening out the woodland while at the same time maintaining a good degree of essential beech cover. Although bramble tends to invade the newly opened spaces, it in turn is naturally replaced by young saplings so that the essential vertical woodland structure is maintained. In some areas, lime tends to be leached out of the soil, resulting in the appearance of bracken and bluebells, while honeysuckle replaces traveller's joy.

Most of the usual species of deciduous woodland birds occur in Buckholt, and other beechwoods, although populations are small, probably because of the sparse nature of the ground vegetation. However, seasonal colour changes in the beeches more than compensates for this. Rides and avenues and groups of beeches, full of the morning sun in May, glow with the green radiance as light gleams through half-open leaves, and dappled shadows on the woodland carpet are rarely still. This beechen beauty is a special Cotswold benediction, one which need not be the prerogative of only those who walk or ride the green glades. A stately avenue of tall beeches graces the minor road which climbs into Turkdean from the south, a breathtaking scene which should make even the most prosaic of drivers take the hill a little more slowly. When autumn's fire burns through the woodlands towards October's end, then is the beech's second annual climax of colouring, a harmony of gold, russet, copper and brown as leaves react to sap's withdrawal, the cooling of the air and the lessening of the light, before they die and fall and become part of the deep litter to lie damp on the woodland floor through a hard Cotswold winter.

If the great beechwoods of the Cotswold scarp claim pride of place through their age, size and continuity, those around the Painswick, Slad and Sheepscombe valleys seem to sit most graciously in the landscape, emphasising

In Frith Wood, near Slad. This high forest beech woodland is now a Gloucestershire Trust for Nature Conservation nature reserve

the sensuous shapes of its surface, cushioning the curves, slopes and folds. Nowhere in the Cotswolds does spring sunlight touch the woodlands with such green magic, autumn burnish so vividly, and November mists veil with such delicate mystery. Yet these, like other beechwoods across the plateau and along the sides of dip-slope valleys, are largely the result of plantings by landowners within the last hundred years or so. Laurie Lee recalls that one of his five uncles, working as a forester for local landowners in the early years of this century for 35s a week, planted many of the trees 'rising in Horsley now, in Sheepscombe, in Rendcombe and Coln . . . his are the mansions of summer shade, lifting skylines of leaves and birds, those new blocks of green now climbing our hills to restore their remembered perspectives'.

Perhaps Frith Wood (877086) above Slad was one of these. Now a Gloucestershire Trust for Nature Conservation Reserve of 55 acres (22ha), it is a good example of an even-aged high forest beech woodland, with slender, straight tall trees along both sides of a narrow limestone ridge. This situation has allowed light to enter from each side, thus encouraging a dense understorey of saplings and shrubs. Near the ridge's crest oak and ash stand above spreading areas of bramble, with dog's mercury carpeting the ground. Old quarries at the northern end are now overgrown with ash, whitebeam and yew, and at the opposite end of the reserve a rich variety of trees includes these together with saplings of beech, elder, hawthorn, hazel and field-maple, wild rose and traveller's joy. The management programme here includes some clear felling of mature beeches, to be replaced by young saplings, thus creating a mixed-age woodland. The B4070 Stroud–Birdlip road through Slad touches the northern apex of Frith Wood, with footpaths and bridleways giving good access.

The Cotswold Way passes through many fine stretches of woodland, including Coaley Wood (788999) above Uley. This Woodland Trust reserve of 55 acres (22ha), bought with the help of grants from the Countryside Commission, the Nature Conservancy Council, and the Heinz/World Wildlife Fund programme, is an ancient woodland with mature beech and ash trees and some derelict coppice. Bluebells, wood anemones and wild garlic dominate a rich ground flora, and, following thinning and felling, some replanting has been carried out. Access is from the B4066.

Another Woodland Trust reserve, Lineover Wood (987187) above Cheltenham, which is also threaded by the Cotswold Way, covers 109 acres (44ha) and takes its name from the Saxon 'lime-bank' and contains examples of the rare large-leaved lime. The upper slopes of this ancient woodland have ash, lime, field-maple and hazel coppice, with a number of mature massive beeches. Conifers along the lower northern slopes have shaded out the ground flora, and these are gradually to be removed, with native broad-leaved trees and shrubs introduced. There is easy access to Lineover Wood from the adjacent A436.

At Crickley Hill Country Park (936163) a rich variety of habitats, including woodland, scrub and limestone grassland, illustrate within a small area (150 acres – 60ha) the range of characteristic Cotswold plants. The woodland is typically beech and was probably planted in the late eighteenth century. A number of large mature trees survive, with some ancient oaks, and an understorey mainly of old coppiced hazel with some holly, which may have been planted with the beech so that their evergreen leaves would provide winter cover for game birds on this exposed site. Ground-cover varies with the extent of shade. Where the leaf canopy is dense the woodland floor is bare, apart from May's brief flowering of bluebells. Where the canopy is less dense, sufficient light penetrates to encourage bramble to take over, but otherwise dog's mercury, sanicle and wood violets are characteristic plants. Some recent coppicing has resulted in quick colonising of rosebay willowherb, like bramble always one of the smartest opportunists in the plant world. Ash trees in the woodland also show how they can succeed in shallow soils, while their appearance in old quarries to the west of the woods demonstrates how their light, wind-borne seeds soon colonise such apparently unpromising habitats.

Beyond the woodland area is scrub and grassland, with the lime-rich scrub showing a good mix of species including ash, blackthorn, elder, hawthorn, hazel, holly and wayfaring tree. Wild rose and traveller's joy add to the tangle, with spreading banks of bramble beneath beech and field-maple of the woodland edge.

In contrast to the woodland of the scarp, the plateau and its valleys, Siccaridge Wood on the north side of the Frome valley below Sapperton provides an example of mixed Cotswold valley woodland with a range of trees and shrubs of all ages. Covering 67.5 acres (27ha), it has been a Gloucestershire Trust for Nature Conservation Reserve since 1984 and adjoins a much smaller and older reserve bordering the banks of the disused Thames and Severn Canal. Footpaths give access to most parts of Siccaridge Wood and the minor road between Sapperton and Bisley passes its eastern extremity. Hazel coppice dominates large areas of the slopes, and mature silver birch trees are often riddled with woodpecker excavations. Spring flowers are characteristic of this type of woodland, with carpets of primroses, wood anemones and dog's mercury, followed by bluebells and wild garlic, and open glades attract butterflies to bask in the sunlight. Management plans include the reintroduction of a coppicing routine for the hazel, cutting trees back selectively on a twelve-year cycle to ensure that cover at a wide range of levels is maintained, although it is intended to leave untouched some areas of dense scrub as shelter for birds and small mammals.

Woodlands in the dip-slope valleys enjoy deeper soils than those of the scarp face, and although beeches do well, confirming that they are the greatest trees in Cotswold landscapes by right of their grave serenity, many woodlands have been changed through human interference, and contain a greater variety of species, resulting in more light reaching the ground and a consequent enrichment of both shrub species and ground flora. Lime-loving shrubs to be found include wayfaring tree, dogwood, hazel and spindle, with traveller's joy, dog-rose and bramble present. At ground level, between seventy and eighty species of herbaceous flowering plants occur reasonably frequently in mixed deciduous woodlands. Although the bare tree canopy of spring encourages and emphasises the early flowers, high summer sees the spikes of rosebay, St John's wort and bellflower adding colourful variety, while meadow saffron's pale mauve flowers, leafless at ground level, add lustre to woodland clearings in September.

Limestone Downland and Commons Vast areas of Cotswold uplands were open country that was used almost exclusively as sheep-walks. Enclosure parcelled out most of the land into hedged or walled fields that are farmed now intensively for arable crops and to a lesser extent for grazing of stock, sheep and cattle, and some has been afforested. A few areas survive as relatively untouched grassland or ancient pasture, places which have been too steep for the plough, or common land where traditional grazing rights are held by local property-owners. But these relics of ancient countryside, cropped for centuries by sheep and rabbits – the rabbits seem to be returning in increasing numbers – with their own special flora and insect life, are tiny islands amid vast stretches of rather lifeless prairie. Some are zealously guarded nature reserves either with no access, or access by permit only, a paranoid protectionist policy that does little to encourage public support for conservation. However, access and interpretation facilities in some nature reserves do exist.

Few restrictions on access apply to the various commons, most of them on or close to the downland edge of the plateau at its highest parts – Cleeve Common, Charlton Kings Common, Painswick Hill, Haresfield Beacon, Minchinhampton and Rodborough Commons, Selsley Common and Stinchcombe Hill. Along some of the steepest parts of the scarp, from the northern limit around to Winchcombe, downland merges imperceptibly into rough grazing, with many plants common to both habitats, easily observed at such popular access points as Dover's Hill, near Broadway Tower, and above Stanton, Stanway and Hailes.

Where such areas are closely grazed by sheep, bent grasses tend to dominate, particularly *Festuca ovina*, but walkers in high summer are more likely to notice the rich variety of colour on the crisp turf provided by the creams and yellows of lady's bedstraw, bird's-foot trefoil, rock rose, hawkbit, mingling with the blues and purples of wild thyme, scabious, betony, carline thistle, clustered bellflower and the frail, sky-blue beauty of harebells, regarded by Richard Mabey as the most perfect of British wild plants. I well remember the quiet joy of a July walk on part of the old Bourton Downs above Hinchwick Manor, a rare surviving area of natural Cotswold grassland, remarkably little-known yet not difficult to find and explore by public rights-of-way. Summer flowers climaxed and a profusion of butterflies – meadow browns, marbled white, skipper, common blue among them – beneath a lark-loud sky with sounds of sheep, produced for me the spirit of Cotswold.

Minchinhampton and Rodborough Commons have been designated a Site of Special Scientific Interest by the Nature Conservancy Council for their species-rich unimproved limestone grassland. Stone-quarrying, both open and underground mining, continued well into the 1930s, and although many of the workings have been filled in, those which remain are of significant geological interest and have their own particular flora.

The Trust manages Minchinhampton and Rodborough Commons to provide a focus for a range of interests and uses. Commoners graze large numbers of cattle and horses; there is a good golf course; a multitude of minor roads, bridleways and footpaths thread the commons. Although the area is on the urban fringe, edged with housing, heavily used by local people, visited by thousands, with the inevitable problems of damage to grassland sward by vehicles, a rich variety of wildlife persists, to inform and delight both casual and knowledgeable observers. Much of the interest of the commons arises from the fact that soils on the plateau are generally deeper than those on the slopes just below, and different plants favour these different habitats. The extent of grazing also affects plants on the plateau, with characteristic downland plants favouring well-grazed areas, but where grasses are coarser, yellow rattle, common spotted orchid, kidney vetch and greater knapweed

Minchinhampton Common (National Trust)

can be expected. Also in the coarser grasses pyramid and spotted orchid occur, suggesting a preference for better soils. One species of particular local distribution, the rare pasque flower, is one that I have so far failed to find. With such a good range of flowers it is scarcely surprising that thirty-two species of butterflies have been recorded on these commons, including marsh fritillary, small blue, chalkhill blue and the Duke of Burgundy.

All the commons mentioned are examples of downland type of grassland, and, where they are not under National Trust ownership, are regulated by local authorities, aware both of their amenity value and of the need for wildlife conservation. Cleeve Common is the largest of the Cotswolds commons, covering about 1,000 acres (400ha) of the highest part of the plateau above Cheltenham, and is controlled by the Cleeve Hill Commoners under an act of 1890. It has a golf course, provides extensive grazing, has training gallops, and is extensively used by the public for walking. Car-parking facilities are available in an old quarry site just beyond the Club House (989272), which is reached from the A46 north of Cleeve Hill, and there is access by minor road from Charlton Kings, which ends near the radio beacons towards the southern end of the common (994248).

Most of Cleeve Common's extent supports a limestone flora similar to that of other upland areas of the Cotswolds, but part of the oolite near the highest part of the common, south-east of the radio masts, is overlaid by a band of sandy rock which has created acid soils close to the surface. A small area has been colonised by heather, adding its bright purple colour in August, with the occasional yellow accents of the tiny tormentil in high summer. The common is largely treeless, although large areas of gorse brighten the landscape in May and June, and, with a few hawthorns, provide nesting sites for a limited bird population, favoured by linnets, stonechats and yellowhammers, while skylarks are ground nesters in the rich tussocky turf. The common's rich flora has yielded over two hundred different species, a quarter of which could be regarded as rarities.

If woods and limestone downland are the most obvious plant habitats, roadside verges and hedgerows play an important role in the Cotswold scene, which is best seen and appreciated away from the main roads. Along them each season is revealed, with the same common plants appearing in the same places year after year – celandines and primroses and violets in the shade, and the frothing cow-parsley that signifies summer's approach. At the crown of the year knapweed and rest-harrow, ragworts, thistle, scabious and, above all, the meadow cranesbill which appears as the wild rose blooms to grace the upland roads, these and scores of other flowers evoke the spirit of Cotswold in the intimate and close-up scene. To catalogue them would nullify their tender charm. They are as much a part of the Cotswolds as the hedgerow ash, the beech clumps and shelter-belts, foregrounds that frame wide views over wold and valley.

7
COMMUNICATIONS

Roads

In the centuries before the Roman conquest the Cotswolds were probably networked with a complex pattern of routes that were used by a sophisticated people who were deeply involved in farming and trading. These early tracks would have evolved in response to the need for going from farmstead to pasture, from one settlement to another, and to trade in flint, stone, pottery, leather and metal. Once such tracks had evolved and continued to be used their beginnings can no longer be identified, and it seems very possible that some of the present Cotswold roads and tracks originated in prehistoric times.

Roman Roads

The Romans imposed upon the landscape the first planned throughways, planned and built to serve military needs. In the Cotswolds these kept, as far as possible, to the higher land, and some of their alignments have been adopted for modern roads; none is so famous as the Foss Way which slices with determined directness from Bath to Moreton-in-Marsh and on to Leicester and Lincoln. South-westwards from Cirencester much of its alignment is no longer in use as a modern road, although there are delightful stretches forming 'green lanes' that are favoured by horse-riders and walkers. From Cirencester to the north-east, however, the A429 follows the Roman road very closely, matching its uncompromising line across the waves of the wolds, usually taking valleys in its stride.

The Foss Way makes a series of straight alignments which take notice of the contours of the land. At deep valleys, such as at Fossebridge (*080113*) and

Broadwater Bottom (*136175*), gradients have been eased by diverting from the line, but until the lower country near Moreton-in-Marsh is reached the road keeps the characteristic quality of a spinal route, rarely dropping below 500ft (150m), and, except at Stow-on-the-Wold and Moreton-in-Marsh, avoided by later settlers, so today there are no villages on the course of the Foss Way across the Cotswolds.

Cirencester was the focal point for Roman roads in the Cotswolds. To its north-west Gloucester was a legionary fortress and, early in the Roman occupation, a main road that ran westwards from London forked at Silchester (Hampshire), with the north-western arm leading to Cirencester and Gloucester. Now a modern trunk road for most of the course from Silchester, identified largely as the A419 but marked on the map as 'Ermin Way', this follows from Cirencester the broad ridge between the Frome and Churn valleys in a series of straight alignments, with a well-preserved *agger* on an impressive embankment up to 5ft (1.5m) above the surrounding downland. Only at Birdlip (*927144*) is a village encountered, and this is now bypassed by the modern road. Below Birdlip the Roman road plunged down the escarpment, easing the gradient in a series of zigzags; the road still demands care by motorists who prefer to take the old descent of Birdlip Hill which is rejoined by the A417 near Brockworth.

Condicote Lane, looking north, near Stow-on-the-Wold. The medieval track crosses the high wolds

Akeman Street was an important Roman throughway across the South Midlands from St Albans via Tring and Aylesbury to Cirencester and Bath. As far as the Cotswold area is concerned, its course is more evident on the map than on the ground, although there are sections which are surfaced lanes, bridleways or footpaths. Running WSW of Asthall (*288112*) in the Windrush valley east of Burford, it is a surfaced minor road after crossing the A361, then a bridleway across the upper Leach valley, and a lane again as it approaches Williamstrip Park. As a good road it continues past the six-road junction at Ready Token (*105045*) and joins the Foss Way 1 mile (1.6km) north-east of Cirencester.

Many Roman villa sites have been identified within 2 or 3 miles (3.2–4.8km) of these main military and supply roads and there seems little doubt that other Roman roads existed in the Cotswolds primarily for the use of local traffic, many of these probably forming part of the basic network of present-day lanes. Since they were not built for military use they did not need straight alignments.

One other route of known Roman origin (if not earlier) is Ryknild Street, an important north-south link through the Midlands, from settlements at Alcester and Wall (on Watling Street) to the Foss Way at Bourton-on-the-Water, and hence to Cirencester and Bath. Although parts of it are now lost, especially near Lower Slaughter, some surviving sections illustrate Roman directness and evoke that special Cotswold magic I associate with the lonely, open landscapes of the high wolds, such as along Condicote Lane, north of its crossing of the B4068 2 miles (3.2km) west of Stow, almost to Condicote village.

Medieval Throughways

Other routes, later than those the Romans made, have lost their original purposes and have declined into local lanes and tracks, but the names of some recall their former use. Salt was an essential in medieval housekeeping, and Droitwich, to the north of the Cotswolds, was an important source. Carriers must have brought great quantities of it to and through the Cotswolds, yet only one named Saltway is recorded on the map.

Place-names evidence suggests that the Saltway crossed the River Avon near Fladbury, continued southwards, east of Bredon Hill, past Ashton-under-Hill, over Alderton Hill to Toddington and Hailes, where a 'saltweie' is named on a charter of 1256. A deviation would here have provided Winchcombe Abbey with its salt. Salters' Lane took the route on to the wolds, where modern maps indicate 'Salt Way' for the minor road that runs southwards along the crest above Sudeley to Roel Gate (*054245*). It probably then went through Hawling and Salperton, by what is now a bridleway to Hazleton, across the A40 east of Puesdown, and, taking a SSE orientation, crossed the Foss Way west of Northleach. Passing Saltway Barn (*100126*) and Saltway

Nathaniel Izod's 'Cross Hands' sign of 1669 above Chipping Campden. Notice his initials on the left arm

Farm (*105108*), it becomes a 'green lane' near Oldwalls Farm (*113098*), soon passes another Saltway Barn (*118092*) and runs south-eastwards to Coln St Aldwyn, and, as a surfaced road, reaches the River Thames at Lechlade, the highest navigable point on the river.

The White Way is a minor road that runs northwards from Cirencester's Spital Gate, along a broad ridge east of the Churn valley, passing between Roman villa sites at Chedworth and Withington and crossing the Coln valley by Cassey Compton. Beyond Compton Abdale the White Way appears to join the Saltway by some long barrows above Hazleton, so it may have been a branch of this Saltway – White Ways were often associated with the carrying of salt – but it may well have been used in prehistoric and Roman times.

Campden Lane, now for much of its winding course across the northern Cotswolds a delightful, secretive track, sometimes footpath, sometimes bridleway, and less frequently a surfaced lane, seems to have been a medieval route between Northleach and Chipping Campden. Motorists can sample its quietness through Hampnett and Hazleton, but northwards from there it is mainly a way for walkers, through Salperton and Hawling, past Deadmanbury Gate and Lynes Barn Farm, offering occasional eastward glimpses down the feeder valleys of the upper Windrush. From Stumps Cross (*075304*) at the B4077 crossing, as a surfaced road it follows the presumed prehistoric route above the edge of the escarpment, by Stanway Ashes and Hill Barn Farm, across the A44 at the 'Cross Hands' and down Westington Hill into Campden. Such a track, named after a likely terminus which itself was an important centre for trade, suggests an important route in medieval times.

When John Ogilby brought out his *Britannia* in 1675 (our first genuine road-book) detailing a hundred roads, among them was that running for 76 miles (122km) from Salisbury to Chipping Campden. Its inclusion implied long historical usage, almost certainly based on the carriage of wool from the Cotswolds to the Channel ports. His map gives the following towns along the route: Salisbury – Marlborough – Highworth – Lechlade – Filkins – Burford – Stow – Campden, adopted today from Highworth, near Swindon, by the A361 to Burford, and then the A424 to Stow, joining the A44 near Bourton-on-the-Hill, before branching at the Cross Hands, the prominent finger-post that was erected by Nathaniel Izod in 1669, its wrought-iron arms pointing the ways to Worcester, Gloucester, Oxford and Warwick. On the section beyond Stow Ogilby's pictorial strip-map names by the roadside 'stone walls', 'a hedge' (more than once) and, by Westington Hill, 'a hedge' and 'a conduit'.

John Ogilby's 'Great Road from London to Gloucester', which was part of the longer route to St David's in south-west Wales, entered the southern Cotswolds at Lechlade and continued to Fairford, but beyond there its importance has declined over the past two hundred years. If the route in Ogilby's road-book is accurate (a doubtful supposition), its westwards course is that of the surfaced lane now marked on the OS maps as 'Welsh Way', by way of Ready Token, Barnsley, across the Churn at 'Perrott's Bridge' (now Brook), north-westwards to join the line of Ermin Street and subsequently descending 'Burlip Hill'. The route thus bypassed Cirencester on the north.

Drove Roads

The name 'Welsh Way' seems to have been recorded first in 1792 on the Enclosure Map for Bagendon parish, but it certainly implies an older origin, possibly in medieval times, as it is known that the droving of Welsh cattle to the markets of southern England was a flourishing trade by 1400. Apart from a few setbacks through disease, the trade expanded, probably peaking in the late eighteenth and early nineteenth centuries. Welsh cattle were not only driven to England as meat on the hoof but also to be fattened on lusher pastures, as there was insufficient good grazing land in Wales. From mid- and south Wales many cattle came to Gloucester, where there was a halting-place near the foot of Birdlip Hill, as well as a 'stance' at Birdlip itself, where two cattle markets were held each year in the village. Large numbers of stock were moved. In 1821 Cobbett encountered two thousand head being driven from Pembrokeshire to Sussex, and Charles Coxwell, an eighteenth-century rector of Barnsley, used to let his pasture at 4d a head to drovers who preferred stopping there rather than at the more popular Ready Token 2 miles (3.2km) to the east. His diary notes that in 1767 he netted £5 17 0d in this way, representing 351 beasts accommodated.

Drove roads tended to avoid towns on their route for the purely practical reason that it would have been a bothersome business to drive large herds or flocks through narrow streets. Villages were often avoided too, as ambling cattle would certainly have been a threat to villagers' crops on their open fields. After enclosures, drove roads would have been confined between walls or hedges, but usually they were left much wider than local parish roads or the new turnpikes that were constructed from the mid-eighteenth century. Where possible, drovers tried to avoid these new roads so that they would not have to pay tolls.

The Welsh Way was by no means the only drove road. Many others were probably made for local traffic and trade, used by farmers for moving stock to markets and by carriers and packhorse trains for transporting goods, particularly wool, over longer distances. Like almost all old roads, drove roads are usually impossible to date. Few, if any, are documented, and it is probable that most of today's Cotswold roads follow tracks that have been used since medieval days, some in Roman times, and others for a thousand years or more. However, some of the main roads can be dated more accurately to the documented days of the Turnpike Trusts, although many of these roads were merely the regularising and improving of existing routes.

Turnpike Roads

In the Cotswolds the first turnpike created by the Act of 1697–8, was the road from Gloucester to the top of Birdlip and Crickley Hills. Others on the lower margins followed during the next fifty years: the present A38 was opened in 1725–6, which was quickly linked from the vale to Stroud, Wotton-under-Edge and Sodbury, together with the present A417 from Lechlade to Cirencester. During the 1740s and 1750s many of the main roads on the upland plateau were brought under toll, possibly as a result of the enclosures of the fields which were then occurring. Enclosure of this open-field country would certainly have helped to confine traffic, both wheeled and on the hoof, between the new boundary walls. Writing in the early nineteenth century, Rudge confirms this, commenting on the total change that had taken place on the hills over the previous hundred years, with

> the downs converted into arable closed fields, and an easy communication is made with the different villages, through a country formerly almost inaccessible to the stranger, and sometimes travelled with difficulty even by the natives.

Cirencester strengthened its focal importance for roads in the south of the area, with Northleach and Moreton-in-Marsh having important east-west roads crossing the Foss Way which was turnpiked in 1751. The present A40 route from Oxford to Gloucester became a toll road in 1746.

Once a main road is created, or an existing one improved, it generates

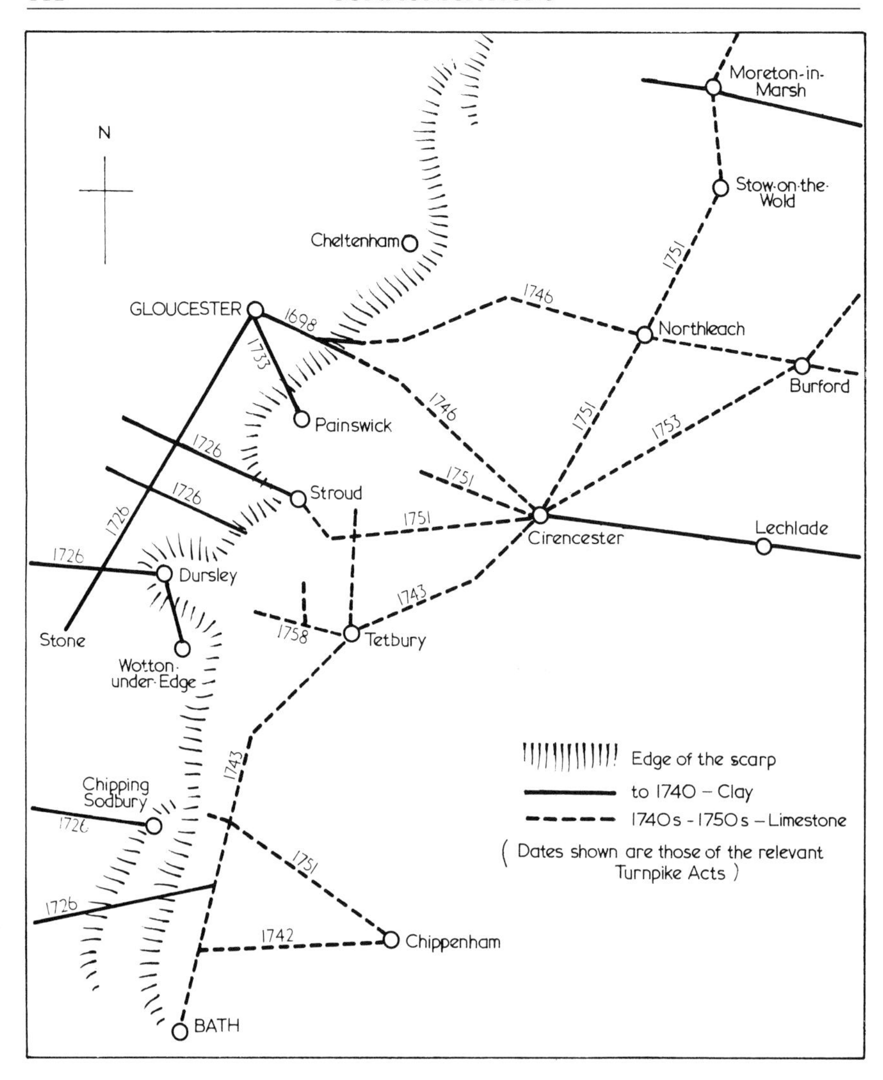

Turnpike development in the first half of the eighteenth century

its own traffic, and in the case of a new road, causes its predecessor to fall into disuse. This happened over two centuries ago; indeed, near Northleach history is repeating itself. Recently a new bypass for the small town has redirected the busy A40 in a long arc to the north, with resultant decrease in traffic through the town centre, and west of the Foss Way crossroads the former A40 is particularly quiet. Before the 1746 turnpike an older road from Burford along the Windrush valley, through Sherborne and Farmington, and apparently missing Northleach, had run westwards along Northleach Down, continuing to Puesdown Inn (*075172*) where it was joined by the turnpike. This is still shown on maps as 'Old Road', and, ironically, now closely parallels the new A40 line. This old road continued, crossing the Coln valley at Shipton, bending sharply at Frogmill Inn (*027184*) before climbing to Kilkenny and heading for Seven Springs and Crickley Hill for Gloucester, or by Dowdeswell for Cheltenham. The present road past Andoversford is a newer route which has had the result of isolating Frogmill Inn.

Further south the 1751 improvement of the road from Cirencester to Stroud, now mainly the A419, made its predecessor redundant. This is now a quiet bridleway along the northern edge of Cirencester Park past Ewe Pens to the Daglingworth crossroads and westwards to Park Corner (962044). A steep descent down Gulph Hill to the Frome valley took it on to Tunley, Water Lane and Bisley, and from there either to Painswick or Stroud.

The Burford Roads Trust was busy in the 1750s, with the Witney route turnpiked in 1751, the Cirencester road (A433) in 1753, and the old northern route through the town from Lechlade to Stow in 1755, when other roads that converged on Stow were also improved. But it was not until the 1780s that the present complex pattern of roads began to be created, partly financed by parish rates, but heavily subsidised by tolls that were collected at the various gates erected by the turnpike trusts along each route. These tolls were mortgaged, or 'farmed', in advance by auction so that the administrators of the trusts knew what income they were likely to have at their disposal to undertake work required. Toll-houses which can be identified today are a reminder of the means whereby this early form of road tax was collected.

Sometimes these toll-houses are just like any other small houses, often with an additional small window in the side wall. More characteristically, they have a protruding angled front bay so that the toll-keeper could see the approaching traffic through the side windows. Many toll-houses have been lost in road-widening schemes and many have been adapted and enlarged to meet modern needs. At Broadway, Turnpike Cottage at the eastern end of the village undoubtedly saw a lot of trade in the late eighteenth century, and this same traffic on the London–Worcester road would also have been halted by the toll-bar across the road at Bourton-on-the-Hill, where Turnpike Cottage recalls its former use. One of the best-known toll-houses, complete with its board of charges, is by the A435 Cheltenham–Evesham road near Oxenton (953306), at present (1989) being modernised. Also retaining its toll-board is the little house at Butterow, below the edge of Rodborough Common (856040), where the 1825 road crosses an older hillside track from Rodborough to Bagpath.

Considering the increased industrial activity in the Stroudwater valleys, road improvements in that area came relatively late. Steep hills had gradients that were too severe for wheeled vehicles, and the surfacing then available could not cope with the downward torrents created by heavy rains. It was a day's journey for a wheeled vehicle to travel from Stroud to Chalford. Minchinhampton must at times have felt isolated on its high plateau, yet the route from Stroud to Cirencester went up through

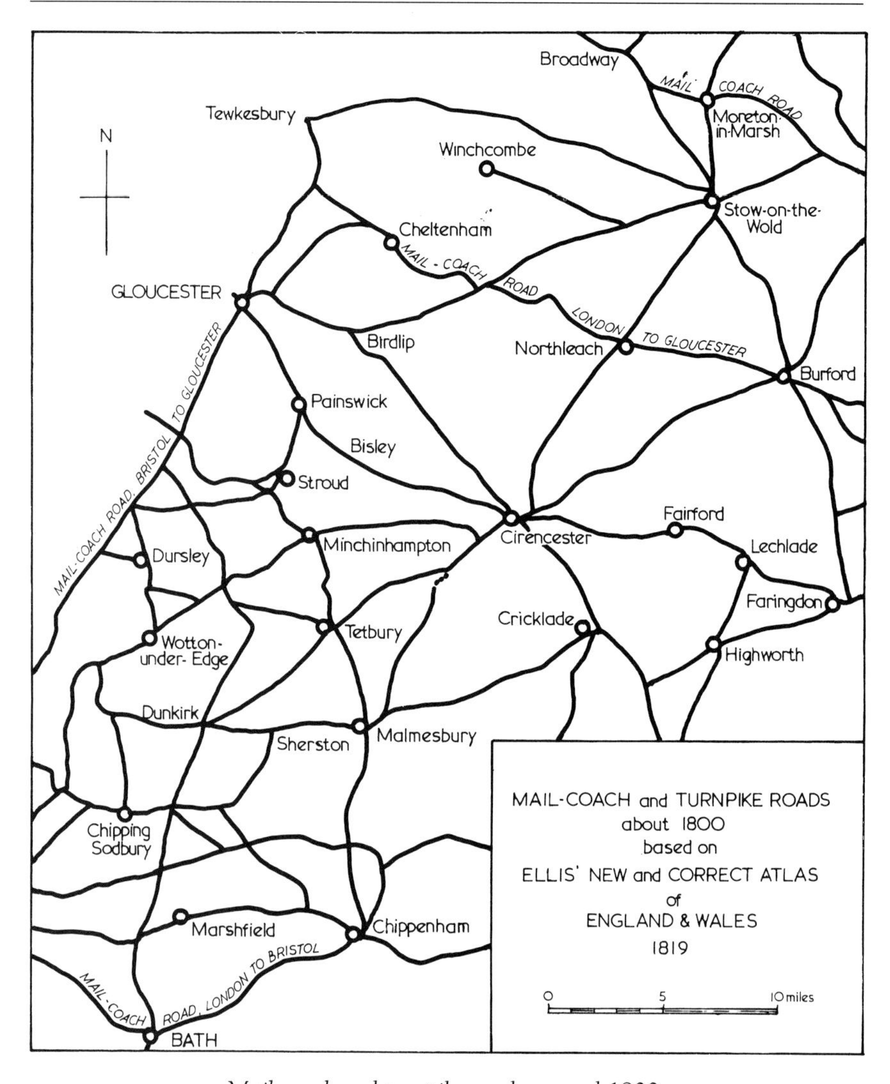

Mail coach and turnpike roads around 1800

Rodborough to Minchinhampton, along the ridge to Sapperton to join the old Cirencester–Bisley road at Park Corner. The route from Chalford followed tortuous lanes through Frampton Mansell to Sapperton. However, in 1780 the Nailsworth Valley Trust initiated many new roads, so that by about 1815 most of the worst routes of the older turnpikes had been superseded and the present pattern emerged.

The most scenic of all Cotswold roads, the A435, is one of the latest turnpikes, the 'new' road up the Churn valley from Cirencester. Made in 1825, it sweeps up the wooded valley in a series of gentle curves, with a gradient almost imperceptible to modern traffic. The Colesbourne Inn by the roadside was built to serve travellers on the turnpike, with public rooms and ranges of stables. The 1820s and 1830s saw the zenith of the coaching trade and left its mark throughout the Cotswolds, particularly in the market towns along the routes of the turnpikes, and also at the roadside inns on some of the lonelier upland sections, which served as staging posts, such as the Puesdown Inn above Northleach. Farther west the Frogmill Inn is now isolated in a 'cut-off' section of the A436, the former line of the main Gloucester road which continued to Kilkenny and Seven Springs. Travellers for Cheltenham changed at Frog Mill, but when the new route through Andoversford superseded the older one through Dowdeswell, the inn was isolated, a position further exaggerated by the more recent taking off of a corner on the A436 Kilkenny route.

Canals

Near the Fox Inn at Little Barrington is a spot known locally as the Wharf, probably marking the place where stone from nearby quarries was loaded on to small barges to be floated down the River Windrush to the Thames for use at Oxford. A short way downstream are the remains of an old sloping stone weir where the water-level could be raised to allow the barges to avoid an adjoining mill-race. These structures are thought to date from the late seventeenth century, about the same time as schemes were being mooted to make the River Frome navigable between Stroud and the tidal Severn. But the needs of local mills for the river's water power soon thwarted such ideas.

However, in 1776, a canal was authorised, and the 8 miles (13km) long Stroudwater Navigation was completed three years later. It ran from Wallbridge, Stroud, to Framilode on the Severn and was capable of carrying craft of up to 60 tons. Early in the project advantages were realised of trying to link the canal with the River Thames, and in 1783 the Thames and Severn Canal was begun, running 28¾ miles (46.2km) from Stroud to Lechlade. Astonishingly, this formidable undertaking was completed within six years and included a short branch to Cirencester. For the first time the Thames and Severn had been linked by an inland waterway.

To raise the canal in its course through the Golden Valley from Stroud, through Brimscombe and Chalford to Daneway required forty-four locks. At Daneway the canal entered the Sapperton Tunnel, 2⅜ miles (4km) long, which, when built by the canal's engineer Robert Whitworth, was the longest known tunnel in Europe. Spoil-heaps of debris laboriously brought to the surface through shafts during its construction were subsequently planted with beech trees. These mounds, still graced with trees, form a characteristic landscape feature which is easily seen from the road south of Sapperton village.

Emerging from the tunnel the canal crossed the Cirencester–Malmesbury road by a single-arched aqueduct, of which the abutments remain. From Siddington (030996) the 1½ mile (2.4km) branch to Cirencester headed northwards, while the main canal continued by South Cerney, Cricklade and Kempsford, to join the Thames by the Inglesham Round House (*205988*) south-west of Lechlade. The first boat went through Sapperton Tunnel in November 1799, the last one in May 1911, but the canal was an unprofitable venture from the start, not only because of difficulties in maintaining water levels in its long summit pound between Sapperton and Siddington because of the porous oolite bed, but because it encountered early competition from the Oxford Canal that provided the Midlands with a shorter route to London. In 1810 the completion of the Kennet and Avon Canal produced a more convenient waterway link between Bristol and London, and within another thirty years railways had entered the scene.

However, the valley section between Stroud and Chalford was used throughout the last century for local trade and deliveries, and an abortive attempt to revive the canal was made early this century, but in 1933 the whole length was abandoned. Parts are still watered and some towpaths are still accessible. The elegant little Round House at Chalford, one of five similar lengthmen's houses along the canal, has been sensitively restored as a private house, which is well appreciated as part of a landscaped area around an old wharf and a filled-in section of the canal. Sapperton Tunnel is now blocked by roof falls; its northern portal is accessible by the former towpath from below the popular Daneway Inn, built in 1784, whose car park covers

Chalford, showing a seventeenth-century house and canal round house of around 1800

Chipping Campden Church

Overleaf
Cam Long Down, from Coaley Wood

In Upper Slaughter

the site of the top lock. Far more dignified, however, is the southern portal near Coates (966006), with its niches, Doric columns, roundels and rusticated arch, all recently restored. Nearby, the Tunnel House, once a regular port of call for bargees and now a popular inn, is easily reached from the minor road between Coates and Tarlton.

Railways

The earliest railway in the Cotswolds, a gravity-operated inclined plane tramroad serving Leckhampton quarry, was built in 1798. Loaded trucks of stone descended a steep slope to the turnpike road (now the B4070) a mile (1.6km) outside Cheltenham, and hauled up empty trucks at the same time. Two further inclined planes were added which continued to serve quarry needs until 1924. Now partly overgrown, their track forms a direct if steep path from Leckhampton to the disused quarries and Charlton Kings Common beyond.

In 1826, as a whittled-down remnant of an ambitious project to link the Midlands and London, a tramroad was opened between Stratford-upon-Avon and Moreton-in-Marsh, with a branch to Shipston-on-Stour. Its course was planned on the advice of Thomas Telford, the only public railway with which he was directly associated, and Brunel inspected it on behalf of the Oxford, Worcester and Wolverhampton Railway Company, who decided to rent it. Initially a horse-operated system, it was brought up to standard gauge in 1853, though still horse-drawn, as steam engines were not permitted at Stratford, and opened as a passenger line. When the Stratford–Honeybourne line was opened six years later the old service ended and the Moreton tramroad almost abandoned. However, it survived until 1904, and was officially abandoned in 1926. Its course east of the Foss Way can still be identified.

Apart from their stone quarries the Cotswolds are largely devoid of mineral wealth. By the time of the railway boom their wool prosperity had severely declined and only in the southern part of the area was there sufficient industrial wealth to attract the attention of railway promoters. Additionally, the hills proved a physical barrier, particularly the formidable escarpment along their western edge. Although the GWR's early interest lay in the line from London to Bath and Bristol, with Brunel's pioneering broad-gauge track completed in 1841, a line from Swindon to Kemble with a short branch to Cirencester was opened the same year by the Cheltenham and Great Western Union, which was later absorbed by the GWR in 1844.

Measured directly, Swindon and Cheltenham are 25 miles (40km) apart, but in order to avoid steep gradients and long tunnels, when they were eventually linked, through Cirencester, Stroud and Gloucester in 1847, the rail distance was 44 miles (71km). Cirencester had thus gained a through

The view from Round Hill, above Winchcombe

station instead of being a branch terminus, and, by digging the difficult 1¼ miles (2km) long Sapperton Tunnel to bring the line into the Golden Valley above Frampton Mansell, the Cotswold backbone was at last breached. The route, still in use, crosses the canal tunnel in Hailey Wood (*961014*) and air shafts mark its course to the north-west. Debris tips were not so tidily dealt with as those from the canal construction half a century earlier.

Brunel also advised on the construction of the line up the Evenlode

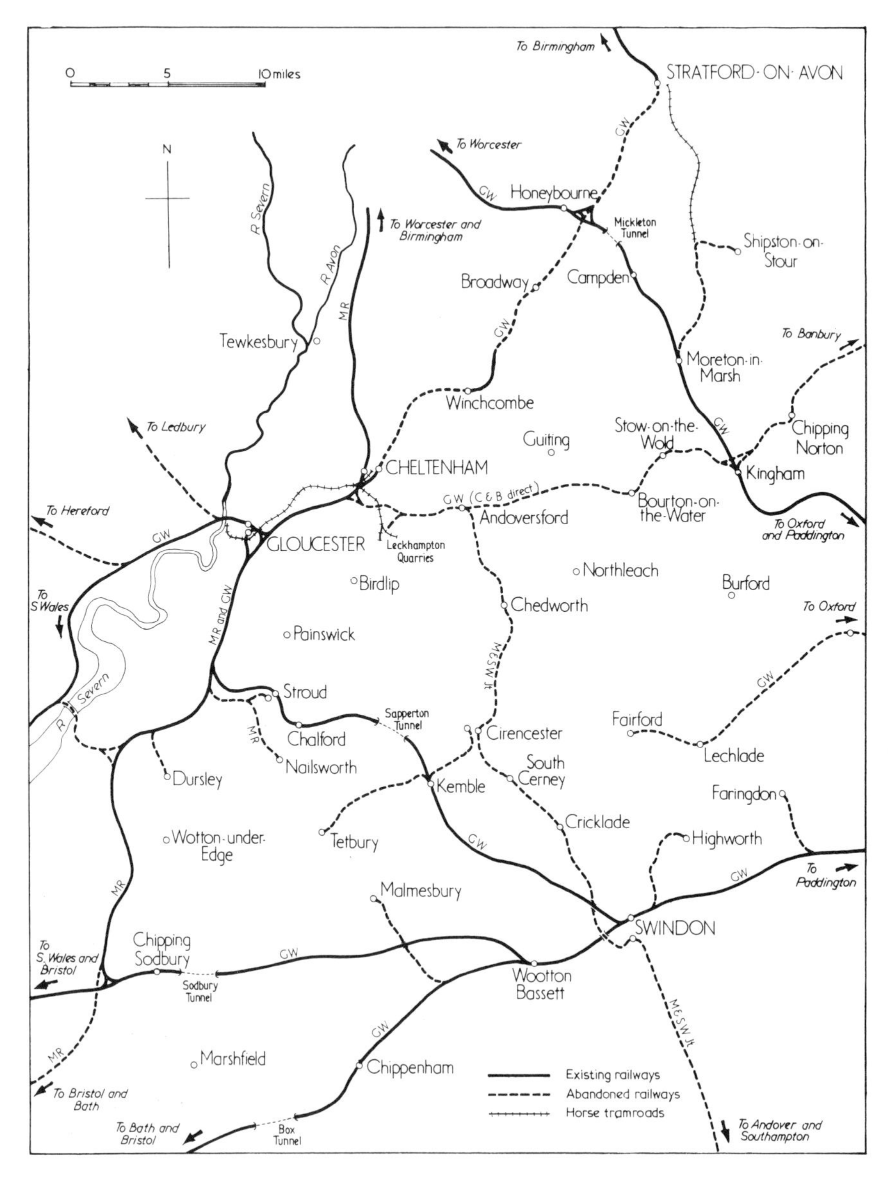

Cotswold tramways and railways

valley for the Oxford, Worcester and Wolverhampton Railway in 1853. The then Lord Redesdale (of Batsford Park) stipulated that every passenger train should stop at Moreton-in-Marsh, which they still do, to the present benefit of local north Cotswold residents commuting either to Oxford and London or to Worcester and the Midlands. Indeed, this and the Swindon–Gloucester line are the only surviving routes serving the main area of the Cotswolds. The GWR absorbed the Oxford, Worcester and Wolverhampton Railway in 1861.

From the Evenlode valley the main Oxford–Worcester line was soon linked by a branch north-eastwards to Chipping Norton (1855) and westwards to Bourton-on-the-Water seven years later, with a single-platform station serving Stow-on-the-Wold a mile (1.6km) south of the town. A route between Banbury and Cheltenham, mooted as early as the 1820s, was now envisaged as a possibility, using the Chipping Norton–Kingham–Bourton branches as a basis. The Banbury and Cheltenham Direct Railway, which extended the branches eastwards and westwards, was opened in June 1881. At Kingham a flyover enabled branch-line trains to cross the main line without upsetting services, and from the Evenlode valley a gradient of 1 in 83 carried the line up to Stow. Beyond Bourton steeper gradients were necessary to take trains across the upland plateau, reaching 1 in 60 near Notgrove to gain the summit at 760ft (231m) north of Salperton, claimed to be the highest point on any GWR through route (the GWR took over the line and railway in 1897). More steep gradients of up to 1 in 63 brought it down to Andoversford, followed by a curving descent through the escarpment, along the Chelt valley and by the A40, towards Cheltenham. The switchback nature of the whole line was such that it took an hour to travel the 24 miles (39km) between Kingham and Cheltenham.

In the years before World War I four trains ran on each weekday, stopping at all seven intermediate stations, but there was a far greater use of the route by mineral trains carrying iron-ore from Oxfordshire and Northamptonshire to South Wales. The main section of the line from Cheltenham to Bourton closed in October 1962, the shorter branches from Kingham about two years later.

A late starter among Cotswold railways was the ambitious project to create a direct north-south link between Cheltenham and Southampton, which was strongly opposed at the outset by the GWR. However, the Swindon, Marlborough and Andover Railway was opened in 1873,with the Swindon and Cheltenham Extension Railway Act of 1881 aiming to pursue its course northwards to meet the Cheltenham–Banbury line near Andoversford. The track reached Cirencester in 1883, and the two companies were amalgamated to form the Midland and South Western Railway. Financial and engineering problems delayed the completion through Chedworth and Withington to Andoversford until 1891, but the line was not an economic success. Trains took twenty minutes to cover the 7½ miles (12km) from Cirencester to Chedworth, but after drastic staff changes in 1892 the company moved out of its bankrupt state and for a short while even showed a profit, probably more from its freight services than passenger use. However, Andoversford hamlet not only became a junction but also acquired a cattle market.

Another project, proposed in 1861 to link Cheltenham with the GWR at Faringdon, never reached fruition, although a branch from Oxford to Fairford was opened in 1873. The last line constructed in the Cotswold region aimed to connect Cheltenham with Stratford-on-Avon and Leamington Spa by a track serving villages along the foot of the northern scarp, bringing particular benefit to Winchcombe and Broadway and joining the main Oxford–Worcester line at Honeybourne. This GWR route opened in 1906 and survived the Beeching axe of the 1960s better than most other Cotswold lines, largely as a relief route to the main line for freight traffic between Cheltenham and Birmingham. When closure did come in August 1976 an intense local effort was immediately mounted, and the Gloucestershire and Warwickshire Railway Society was formed to try to purchase as much track-bed as possible.

In 1981 a Light Railway Order was applied for. The society established a base at the restored former GWR station at Toddington, where locomotives and rolling stock are on display in the old goods-yard. Over 3 miles (4.8km) of single track have been relaid, and a service operates from Toddington to Winchcombe on Sundays from March to October, bank holidays, Saturdays throughout the summer and on additional days during July and August. Most trains, especially at weekends, are steam-hauled, and by 1990 the track is expected to be extended another mile, including Gretton Tunnel, to emerge at the next halt, Gretton Meadow. So once more the sound of steam echoes across the pastoral softness of the north Cotswold landscape.

8
EXPLORING THE MARKET TOWNS

Towns featured in this chapter have deep historic roots and most were founded for commercial purposes. Their fortunes have fluctuated, some succeeding more than others. Today, most have reasonable car-parking facilities, usually and sensibly away from their historic cores. All are worth exploring, and each town is small enough to do this on foot. Use your legs and use your eyes. Look at the shapes and sizes of streets, of buildings, of groups and spaces and you will begin to realise that townscapes are a series of personal statements made by different individuals at different times, and the most successful ones were made without the interference of planners. Look at details of masonry, treatment of doorways and windows, of chimneys and the rhythm of roof lines. Admire the texture and colour of stone in sunlight, and perhaps ponder on the logistics of building houses, inns and workshops centuries ago, always remembering that towns did not make themselves. Each is the product of decisions and choices either by an individual or as the result of different decisions at different times. Above all towns were, and are, for people; as resident or visitor you become, if only for a brief while, part of the river of humanity which has flowed through them, giving them life.

In most towns the main street, usually High Street, contains buildings which enfold the history of Cotswold town life over at least four centuries, but the town's layout goes back much further, to medieval, Saxon or even Roman times. Details of buildings may have changed as architectural styles evolved to meet changing fashions, or buildings themselves acquired different uses. In most towns stone dominates the street scene, with only a few examples of visible half-timbering surviving. Thus there is

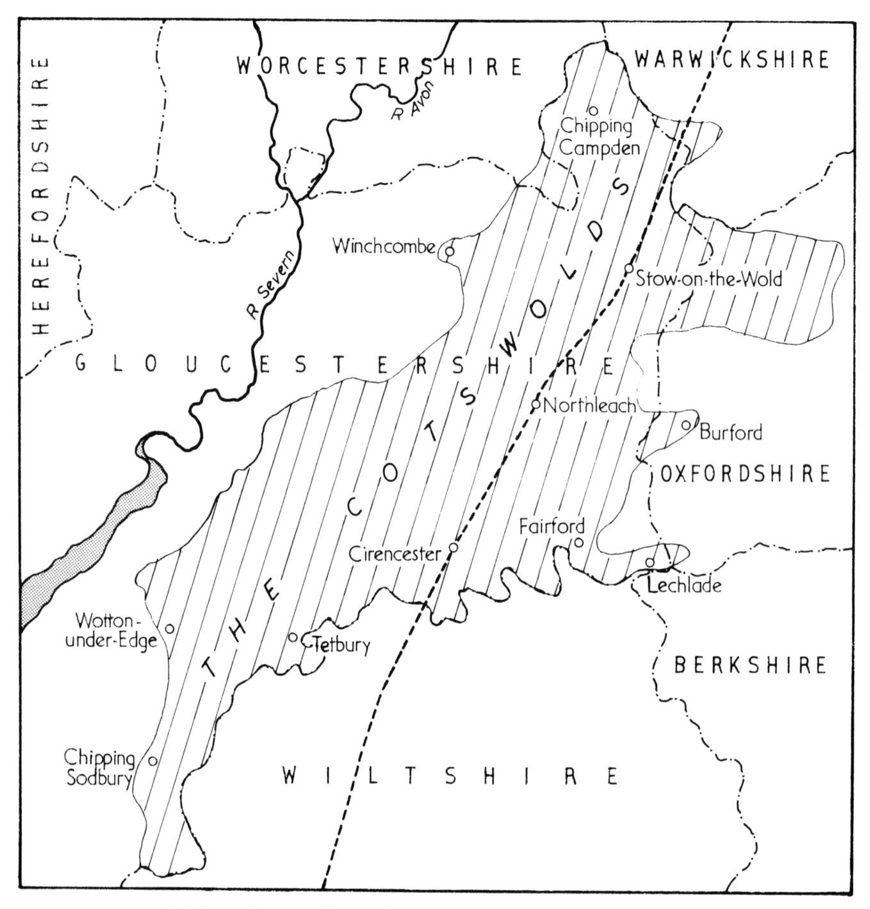

Medieval boroughs and market towns of the Cotswolds

a noble harmony of colour and texture creating an ambience which makes Cotswold towns unique and merits their designation as Conservation Areas.

Most of the selected towns are on main A roads: the Foss Way (A429) links Moreton-in-Marsh, Stow-on-the-Wold, Northleach (a mere whisker away) and Cirencester with Tetbury to the south-west down the A433. Burford is on the A361 coming north from Lechlade and is itself linked to Stow by the A424 and to Northleach by the A40. Painswick and Winchcombe enjoy, or suffer, a presence on the A46 south and north of Cheltenham, while the towns at the southern and northern extremities, Wotton-under-Edge and Chipping Campden – surely the jewel in Cotswold's crown – are on the B4058 and B4081. In this team of eleven only the alphabetical first, Burford, is not in Gloucestershire, but owes its allegiance to Oxfordshire. If there has to be a twelfth man, however, it would also come from Oxfordshire, for Chipping Norton deserves an innings.

Burford

A small Saxon settlement by an important crossing on the River Windrush was boosted into the status of a seigneurial borough around 1100 by Robert fitz Hamon, Earl of Gloucester, who laid out a broad street that climbed southwards up the hill from the river. Long narrow burgage plots opened out along each side, ending in a back lane, with similar development along the Oxford–Gloucester road, crossing High Street where its gradient eases. Within this simple framework Burford's life has continued for nearly nine hundred years. By their foundation market charter, Burford's burgesses had one of our earliest merchant guilds, the right to a weekly market in the wider High Street below the crossroads, on level land, as well as fairs, which were attended regularly for the next three centuries by wool-buying Italian merchants.

When a stone bridge replaced the ford, more trade ensued, mainly wool and cloth, but also wine, butter, livestock, fleeces, leather goods, timber and charcoal from nearby Wychwood Forest. Burford flourished and became wealthy, and until the seventeenth century it continued to be governed by an alderman and burgesses. During Edward VI's reign (*c*1550) it was described as 'a very great market town replenished with much people'. Prosperity peaked during the fifteenth and sixteenth centuries – reflected in the beautiful rebuilding of the parish church – from wool trade profits, although individual benefactors are not known. Pevsner devotes seven pages to the church, a sure sign of its architectural merit and interest.

Nearby, in Church Lane, the Great Almshouses were founded in 1457 by Richard, Earl of Warwick, and their rebuilding in 1828 fortunately left the front unchanged. Also in Church Lane is a range of Simon Wisdom's grammar school founded in 1571, almost contemporary with the neat little Tolsey, or Court House, at the corner of High Street and Sheep Street. Below the Tolsey, Falkland Hall of 1558 was possibly Burford's first major house to be built wholly of stone.

Medieval inns, The George, The Bull, The Bear, and along Sheep Street The Lamb, were conveniently grouped for travellers and merchants. Some have changed function, some their façades as well and The Bull now has High Street's only brick frontage. On the west side of High Street cottages line the sides of former inn courtyards, corridors of calm a few yards away from traffic turmoil. Timber-framing, often with jetties, is usually medieval, and four-centred archways indicate entrances of fifteenth- and sixteenth-century date.

Sir Lawrence Tanfield, who had bought priory lands in 1584 to build a house on the site, obtained the lordship of the manor and successfully took Burford's burgesses to court for usurping manorial rights. The Merchants' Guild lost its powers and some of the cloth trade vanished, the clothiers moving to Witney. Quarrying and saddlery flourished, yet prosperity continued for another century and more, with more houses large and small being crammed into High Street and its neighbours, resulting in the almost continuous frontages we see today. In 1700 Witney Street saw the huge baroque mansion appropriately called the Great House loom majestically above neighbouring modest cottages and inns. Another baroque mansion, its rusticated front having six huge pilasters, was built in 1715, and was gutted and converted in 1849 to become the Wesleyan Chapel.

When Byng visited Burford in 1781 he found it 'a poor declining place, having lost the clothing trade, and almost the saddlery business'. Thirty years later the Oxford–Gloucester turnpike was realigned south of the town, taking some through coaching traffic away, but the older inns in and around High Street continued to flourish on local trade and freight traffic. The Industrial Revolution bypassed Burford, as did the railways, so it maintained its importance as a roadside town. There was scarcely any new building since the early eighteenth century, although existing buildings were refronted, enlarged, modernised or divided. Thus the town preserves its medieval, Tudor and seventeenth-century character. The market area of High Street was too narrow to allow island development, the River Windrush effectively prevented a northwards spread, and the bridge still marks an instant transition from town to country. Old buildings enjoy a new lease of life with their ground floors adapted as estate agents' offices and shops, especially those selling antiques. The former eighteenth-century Greyhound Inn in Sheep Street, has been, since 1947, the editorial offices of Britain's most authentic and prestigious rural voice, the bi-monthly magazine *The Countryman*.

Burford has become a town for tourists, whose favourite activity seems to be walking up one side of the High Street and down the other, browsing and sometimes buying. Few seem to reach the top of High Street where pollarded limes, grass verges and cottages where people actually live create an entirely different scene. From here, looking down, or from Simon Wisdom's weavers' cottages by the bridge, looking up, High Street looks its best. But Burford desperately needs a north-south bypass to improve its quality of life, and it would assuredly benefit from access to the lovely Windrush. There are no riverside paths to the west and only one short stretch towards Widford on the east.

Chipping Campden

Many roads converge on Campden, none of them of 'A' classification, but my favourite approach is from the south, either by Westington Hill or on the lane that climbs from Blockley past the edge of Northwick Park. As this descends from over 650ft (200m) it reveals a landscape of calm, unshowy loveliness, with fields, farms, trees and hedgerows. Broad Campden is below the brow, with Campden's clustered roofs beyond, varying in shade according to the light's angle and brilliance. From here you see the context of the town, the glory of its church tower tucked away at its eastern edge, and you wonder if the reality of nearness can match the distant view's enchantment. It can and does. John Masefield distilled its essence:

On Campden wold the skylark sings,
In Campden town the traveller finds
The inward peace that beauty brings
To bless and heal tormented minds.

Arguably the most beautiful town in the Cotswolds, and therefore in England, Campden's situation emphasises the part played by geography in producing a shallow, curving valley with a small, probably late Saxon village on its north side. Its lord, Hugh de Gondeville, obtained a market charter about 1180 and laid out the High Street along the line of an important trading route, with long narrow burgage plots fronting both sides. Widening to accommodate a market place near the mid-point of its gentle curve, High Street has witnessed the changes and developments that eight centuries have brought and contains stone-built houses that span the last six of these.

The oldest property, Grevel's House, with its distinctive, two-storey bay window, and Woolstapler's Hall opposite, both late fourteenth century, would then have been the only stone buildings in High Street, all others being little more than thatched hovels. A few buildings, probably of Tudor times, have timber-framed upper storeys, but most are of the abundant, honey-gold local stone, occasionally tinging on brown, which is vibrant after it has been rinsed by rain or can appear silvery in the moonlight.

Walk southwards down the east side of High Street and return on the higher side so that the gentle curve focuses on the church tower. White paint gleams, and flowers and pot plants contrast with warm stone. Front rooms of houses, flat or angle-bowed, match neat, small shop windows of real shops that supply domestic essentials – antique shops are fewer than in Broadway. A narrow strip of grass with small trees breaks the line, but the stone frontages are continuous, except for occasional dark alleys between houses. The street has evolved, and, down the centuries, has been home for artisans, tradesfolk, craftsmen, shopkeepers, innkeepers and wool merchants.

Sir Baptist Hicks' lovely Market Hall of 1627 was intended for the sale of butter, cheese and poultry. Gabled, open-bayed and with its stone-cobbled floor, the hall is a marvellous focus, sharing its island site with a memorial cross and rebuilt Town Hall. Hicks' own mansion, near the church, was destroyed during the Civil War, but its Jacobean gateway and the almshouses which are high-perched above the road south-west of the church (1612) are dignified survivals of Hicks' taste and philanthropy. The church is superb, a majestic monument to the wool-merchants of the fourteenth and fifteenth centuries whose benefactions paid for it, and who lie, commemorated in brass and stone,

Above *The High Street, Chipping Campden, looking north*

Opposite *Market day* in Cirencester

ICEBERG
MEVA

in its cool interior. Smiling ploughboy cherubs on churchyard memorials greet emerging worshippers and visitors, and a stone owl marks the grave of furniture-designer Gordon Russell, who lived and worked in Campden.

Signs hang; chimneys and gables carry the eyes to Cotswold skies; mullions, date-panels, sundials, doorways deep-set and shadowed add character, and all details delight. Everything is balanced, blended and beautiful in its harmony, so that it is hard to realise that, according to local Poor Law papers, poverty had been a serious problem for two hundred years. By the end of the last century many houses were decayed, the streets were deserted and a quarter of the town's two thousand population had left. No railway came to revive it, but C. R. Ashbee did in 1902, bringing craftsmen from their unhappy London environment and setting up the Campden Guild. Although this lasted for only a few years it did help rejuvenation, establishing the town as a centre for arts and crafts. In 1929 F. L. Griggs, Norman Jewson and others set up the Campden Trust, bought and restored empty High Street properties and initiated an early awareness in the conservation of buildings. What we see today is the outcome of those men's vision.

Chipping Norton

At about 650ft (200m) exposed to the cold winds of winter, Chipping Norton's large triangular market place is the smile on the town's friendly face, for it is full of life, colour and activity on Wednesdays. Relatively little is known about the growth and fortunes of the town, although it was probably founded in the mid-twelfth century by William fitz Alan, then lord of the manor. By 1224 it had acquired the Chipping (meaning market) part of its name, and in 1607 it gained its borough charter.

Near a green and breezy recreation area to the south of the market place, and enjoying quiet seclusion, St Mary's Church is witness to the town's prosperity which was based on the wool trade. Its soaring, elegant nave was rebuilt in 1485 at the expense of a local merchant, John Ashfield, although he is not commemorated among the many woolmen whose memorial brasses, taken up last century, are now displayed on wooden panels in the north aisle. The great east window in the south aisle traditionally came from Bruern Abbey.

'Chippy's' heart is at the market place, really a widening of the High Street. The sloping site results in its being on different levels, with High Street terraced along the upper side. Banks now occupy former eighteenth-century merchants' houses, and the White Hart has a proudly baroque front. Much refronting of properties (1720–80) points to Georgian prosperity, but too many hideous shop fascias, mainly those of chain and group stores, mar the overall effect. Antique and some other individual shops show more care. Gabled buildings in Middle Row and West Street show traditional seventeenth-century Cotswold gables in buildings with modern uses, while the idiom is more apparent in a row of almshouses in Church Lane, 'The work and gift of Henry Cornish, gent, 1640'. Eight gables and tall chimney stacks make a marvellous rhythm, but beyond the town is its most memorable skyline, the gleefully eccentric chimney, dated 1872, rising from the massively Victorian Bliss Valley Tweed Mill, built as though it were a great mansion in a park.

Cirencester

In the south Cotswolds all roads seem to converge here as they have done since Roman times. The Saxons established the first market, which was renewed and enlarged by the Normans who recognised the value of good communications. Henry I refounded the Augustinian abbey in 1131, which subsequently formed the royal manor of Cirencester, and exercised great influence on the medieval development of the town and its fortunes until the Dissolution. By then the abbey had become the largest community of its order and the wealthiest Augustinian foundation in England. Now, apart from a Norman gateway and a short stretch of precinct wall, all traces have vanished.

Roman Corinium, founded about AD75, was planned on a grid of straight streets. Medieval Cirencester, covering only a small part of the original town, seems to have avoided straightness. Only Gosditch Street, Dollar Street and Gloucester Street, aligned on Ermin Street, retain Roman directness, and, with Spitalgate Lane, effectively formed a western boundary to the abbey lands. The parish church abutted on the south. After the Dissolution the abbey and its lands were acquired by Dr Richard Master, one of Queen Elizabeth's physicians; his house was demolished in 1964 and flats were built on the site. Today, the Abbey Grounds, with swans on the landscaped River Churn, create a delightful and large open space for public enjoyment. Thus, from early medieval times, any town expansion north of the parish church has been restricted.

South of the Market Place, Cricklade Street represents the continuation of Ermin Street, while Castle Street leads south-west along the line of Foss Way, now the Tetbury road. Medieval Cirencester is largely concentrated in a compact area within the western angle between Ermin Street and the Foss Way, and along Cricklade Street and Dyer Street south and east. The parish church of St John stands pivotal at the town centre, dominating the Market Place, the largest and most handsome of all Cotswold wool churches, earning nine pages in *Pevsner* (really by David Verey). Twelfth century in origin, most of what we now see covers the period 1350–1530, the last date showing the complete rebuilding by the parishioners in its glorious Tudor style. Almost a century earlier, c1460, the soaring Perpendicular tower had been completed, and in 1490 the great south porch was added, paid for by the abbot and designed as an office in which to conduct secular business. At the Dissolution it became the Town Hall, and in the eighteenth century it was handed over to the vicar and wardens.

Only one pre-Reformation secular building survives, St Thomas's Hospital, known as the Weavers' Hall, in Thomas Street, founded in the fifteenth century as an almshouse and, modernised inside, still used for that original purpose. Elsewhere, seventeenth-century gabled houses, individually or in short terraces, share street frontages with taller, formal, eighteenth-century houses reflecting the town's continuing prosperity. The best examples are all encountered on the Cirencester Town Walk, described in an excellent and useful leaflet of the same name, with map, and produced by the local Civic Society. I advise anyone interested in buildings to follow its suggested route, which takes between an hour and an hour and a half, starting and finishing outside the south porch of the church. From there you may be satisfied merely to watch the flow of life in and around the Market Place, which is filled with stalls on Mondays and Fridays, with cars at all other times. Eighteenth-century façades, pastel-painted and modest, with ground-floor shops, create an elegant frame to the Market Place's bowed curve. Behind, some timber-framing can be discovered, as can modern developments in brick and slate. Fascia-boards, windows and roof-lines all contribute to the pleasing effect and the 1860 Corn Exchange on the south side is a nice counterpoint to the church opposite on which all lines and curves converge.

Cirencester seems to be the right size for a town, with a population of around fifteen thousand. It certainly feels right, with a friendly atmosphere, a fashionable quality, a justifiable air of well-being and few jarring visual notes. It retains market-charter character, serving a large surrounding rural area, yet does not aim too much for tourists, although the superb Corinium Museum is a real attraction. So is Cirencester Park with its many square miles of formal parkland, probably the finest example of geometrical landscaping, with great avenues and rides and splendid trees. Pope helped the first Earl Bathurst to design it in 1720–70, and it is open to the public for walking and riding, but vehicles are prohibited. The mansion (1714–18), hidden behind the enormous yew hedge by Park Lane, is not open. Along the Tetbury road is the Royal Agricultural College, founded in 1846 by progressive local farmers under the chairmanship of the then Earl Bathurst. Ever since, this independent organisation has profoundly influenced farming, not only in the Cotswolds, but throughout the country.

Lechlade

With its feet very much in vale country Lechlade can rightly be regarded as a cornerstone of south-eastern Cotswolds. Just within Gloucestershire it fronts three other counties, Oxfordshire, Berkshire and Wiltshire, and is washed by two Cotswold rivers, the Leach and the Coln, which join the Thames south-east and south-west of the town respectively. Geography, therefore, has given it advantages, added to which it was for centuries the highest navigable point on the Thames, one of the main trade arteries from London to the west. Of almost equal significance was its being on a busy north-south route, represented now by the A361, from Chipping Campden to Salisbury, a road recognised by Ogilby in his 1675 road-book and turnpiked eighty years later. The east-west road, the A417, from Oxford to Cirencester and Gloucester passes through the town, and surprisingly Lechlade failed to capitalise on the advantages that river and road traffic brought it. Fairford, only 4 miles (6.4km) to the west, developed like Lechlade as a market town from the early thirteenth century, and neither prospered at the expense of the other, although trade in river-borne commodities gave Lechlade the edge later. Today, Lechlade suffers from being at the junction of two busy roads.

St Lawrence's is one of the great, if lesser known, wool churches, which was built of Taynton stone in the late fifteenth century. Brasses commemorate merchants; in 1815 Shelley was inspired to compose 'A Summer Evening Churchyard, Lechlade', which is more of a Gothic dirge than an ode to beauty. Halfpenny Bridge (1792) still retains its toll-house, although traffic on the A361 passes freely. St John's Bridge to the east has medieval origins but is largely a rebuilding (*c*1830).

Good seventeenth- and eighteenth-century houses front High Street and Burford Street, many having arches big enough for waggons or coaches. The most characteristic feature of the town is the large number of neat little summer-houses and elegant gazebos that adorn the gardens. Lechlade life was quiet and leisurely before the surge of motor traffic.

Moreton-in-Marsh

Although the Abbot of Westminster was granted a weekly market in 1226 in his manor here, and it did not appear to have become a borough, it did have non-agricultural tenements referred to as burgages, and their pattern survives along and behind High Street properties. This very wide street aligned along the Foss Way continues to serve as a busy market place on Tuesdays. As a centre of the wool trade in the northern Cotswolds Moreton never succeeded to the extent that Stow did. Perhaps the century start enjoyed by Stow, only 5 miles (8km) down the road at a more important junction of roads, always gave the higher town an advantage. The arrival in 1853 of the Worcester–Oxford railway encouraged some growth, which resulted in an increase in trade at the livestock mart and promoted Moreton's hopes, but only in the last third of this century, with its surge in motor traffic and the visitors that it brings, has Moreton really flourished.

Today Moreton is a cheerful, busy place. The trees that line High Street break up the lines of cars that park there and make the street appear narrower than its real width. The church, originally a chapel-of-ease for Bourton-on-the-Hill, largely an 1848 rebuilding, hides away east of High

Street and marks the nucleus of the original village by the Roman road. It is not a wool church, and few buildings in the town relate to any medieval prosperity. Curfew Tower, at the corner of Oxford Street, probably dates from the sixteenth century. Possibly the oldest structure in the town, it consists of a small stone tower with a gabled turret, a clock dated 1648 and a bell apparently dated 1633. On the wall a copy of the 1905 market tolls gives a glimpse of those leisurely Edwardian days that are beyond the memory of most of the hurrying visitors.

Elegant eighteenth-century frontages grace both sides of High Street, all in the golden stone from Bourton quarries nearby, with The Steps, The White Hart and the Manor House Hotel particularly pleasing. Moreton has been a travellers' town for at least 1,700 years, and the tradition continues, with a variety of good accommodation, good shops, including the inevitable antique shops, an excellent book-shop and friendly restaurants. Most buildings are two-storey, with only a scattering of three-storey ones, and a north-south alignment ensures that, given sunshine, one side of High Street or the other present a bright face for some time each day. The island group in the middle holds centre stage, dominated by the remarkably fine Redesdale Market Hall, a successful essay in Victorian-Gothic of 1887. Oxford Street contains more worthwhile buildings, particularly the neo-Greek Congregational Chapel (1860) and the slightly earlier Infants School with its nice Victorian lettering in an inscription.

Northleach

The recent completion of the A40 bypass to its north has not only returned a relative peace to Northleach but has probably enhanced its survival value as a small, relatively unspoilt Cotswold market town. About 1220 the Abbot of Gloucester took 50 acres (20ha) from his manorial land at Eastington in the upper valley of the Leach, near the Foss Way and other existing trade routes, and in 1227 was granted a charter to hold a weekly market and annual fair. Based on a triangular market place twice as large as the present one, and having 80 burgage plots along its north and south sides, each about 2 poles (11yd – 10m) wide and 20 poles (110yd – 100m) long, the town quickly flourished through its wool trade.

Cirencester, Gloucester and Winchcombe abbeys grazed their flocks on the surrounding hills and huge quantities of wool were sent to European countries. From the mid-fourteenth century this export trade was concentrated in the hands of a few merchants, who were members of the Staple, and Northleach was a wool-collecting centre until the Dissolution, when the wool trade declined and there are no more records of the activities of

The south view of Northleach Church. The tower dates from 1360–1400 and the south porch is early fifteenth century

the Northleach wool-merchants. Northleach became a country market town whose mid-sixteenth-century tradesmen included glovers, weavers, collar-makers, smiths and brewers, supplemented on market days by stall-holders from Bourton, Stow, Great Rissington and Winchcombe.

Islanded buildings to the south and east of the small sloping Market Place represent in-filling of the original area with permanent shops, houses, and work-places. Some, like the Old Wool House, the Sherborne Arms and, by The Green, the Tudor House, show their sixteenth- or seventeenth-century origins. A narrow street near The Green is delightfully called The Peep. The road from the south-east corner of the Market Place leads to Mill End, where two mills existed at the time of Domesday. The Allen Almshouses by the stream form a pleasant terrace.

Northleach's great church, paid for by local wool-merchants, stands slightly aloof beyond the western side of the market place yet commands the townscape. Lofty, light and graceful, it was completely rebuilt during the second half of the fifteenth century. Its masonry and the statuary of the south porch are fine enough to grace a cathedral, while inside woolmen and dealers gaze piously from gleaming, costly memorial brasses, usually incorporating merchants' marks. Feet rest on sheep and woolsacks, and slender-waisted wives, also depicted in Tudor dress, share the silent dignity. Churchyard memorials show fine carving and inscriptions to complete the setting for this most memorable of Cotswold wool churches.

The London–Gloucester turnpike came through the town in 1746, and most of the larger buildings along High Street were refronted then or soon afterwards. Seen from the top of the Market Place, roofs of buildings opposite still indicate the original width of burgage plots, even when some of these have been combined. Footpaths to their north, and by the side of the River Leach to the south, give views of the backs of these plots, illustrating their length.

Few other buildings in the town have great architectural merit. A clutch of former coaching-inns by the Market Place add distinction; the Dutton Almshouses of 1616 to house six women have recently been modernised to provide comfortable homes for four; beyond Northleach's western end, by the Foss Way crossroads, the 1790 House of Correction became a police station, and now, suitably adapted, houses the Cotswold Countryside Collection, artefacts illustrating the agricultural history of the area, rural and social life, plus indoor displays and, during the summer, outdoor events (open from April to October). An excellent local history leaflet outlines Northleach's history, gives details of town walks and buildings, and is good value for money.

Painswick

Whether it is described as a large village or a small town is immaterial, for Painswick is unique in the Cotswolds. Sensibly sited on a well-drained spur of high land between Painswick Beacon and Stroud, Painswick received a market charter in 1253, and New Street, now carrying the A46 through the heart of the town, was intended for development as the borough, although it has no burgage plots like those of other planned towns.

Although a few Tudor buildings survive, Painswick's prosperity as a clothing town rather than as a wool town occurred during the seventeenth and eighteenth centuries, peaking at a time when the new Classical Renaissance in architecture influenced the visiting clothiers and merchants to improve or even rebuild their provincial houses by introducing elegant façades, with sash windows, pediments, pilasters and intricately carved door-cases. Local limestone from quarries on the Beacon – creamy-coloured when fresh and weathering to a wonderful silvery-grey – was cut and worked to yield marvellous detail, creating endless patterns in texture, light and shade, so that a walk along the narrow streets is full of joyous discoveries.

New Street has some of the best houses, including Hazelbury House, the Falcon Hotel and the fifteenth-century building housing the post office – the only exposed timber-framing in the town (the churchyard lychgate of 1901 reused timbers from the belfry). Bisley Street, a continuation of Gloucester Street into the town, has some Tudor houses, with The Chur and The Little Fleece of fourteenth-century date – the latter (now National Trust) is a bookshop and its upper floor was a weaving room. Semi-circular arches, some blocked, some now windowed, some open, were packhorse entrances to courtyards behind.

Painswick houses front directly on to pavements, with small patches of brightly flowered gardens tucked away in odd corners, yielding unexpected accents of colour. As a consequence the large churchyard surrounding St Mary's Church takes on the attributes of an important open space in the centre of the town. Enhanced by its famous yews – supposedly a total of ninety-nine, the oldest having been planted in 1792 – the churchyard is embellished by the finest collection of tombs and monuments in the Cotswolds, if not in England. Dating from 1603 to 1841, so far as their inscriptions are decipherable, they commemorate Painswick's clothiers, merchants and traders, mainly of the seventeenth and eighteenth centuries. Many were carved by the Bryan family of masons, whose ornate house was in Bisley Street. Designs sometimes took the form of domestic articles – tea-caddies, pepperpots, wine-coolers, octagonal, cylindrical, some with knobs on, and decorated with carvings of shells, lyres, skulls, hearts, ovals, ribbons and swags. Two 'Tomb Trail' leaflets identify many of the memorials and the craftsmen who created them.

Streets web from east of the churchyard, where Loveday's House, now the Vicarage, is a good example of a small eighteenth-century house with rich detail, although its windows have lost their glazing-bars, contemporary with Dover House in Vicarage Street which leads down to the valley where Painswick's many mills successively used the waters of Painswick Brook, which is now scarcely sufficient to float a tadpole. Modest structures all, most have been converted into private houses or flats, but seventeenth-century

Stow-on-the-Wold

date-panels point to their long history, which ended so far as clothing was concerned between 1820 and 1840, although some became pin mills or flour mills a few decades later. A self-guided walks leaflet encourages people to walk along the Painswick stream, observing the mills.

The Annual Exhibition of the Guild of Gloucestershire Craftsmen takes place at the Painswick Institute in August, attracting thousands of visitors. On the Sunday on or following 19 September, the patronal festival is marked by the colourful Clipping Ceremony, when flower-garlanded village children join hands and 'clyp', or embrace, the church, circling in procession around the church, and then are joined by a large congregation for an open-air service on the north side of the church.

Above the town 250 acres (100ha) of common land on the Beacon invite walking and riding (and provide a golf course), with rewarding all-round views. The Iron Age hillfort at the crest is a reminder of early settlers. Today, we are the inheritors of the architectural good taste and good manners that the clothing prosperity generated.

Stow-on-the-Wold

Eight roads converge on Stow, which, at over 750ft (229m), is the highest town in the Cotswolds. The importance of the road junction made Stow a natural site for a market, and in 1107 Henry I granted a 'port', or market, to the Abbot of Evesham, the manorial landowner on his Maugersbury estate. It was a purely entrepreneurial and commercial proposition, for Stow had no castle, fortification or abbey.

The Foss Way was diverted into the large rectangular market square, still the lively heart of the town, which is bypassed to its west by the A429 along the Foss and crossed by the important east-west roads away from the town centre. Streets leave The Square at three of its corners, only the north-eastern one creating a more intimate closed grouping, enhanced by the small area of green, with a few small trees acting as a foil and foreground, its stocks replacing earlier ones whose ancestry probably dates to late medieval times. Earlier this century the grassed area, which was grazed by sheep, was much more extensive than it is now. Stone-built houses, shops and inns face inwards to The Square, whose most prominent element is, regrettably, the uninspiring St Edward's Hall. Dating from 1878 and built in the Gothic Revival style, it became a favourite tethering-place for horses before the motor age. To its south the town cross is more medieval although it does bear a headstone of 1878. Apart from the police station at the north-western corner of The Square, almost all the buildings in The Square and its radiating streets are seventeenth and eighteenth century.

The best range forms an almost continuous frontage down the eastern side, dominated by inns and hotels, with the King's Arms taking pride of place. Known to have been used as an inn in 1647, it became a busy and important post house and coaching-inn during the early decades of last century. Just above it, Ross House, formerly The Plough, has a particularly fine canopy over its doorway. The Talbot, on the south side of The Square, dates from 1714 and was once the Corn Exchange, although all that remains from such use is the small brass 'letter-box' on its walls, through which farmers placed their sample packets of grain. Beside The Talbot narrow alleys run through to Sheep Street, following the lines of former burgage strips (although Stow was never a borough, its medieval plan kept to traditional burgage plan). The Talbot Yard is now an attractive intimate precinct.

Stow's most attractive elevation adorns St Edward's House, on the west side of The Square. Its early eighteenth-century front with fluted Corinthian columns was probably an addition to an older structure behind. To its north, the Crooked House is thought to date from 1450, its tilt supposedly the result of subsidence of old foundations. The west side properties tend to hide the parish church which lacks the unity and appeal of those at Campden and Northleach. Wool prosperity at Stow seems not to have been transmitted into fine architecture and a mix of styles results in a fragmented building.

Near it, in Church Street, is St Edward's Grammar School, which was founded in 1475 but rebuilt in 1594. This modest late Tudor building has good six-light windows and two unusual, perforated ventilation stones, and is now used as a masonic hall. Digbeth Street, which leaves The Square at its south-eastern corner, also has a Tudor building, with an arched stone doorway and stone mullioned windows, which is contemporary with the grammar school. Beyond, at the corner of Sheep Street, the Royalist Hotel contains wooden beams which radio-carbon tests have dated to the late tenth century. Although the date on the porch is 1615, the building is considerably older, possibly fifteenth or sixteenth century, and, unusually for Cotswold, was timber-framed, but this is now hidden behind roughcast walling. Prior to its present use, it was known as The Eagle and Child, and has been a hospice, a religious house and, more recently, a pair of private houses.

Sheep Street, the road out towards Oxford, is lined with modest artisans' houses, some of which are now shops. More burgage plots extend behind them for about 100yd (91m), with stone-walled alleys called tures leading to Back Walls. Small workshops in some of these are reminders that in medieval times these burgage plots would have seen a lively activity, with many trades involved.

Tetbury

Its situation between the arable and dairying country of the vale to its south and the wool-producing Cotswolds to the north, with good roads between, made Tetbury an obvious site for a market town. Today, all streets converge on the Market Place which was laid out by 1200. Its original large triangular space is intruded upon by the great wool market house which was built on eighteen stout stone pillars, unusually, during the Commonwealth in 1655, when there was, apparently, 'a very considerable weekly market on Wednesday, which chiefly consists of yarn'. The market still flourishes, with stalls in and under the Market House displaying a wide variety of goods. A Women's Institute market on Friday mornings is more specialised and undeniably popular.

Chipping Street leads northwards to The Chipping, now a car park and formerly the site of an important cheese and bacon market, but its market house has gone. Running down from its north-east corner, Chipping Steps, which are cobbled and of medieval origin, give a flavour of earlier days when this was the main packhorse route from Cirencester into the town centre. Stepped roof-lines of cottages down their eastern side add particular appeal, although the buildings are modest compared with many in the town.

Around The Chipping itself, especially along its tree-lined western side, three-storey houses show the elegance associated with eighteenth-century prosperity. The Priory, a large house of 1767 at its north-western corner, with two medieval windows, occupies the site of a short-lived Cistercian priory which soon moved to a fresh site at Kingswood, near Wotton-under-Edge. Further monastic remnants exist on the opposite side of The Chipping, at Nos 5, 13 and 15. A Tudor arch between Nos 5 and 13 leads into a passage with an earlier arch, beyond which is the Malthouse, used during World War II by US forces planning their part in the Normandy landings.

Fine buildings around the Market Place, mainly three-storey, include the whimsically named hotel The Snooty Fox. Formerly the White Hart Hotel, it was rebuilt around the middle of the last century and has a ballroom for the Beaufort Hunt on its first floor. Closing the eastern end of the Market Place, more handsome Georgian buildings include the Talbot Hotel, with seventeenth-century gables down its eastern side, and the classical idiom continues eastwards along Silver Street to The Green at the end, where Barton Abbot's eighteenth-century wing has been added to an older house which bears a date-panel 'JW 1776'.

St Mary's Church of 1781, apart from its medieval tower and late-Victorian rebuilt spire, is a graceful essay in Gothic Revival architecture. Huge windows ensure a flood of light which is scarcely broken by the tall, slender nave pillars – narrow clustered columns, iron-cored but wood-encased. A magnificent plaster ceiling enhances the quality of light, but diminishes those elements of mystery enjoyed by dark, medieval roofs, while splendid chandeliers, each of thirty-six lights, exude the impression of Georgian opulence which characterises much of Tetbury.

Church Street carried the Bath road up into the Market Place. Most of the former merchants' town houses now have ground-floor shops or are business premises, with some façades concealing timber-framing while others are jettied over pillared arcades, as with the former Eight Bells Inn, which is now a shop. Almost opposite, No 17 has two projecting gabled wings which bear the initials of Richard Talboys, one of the town's important personalities in Jacobean times.

Long Street curves gently north-westwards from the Market Place, with the best surviving continuous frontages in the town, although the most impressive ones are on the north-facing side and are invariably seen in shadow. Although the Classical idiom predominates, many seventeenth-century gabled buildings survive, most of which are three-storey, although one has four storeys. This is evidence of the continuing prosperity that was enjoyed by Tetbury, probably through the influence of the Stroud clothiers, while at Cirencester and in the main Cotswold area trade had declined.

Gumstool Street, which runs north-eastwards from the Market Place, carried the old coach road from Cirencester into the town, with the Crown Inn (1693) prominent at the top, and the starting-point each Spring Bank Holiday Monday for the celebrated Woolsack Races, when competitors, each carrying a 65lb (30kg) sack of wool, race downhill to the cattle market and back. The races form part of Tetbury's festival, when local stallholders wear medieval costume, and mummers, Morris dancers and jesters help to re-create a colourful cameo of the town's past. Today, the friendly town prospers on its small businesses, offices, workshops, shops, two industrial estates, and a companionable, comfortable atmosphere within the historical ambience which is imparted by the fine buildings of grey Cotswold stone and the undoubted kudos associated with the fact that HRH The Prince of Wales's country home, Highgrove House, is just across the fields south-west of the town, and the Princess Royal's home, Gatcombe Park, is nearby.

Winchcombe

This small town on the busy A46 a few miles north-east of Cheltenham has roots that go deeper than those of most Cotswold towns. Its strategic situation enabled it to control northern access to the hills and by the eighth century Winchcombe was not only a seat of Mercian royalty but also the home of a great abbey, refounded under the Benedictine order in 969, which flourished, apart from a period in the mid-fourteenth century, until its Dissolution in 1539. Few abbeys of such importance have so successfully vanished without a trace of survivals, the result of effective demolition by Lord Seymour of Sudeley. No serious excavation of the abbey's site east of the parish church has been attempted.

Winchcombe became a borough by the eleventh century and at Domesday was one of only four boroughs in Gloucestershire, with a probable population then of almost a thousand – large by the standards of those days – and its free burgesses would have included craftsmen and traders. The comings and goings of its monks to and from their vast wool-producing Cotswold estates, together with the pilgrims and the Tudor visitors to nearby Sudeley Castle, must have ensured a round-the-year liveliness and prosperity in the town.

A list of market tolls in the early Middle Ages covered a wide range of products, while the growth of the wool trade during the thirteenth and fourteenth centuries, although controlled by the abbey, undoubtedly benefited Winchcombe. By about 1400 the abbey tightened its control over the market and the affairs of the town. In the 1460s, Abbot William initiated the building of a new parish church, starting with the chancel, but he left the parishioners to complete it, with the financial help of Sir Ralph Boteler of Sudeley, whose features may be those of one of an impressive array of carved heads and grotesques that adorn the outside walls.

A few late-Tudor buildings survive. The George Inn, opposite North Street, which was built by Winchcombe's penultimate abbot in the early sixteenth century for pilgrims, retains his initials 'RK' (Richard Kidderminster) in the spandrels of its doorway. Its timber-galleried courtyard also dates from that period, but later alterations have changed much of the inn's character. More half-timbering, probably of the late sixteenth century, exists both in High Street and in its northwards continuation, Hailes Street, where Nos 21 and 23 were, last century, The Sudeley Arms. However, the so-called Tudor House, on the west side, is manifestly Victorian-Tudor and of stone.

To its west, High Street was widened in 1835, taking in part of the abbey grounds, and its nicely grouped eighteenth- and nineteenth-century houses stand on much older foundations. Nearby, at right angles, multi-coloured stonework and many small gables of the Dent Almshouses of 1865 represent Sir Gilbert Scott's contribution to the town. Three centuries earlier, and in a narrow lane behind the free-standing Jacobean House, which was built in 1618 to house the King's School, with the master's accommodation on the first floor, the Chandos Almshouses are the genuine Tudor article.

This wide area opposite the church may have served as a market place. To the west, Gloucester Street is rich in old buildings, which are mostly of stone but a few with half-timbering. Curvature of the streets imparts unplanned but graceful rhythm, revealing textured surfaces and lively roof-lines. There is little to displease and much to delight. No 23 houses the Winchcombe Railway Museum, and opposite, the Rabbit Box House shows carvings on its string course of a Tudor Rose and a rabbit. The Old Corner Cupboard, dating from about 1550, has a stone buttress, mullioned windows (one of seven lights), and a Tudor doorway with an oak studded door, with, oddly, a bust of Disraeli above.

Wotton-under-Edge

Steep-sided hills, many clothed with beechwoods, crowd in and enfold Wotton on the north and east, with the grey town set at the mouth of Tyley Bottom. Formerly part of the Berkeley estate, the town regained its borough status in 1253. By the early 1600s, the clothing trade was well established here, with mills along Dyers Brook that runs through Potters Pond at the lower, eastern edge of the town. Half of Wotton's workforce was employed in the clothing trade; among the others were shoemakers, bakers,

One of the many fifteenth-century gargoyles which adorn the church at Winchcombe

butchers, glovers, inn-keepers, carpenters, smiths, masons, millers, tanners and carriers – a typical trading galaxy of a thriving country and market town in the seventeenth century.

Wotton flourishes today. The old street pattern of the thirteenth-century planned town survives along the east-west double spine, where Old Town and Gloucester Street are paralleled by Long Street and Bradley Street, with Church Street and Bear Street forming cross-links. St Mary's parish church, off Culverhay, a northward continuation of Church Street, is mainly thirteenth century, with perpendicular tower and a historic organ (played by Handel) from London's St Martin-in-the-Fields, a gift from George I in 1726, which was bought by Wotton's vicar in 1799. Gimson's Cotswold craftsmen made the altar, reredos and communion rails, and the early Berkeley brasses are famous.

Exploring Wotton from the church is easy. Verey rightly states that there is 'nothing architecturally outstanding, and no horrors'. Modest eighteenth-century town houses of clothiers and merchants line the streets, with a few gabled seventeenth-century buildings. Most now have shops on ground floors, but few sell antiques. Continuous frontages along narrow pavements and a fractured skyline of gables maintain liveliness, with the Tolsey's cupola a contrasting accent. Some brick frontages intrude. On no account miss the Perry and Dawes Almshouses in Church Street, and heed the welcoming inscription above the entrance. Wotton is by far the most workaday and untourist-orientated of the Cotswold towns; it looks, feels and *is* friendly, and, with its present population approaching 5,000, is the largest town in this survey apart from Cirencester.

9
EXPLORING THE COTSWOLDS

This chapter is concerned mainly with the motoring visitor and the walker, while the cyclist should also find plenty that is relevant. A glance at a motoring map on the relatively small scale of 3 or 4 miles to the inch shows a good network of main roads threading the Cotswolds, supplemented by an intricate web of minor ones. For serious exploration, however, such maps are inadequate. By far the most useful is the Ordnance Survey Tourist Map, at 1in to the mile, which covers about 90 per cent of the area, but does not touch the sector south-west of Stroud and excludes a narrow strip along the eastern margin, with Chipping Norton just off the edge. This map shows places of special interest, historic houses, viewpoints, parking and picnic areas, together with camp and caravan sites. Rivers, woods and contours are clearly picked out, and footpaths marked – the two long-distance ones very prominently. For general exploration this map cannot be bettered, although walkers may prefer the 1:50,000, and more likely the 1:25,000 maps of the Landranger and Pathfinder series published by the Ordnance Survey.

With eight roads converging on both Cirencester and Stow-on-the-Wold and six on Burford, these are excellent centres for motor touring, although distances between neighbouring market towns are so modest that, apart from the south-west, the choice is really much wider. Many visitors may, indeed, opt for Cheltenham as being at the focus of a semi-circle whose base runs from Broadway to Stroud.

Most 'A' roads, except the A46 along the foot of the scarp, tend to follow the upland ridges. They are mainly wide and well-surfaced, and some carry heavy traffic. These include the A44, A40, A429, A417, A433 and A461. Most villages lie off these main routes and to appreciate such places minor roads need to be taken. Most of the minor roads are narrow and winding, sometimes wide-verged, and often quite narrow between hedges or walls. Occasional short steep sections may be expected. Arable farming nowadays needs machinery, tractors seem to become ever larger and frequently tow trailers or other equipment. The Cotswolds are not predominantly dairying country so the twice-daily movement of cows for milking is not usually encountered. However, horse-riders are, so be prepared to meet these at any time. David Nicholson's large training establishment is at Condicote, near

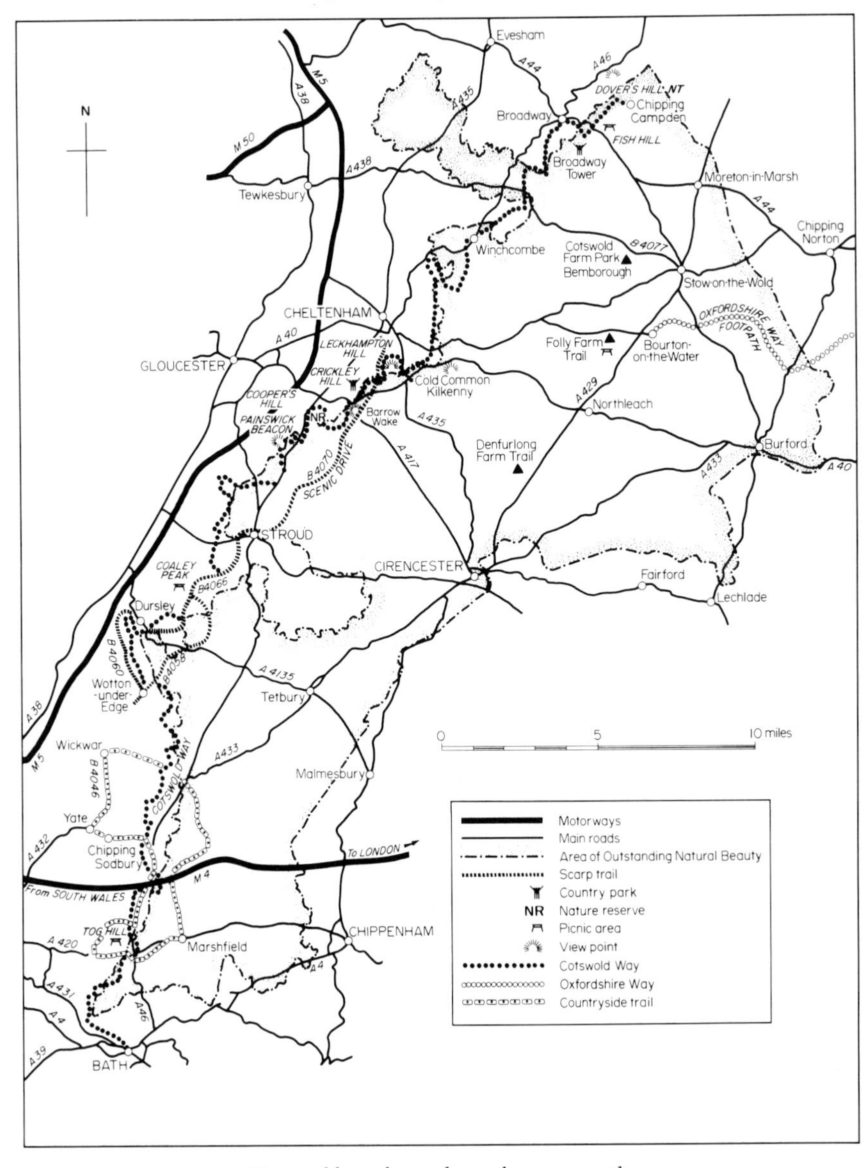

Cotswold roads, paths and nature trails

'Shakespeare Cottages', Broadway. Sixteenth century in origin, they were condemned in 1930 as being unfit for habitation, but were modernised in the late 1940s

Stow, and strings of his horses are often out on exercise in the nearby lanes. Consideration shown is always courteously acknowledged by a friendly wave from the stable lads who ride them.

The tours described are merely suggestions and vary in length from 30 to 70 miles (48–113km). Qualities of scenery, buildings, villages and places of interest are the criteria, not mileages. Each is a circular tour from one of the centres named, but obviously any other starting-point can be used where it is more convenient. Most of the popular villages have pubs serving refreshments or bar meals, and former coaching-inns on many main roads now provide excellent meals. (The largest and most ostentatious places do not necessarily offer the best value for money.) In planning a tour which incorporates a visit to a National Trust, English Heritage or other property with restricted opening times, it is advisable to check these beforehand at one of the Tourist Information Centres available in each of the main market towns.

1. Stow-on-the-Wold – Moreton-in-Marsh – Blockley – Chipping Campden – Willersey – Broadway – Ford – Stow-on-the-Wold

A tour that incorporates high wold landscapes, fine views from the northern section of the escarpment, beautiful villages and towns.

Take Foss Way, A429, north to Moreton, where car parking can be difficult on market days (Tuesdays). Turn west along A44 to Bourton-on-the-Hill. Batsford Park Arboretum lies north of the road near foot of the hill. Beyond the top of the hill, right on B4479 to Blockley, following signposts to village which lies off the B road. Follow signpost north to Chipping Campden, passing Broad Campden on the way. Chipping Campden merits a long stop. Everything pleases. Short detour to Ebrington, Hidcote and Mickleton would be justified; otherwise take B4035 north-west out of Campden, to descend the scarp to Aston-sub-Edge, joining A46 and turning south-west through Weston-sub-Edge and Willersey to Broadway. Allow generous time for a walkabout here. If Broadway Tower is to be visited, take A44 east, and turn right at top of Fish Hill. (Fee payable at Broadway Tower Country Park.) From either Broadway or the Tower, follow signpost to Snowshill, where there is a NT car park at northern edge of village.

Continue south along narrow, unclassified road to Ford, east on B4077 to Stow. If Cotswold Farm Park is to be visited, turn right at crossroads east of Ford.

2. Stow-on-the-Wold – Chipping Norton – Burford – Bourton-on-the-Water – Stow-on-the-Wold

A tour into the Oxfordshire Cotswolds also incorporating pastoral scenery in the Evenlode and Windrush valleys.

Take A436 east from Stow and in 2 miles (3.2km) fork right into Oddington, detouring in village to see the old church (signposted). Rejoin A436, detouring (left), if required, for Adlestrop, but in any case fork right for Cornwell and eventually reach Chipping Norton by A44.

Leave the town by B4450, south-westwards, for Churchill, right for Kingham and Bledington, and by an unclassified road through Idbury, joining A424 south into Burford. Allow plenty of time to explore the town before making another diversion, A361, to Fulbrook and narrow lane to Swinbrook and Minster Lovell. Return to Burford along A40, descend north through town again, across river, taking minor road west to Taynton and Great Barrington. Make a short 'there-and-back' detour to Little Barrington before heading north along ridge road above Windrush valley, and in 4 miles (6.4km) turn left into Little Rissington, continuing into Bourton-on-the-Water and returning to Stow by A429.

3. Stow-on-the-Wold – Northleach – Sudeley Castle – Winchcombe – Hailes Abbey – Stow

High wold country with upland roads and lanes, wide views, splendid churches, a castle and a monastic ruin.

Take A429 south, turning left ½ mile (800m) beyond Bourton bridge and follow minor road south via Clapton-on-the-Hill to Sherborne, enjoying wide views eastwards across the Windrush valley. In Sherborne turn left, above the Sherborne Brook, to Farmington and Northleach, where morning light is best in which to appreciate the sight of the church above the Market Place.

Take the main road westwards, crossing Foss Way at the traffic lights by the Countryside Collection Museum in former prison. In 2½ miles (4km) turn left, down into Compton Abdale, climbing beyond to rejoin A40, continuing to and along the Andoversford bypass. 1 mile (1.6km) after the A436 crossroads turn right into Whittington, right in the village, and second left in a mile, along a minor road northwards past Charlton Abbots and Humblebee Wood (Cotswold Way footpath sign to Belas Knap) to join A46 west of Winchcombe, where a short detour west for 2 miles (3.2km) is worthwhile if you wish to visit Cleeve Hill. For this, turn left at the Golf Club crossroads and park in an old quarry immediately past cattle-grid near Club House.

Returning to Winchcombe, make short detour to Sudeley Castle, if desired. Continue to top of hill for fine views, and turn sharp left, north descending to Hailes Abbey. Rejoin A46 and go north to roundabout at Toddington. Turn right, B4077, to Stanway, detour if required to Stanton, but rejoin B4077 up long winding hill to Stump Cross. In 1 mile (1.6km) fork right at crossroads before Ford, continue through Kineton to A436. Turn left and fork left into Naunton, rejoin A436 but soon turn right for Upper and Lower Slaughter before returning to Stow.

4. Cirencester – Seven Springs – Cheltenham – Winchcombe – Roel Gate – Compton Abdale – Chedworth Roman Villa – Cirencester

Follows the Churn valley and touches Cheltenham, largely on main roads, but the return from Winchcombe follows lonely minor roads over the central wolds, finishing with a visit to Chedworth.

Take A435, winding gently up the lovely Churn valley, pausing to see North Cerney church early on, with a possible detour to Elkstone from Colesbourne or Cowley (very narrow unclassified roads). At the important Seven Springs crossroads turn right on A436, with perhaps a pause at the Kilkenny viewpoint and picnic site, before swinging north to Dowdeswell, down A40 towards Cheltenham. Shortly after this joins A435 at Charlton Kings, turn right at traffic lights (signposted Prestbury) and in 2 miles (3.2km) join A46 in Prestbury, continuing to Cleeve Hill (detour at top of hill to visit the Common) and Winchcombe, which merits exploration.

Take minor road from centre of town (*not* the Sudeley Castle one) and climb south-eastwards up Round Hill, fork right, heading due south, with splendid view to right (west). Keep straight on, along the Salt Way, past Roel Gate crossroads, across A436 and in another 2 miles (3.2km) across A40, descending to Compton Abdale and up the hill beyond. This is now the White Way, with more wide views. If you wish to visit Withington turn right at Cassey Compton in the valley. If not, fork left for Chedworth Roman Villa. Return to Cassey Compton to rejoin White Way, heading southwards for Cirencester.

5. Cirencester – the Duntisbournes – Sapperton – Chalford – Bisley – Painswick – Crickley Hill – Elkstone – Cirencester

A shorter tour through the complex but beautiful countryside between the Churn and Frome valleys, mainly on minor roads which are narrow and winding.

Take A417 north from Cirencester, turning off left at the northern end of Stratton, to Daglingworth and the charming Duntisbourne villages and churches. From Duntisbourne Abbots turn back south-westwards to follow the ridge road southwards to Sapperton, with its fine church and Gimson, Barnsley and Jewson associations. Pick up A419 and head westwards into Chalford, which can be explored *only* on foot, starting along High Street. Limited car parking by main road near church or below canal round house.

Take minor road near church northwards (signposted Bisley). Steep climb out of Golden Valley, but Bisley soon reached. Enjoy a village walkabout before heading north out of Bisley (signposted Birdlip or Cheltenham). In 2 miles (3.2km), at The Camp, turn left, soon joining B4070 (signposted Stroud). In 1 mile (1.6km) at Bull's Cross (layby and good views), turn right down very narrow road (signposted Painswick). Slad, incidentally, is 1 mile (1.6km) south of Bull's Cross.

Painswick deserves a long stay (free car park in Stamages Lane south of the church). After savouring, follow A46 north, and in 3 miles (4.8km), if

Duntisbourne Leer

desired, turn left for Prinknash Abbey. A46 continues to Brockworth roundabout, turn right on A417, up Birdlip Hill to Air Balloon Inn roundabout. Keep left, and immediately left again, for Crickley Hill Country Park (free parking, various trails, good views). Return to roundabout and take A417 for Cirencester. If not visited already, in about 3 miles (4.8km) turn off for Elkstone and its exceptional church.

6. Cirencester – Tetbury – Wotton-under-Edge – Uley – Coaley Peak – Selsley Common – Minchinhampton – Cirencester

A tour of the south-western sector of the Cotswolds mainly along A and B roads, but becoming complex at the end.

Take A429, soon A433, from Cirencester to Tetbury, well worth a close exploration. A4135 west, past Beverstone, across A46, and in 3 miles (4.8km), where this forks for Dursley, keep ahead on B4058 to Wotton-under-Edge. Car parking near town centre. Give generous time to this most workaday, unshowy, friendly town.

Return up B4058 to the Dursley fork. This is the point from which, if desired, Ozleworth (church) is most easily visited, by minor road south, 2 miles (3.2km). Just east of the road junction, heading east, follow 'Scenic Route' signpost, forking left and turning left at first crossroads into Uley, joining B4066 up through village. Detour to Owlpen strongly recommended. Follow B4066 from Uley to Coaley Peak picnic site (extensive views, walks, Cotswold Way). Continue on B4066, crossing and descending Selsley Common, joining A46 near Stroud. Turn right, immediately fork left and go across the next main road, following the sign for Rodborough. Climb to Rodborough Common, and in the maze of lanes and roads which follow, aim for Minchinhampton, crossing the broad common on the way. Turn left into the town (church tower is a helpful beacon), and after looking around head eastwards for Cirencester.

Walks

Although no OS Outdoor Leisure Maps on the 1:25,000 scale have yet been prepared for the Cotswolds the area is covered by the OS Pathfinder Series at the same scale. Each sheet covers an area 12½ × 6¼ miles (20 × 10km) – about 75 sq miles (194km^2), is very handy to use and includes all necessary details useful to walkers including footpaths, bridleways and field boundaries. Additionally, there are increasing numbers of walks guides and leaflets, which are published privately but of varying quality.

Local authorities are statutorily obliged to identify where public footpaths leave the highway, but this is not always the case in practice. Across-country paths should be identified by yellow waymarks, bridleways by blue ones, but far too often no such waymarking occurs, either through local authority inaction or, more likely, because farmers and landowners have not given the necessary permission for such waymarking to be undertaken. Thus, while you *know* you have the right to use a waymarked track, the absence of waymarking does *not* imply that there is *no* right-of-way. If the OS map indicates a right-of-way, even though it may not be apparent on the ground, or may be obstructed (illegally, of course), it does exist and you may use it. An important High Court ruling (11 December 1987) relating to a section of the Wildlife and Countryside Act (1981) confirmed that the showing of a path or bridleway as a right-of-way on the definitive map, as given on the recent OS maps, is conclusive evidence of its existence as a public right-of-way.

In the Cotswolds many footpaths cross or follow the edges of fields, whether arable, pasture or meadow. It is, therefore, essential to keep to the line of a path to minimise any possible damage to growing crops. Even if the line of a path crosses, say, a field of growing corn, you are entitled to follow the route even if it means treading on the crop. If this is physically impossible, as it could be with mature oil-seed rape, you have no option but to try to walk around it. Paths running around the edges of fields should, incidentally, never be ploughed.

Gates should be left as you find them, which usually means closed. Wandering stock can become mixed with others, mate prematurely, upset cropping regimes, stray on to roads, or even spread infection. Courteous behaviour to landowners and farmers costs nothing. One wishes it was more often reciprocated and that walkers were shown more consideration. The law now allows farmers to graze some breeds of beef bulls with cows or heifers in fields crossed by footpaths. It is advisable to give them a wide berth and not to provoke them. Dairy bulls, usually Friesians, should not be grazed in fields crossed by public paths, and in any case should be avoided. In all my Cotswolds walking this is a problem I have not yet encountered. Much more to be expected is the natural curiosity shown by young bullocks towards humans. Unless provoked, such beasts will merely approach you and nothing more. They really are much friendlier than you would think! If you walk with a dog keep it under control, preferably visibly on a lead. This helps to reassure farmers that you are a responsible and thoughtful person.

A similar attitude of common sense should apply to your clothing, which should be comfortable and practical. The Cotswolds are not wilderness country, but some paths, especially on the western escarpment, have steep areas,and in wet weather most paths can become very muddy; Cotswold mud is particularly glutinous. Bridleways suffer from mud, too, and where well used, present problems for walkers. I have vivid memories of battling along sections of the Cotswold Way through Witcombe Wood, Brockworth Wood and Standish Wood which were almost impassably churned up by hooves. All of which is intended to show that, in any but the driest conditions, walking boots are the most sensible form of footwear, although strong shoes or trainers may be adequate for straightforward field paths.

Since the Cotswolds are largely under 1,000ft (305m) OD, only when there is very low cloud or thick mist is visibility likely to be so impaired that a compass becomes necessary. However, I have found one useful in some woodland, given a choice of routes and no waymarking, to help me to decide the correct path to take. Lightweight binoculars are more useful, not only for observing wildlife but for locating, on the far side of a field or on a hillside, a stile or a gap in the hedge which indicates, in the absence of a visible footpath, a point at which to aim.

The Cotswolds offer many miles of good, usually fairly easy, walking. Mixed and varied landscapes of wold and field, woodland, copse or riverside present new scenes every few hundred yards. Stiles and gates, no matter how rustic or shaky, are welcoming pointers along the route. Where they are used, yellow or blue waymarks are discs of reassurance. Quiet countryside provides scope for observing, listening, appreciating: flowers, bird song, the rustle of leaves, the kiss of grass, the wind-waved corn, bare winter branches against the sky, or clouds that mimic mountains.

Farmed landscapes are remote, so walking through them can be very lonely. Be prepared not to meet a soul, unless you are on the Cotswold Way. Except at certain times and seasons you are not likely to meet anyone working in the fields with whom to exchange a word. Any farm worker will probably be on a distant tractor. Most villages seem deserted on weekdays, except the popular 'honeypots'. Only at weekends and during school holidays are there many signs of life. I have rarely seen village children on country paths, nor have I met country folk on the parish paths unless they were exercising dogs; yet I have always been aware that the paths I have walked have, for the most parts, deep roots bearing the imprint, or footprints, of generations of country folk going about their daily lives, walking from farm to village, hamlet to village, to market town, or to work, to church, to the pub. Richard Jefferies, that most mystical of walkers, truly wrote, 'They only know a country who are acquainted with its footpaths. By the roads, indeed, the outside may be seen, but the footpaths go through the heart of the land.'

Neither of the two long-distance footpaths which affect the Cotswolds has yet been officially designated by the Countryside Commission. The Cotswold Way, which follows the escarpment for 100 miles (161km) from Chipping Campden to Bath, uses existing rights-of-way and owes its existence to efforts of the Gloucestershire Ramblers' Association and is supported by the County Council. The Oxfordshire Way is a 65 mile (105km) route initiated by CPRE Oxfordshire branch that links the Cotswolds AONB to the Chilterns AONB, from Bourton-on-the-Water to Henley-on-Thames. Only about one-fifth of it comes within the area covered by this book. Both walks are suitable for walkers of all abilities and are enjoyable at any time of the year. The high-level nature of the Cotswold Way offers spectacular views and although it, as well as the Oxfordshire Way, provides challenges for serious and fit walkers, they can be sampled in sections which, by using other rights-of-way, can be incorporated into circular walks. Some suggestions for these are included in the detailed walks that follow.

1. Bibury Circular (5½ miles – 8.8km)

A pleasant, easy walk in and above the delightful Coln valley, starting and finishing at the car park south of the bridge at Bibury.

Cross the river by the new footbridge and follow the main road southwards by the river and up the hill through the village. At the end of the village turn right along the bridleway (signposted Bibury Court Farm). Go down to Bibury Mill, cross the river and keep right, heading almost due south along the surfaced track, between fenced parkland pastures and passing many gates bearing 'Private: No Footpath' notices. Follow the obvious track ahead, climbing into woodland and heading away from the river. Where the main track eventually swings right, keep ahead through a gate on a grassy track along the right-hand edge of a wood. Notices remind you that the bridleway you are on runs through Bibury Court Estates, and as the track descends to and through riverside meadows, further notices warn you to stay away from the river bank in order not to disturb fishes (or sensitive anglers). Apart from the unnecessary notices, this is a very pleasant part of the walk along the valley of the Coln.

Entering mature woodland, where the bridleway can be very muddy, the route is obvious, enters parkland, and reaches the road at the river-bridge at Yew Tree Cottage, south of Coln St Aldwyn, so a visit to this village necessitates a 'there-and-back' detour.

The return route almost turns back on the outward one near Yew Tree Cottage where a 'Bridleway' sign points up a grassy track that climbs through the parkland beeches. Veering right and passing through a gate, cross a field and aim between a house and barn ahead. Continue straight ahead, keeping the house on the right, and aim to the right of a double power post, across a field, towards its far corner with another house on the right. Turn right on the road and, in a short distance, a signposted footpath on the right sets you on a good track which soon descends, through gates, into a small valley, climbs past a small wood, where you keep right at the top, following a hedge and heading generally north-westwards. Eventually, when the new houses at Arlington come into view ahead, yellow waymarks appear, directing you right along footpaths towards Arlington, where you join the main road into Bibury.

2. Seven Springs – Charlton Kings Common – Leckhampton Hill – South Hill – Coberley – Seven Springs (6 miles – 9.6km)

An invigorating upland walk along good tracks, with wide scarp and wold views, passing famous quarries and an attractive village.

Walk north-eastwards along the A436 to the busy A435 crossroads, turn left and immediately take the minor lane on the left, climbing past Windmill

Farm. Where this lane turns left, keep straight ahead following the 'Cotswold Way' sign, along a bridleway, through a small wood, and eventually emerge on Charlton Kings Common. The path follows the scarp edge through grass, gorse and brambles, with glorious views northwards along the Cotswold edge and over Cheltenham. The hollows and rough ground below the scarp are the overgrown remains of old quarries. There is a multiplicity of paths, but the general direction is westwards, either contouring the hill, or by aiming for the triangulation point on the hillfort 961ft (293m). Follow the path signposted 'Devil's Chimney' – well worth the small detour necessary to see.

Now heading southwards, with wide westward views, descend to a minor road near the disused Salterley Quarry. Turn left and follow this up the hill, turning right at the top, signposted Shurdington Hill, and follow this bridleway (muddy after rain) down to the road by the club house of the Cotswold Golf Club. Continue down the road to the A436, cross this and take the farm track opposite, which curves and climbs gently, through arable fields, between two circular clumps of trees on South Hill. Picking up the left side of a wood, at the hill-top turn sharp left, still between arable and passing on the right Cuckoopen Barn Farm at 915ft (279m). The long gentle descent that follows is sheer delight, with wide views over wold landscapes, with Coldwell Bottom to the right and Coberley village a mile (1.6km) ahead to the east. Go ahead where the bridleway joins the road, by the 'free-range' pigscape of Close Farm. Turn left off the road, through the gate identifying Profort Farms Ltd, and follow the yellow waymarks over stiles, across a tiny valley, into Coberley. Continue straight ahead through the village, northwards, past the school, along a waymarked bridleway. At the end of the second field, where this swings left, take the narrow fenced footpath on the right, which soon joins the A436 opposite Seven Springs House, from where it is a short distance to the car park.

3. Hinchwick Manor – Smallthorns – Buckle Street – Hornsleasow – Hinchwick (7½ miles – 12km)

Splendid upland walking, mainly on the high Cotswold plateau at 650–800ft (200–250m), finishing along a beautiful dry valley.

The walk starts and finishes near Hinchwick Manor, about 1 mile (1.6km) north of Condicote which is reached by a minor road running north from B4077, 2 miles (3.2km) west of Stow-on-the-Wold. Car parking on roadside waste ground a short way east of the 'T' junction at Hinchwick Manor.

Take the bridleway northwards, soon climbing steeply into deciduous woodland (the only serious climb of the walk), and, at the top, by some new planting, keep left, continuing through woodland for another ½ mile (800m), emerging on to open pasture above the dry valley along which the walk ends. Contour the hillside, but try to gain height gradually, along no distinct track, but aiming for a boundary fence ahead. On reaching this (and a blue bridleway sign), follow it into a dip where another blue waymark points the way through a gate, north-eastwards up a small hollow-way, to more waymarks indicating right and left at successive field boundaries. Follow the left edge of a narrow shelter-belt to emerge on a good track with Bourton Hill House away to the right.

Turn left and walk westwards for ½ mile (800m) always with a wall, hedge or fence on the right. Go through two gates, with sweeping views to the south and ahead, and look for the yellow waymark on a gatepost indicating the path to the right to Bourton Far Hill Farm. Take this, through rough pasture, to emerge on a bridleway behind the buildings. Turn left along the farm lane north of a shelter-belt. Cross a road at Smallthorns Farm, continuing westwards along a public bridleway (sign), behind the excellent range of buildings, into a small paddock and through two gates into arable fields, where the path has been distinctly left unploughed. Continue ahead to Snowshill Hill, a large farming complex, where the way runs right and left between extensive buildings, through a gate, and into parkland pasture. Follow its causewayed course into arable, where again the path forms a prominent headland between ploughed fields and eventually reaches Buckle Street at the walk's western limit.

Turn left along the road, and soon left again on to a bridleway, with a wall on the left, and into woodland. Beyond the wood the track continues through pasture, always with a wall on the left, reaching a road below Middle Cottages. Turn right and, just beyond some more cottages near Hornsleasow Farm, follow a green lane on the left that curves past the farm buildings and join a metalled road in 300yd (270m). Turn left and follow this road for 500yd (465m). Where it curves left, take the bridleway ahead into a thicket, past an old quarry, and then into woodland. At the end of the woodland the way is down the dry green valley that curves between increasingly wooded banks, until Hinchwick Manor is seen ahead.

4. Wyck Rissington Circular (7 miles – 11.2km)
Links the Windrush and Evenlode valleys, involves some climbing and walking through varied landscapes. Uses part of the Oxfordshire Way. Starts and finishes at Wyck Rissington, 3 miles (4km) south of Stow-on-the-Wold, and offers a shorter route and a longer one.

Park on the grass verge at the northern end of the village and walk through the village as far as the church on the left. An 'Oxfordshire Way' (OW) sign points the direction through the churchyard to its eastern edge, across a drive, into pasture, and slanting diagonally up the hillside. After a rather scrubby field, aim right through a tall hedge, across a gully, and head directly uphill with a hedge on the left. Follow OW signs to the top and turn right on the ridge road. In ¼ mile (400m), just past the Wyck Rissington turning, turn left opposite Court Hayes Farm on to a signposted bridleway, with easy walking to the main Stow road, A424. Turn left and almost immediately right, down the Gawcombe road, soon keeping straight ahead down the private drive to Gawcombe House, with its ornamental lakes in parkland to the right.

Continue down past extensive farm buildings, right and left by farm cottages, past two large barns, with the OW track gradually descending into the broad Evenlode valley, with widespread views. A yellow waymarked footpath on the left indicates a shorter route below a hedge, crossing Westcote Brook and leading northwards to Icomb, a mile (1.6km) away. The main track goes ahead, crosses and then parallels Westcote Brook along its northern side, curving along the edge of arable fields, through pleasant intimate landscapes. On reaching cross-tracks by a prominent concrete bridge the OW, and a longer route, goes ahead to Bledington where, by following the road northwards through the village and ¼ mile (400m) beyond a white-railed road-bridge, a signpost on the left indicates a good footpath across fields to Icomb, via Pebbly Hill Farm. Our route turns sharp left at the concrete bridge and follows a hedge northwards, soon becoming a farm track and bridleway to Pebbly Hill Farm.

Before reaching the farm a waymarked footpath on the left points the route, by a series of field paths, westwards to Icomb, joining a farm track where the shorter route comes in on the left before gently climbing to the village which is reached near the church. Continue through Icomb, past the war memorial, and, where the road forks right, cross a stile ahead into a paddock, across a horse-jump fence and through a metal kissing-gate towards a pasture, rising to the conifer copse on its crest. Keep left of this, over a stile into an arable field, crossing this diagonally to a gate, and over the road into a lane leading to Icomb Hill Farm.

Pass between farm buildings, through a small plantation, and two gates into an arable field. Follow the hedge round left and pick up a waymarked path that soon emerges on the main Stow road. Cross into woodland, joining the drive to Wick Hill House Hotel. Descend and fork right on a bridleway, passing an old orchard, through a gate, and continuing down pleasant pastureland with woods on your left, past the Lodge and on to a fenced drive to complete the walk at the wide green in Wyck Rissington.

5. Bourton and the Slaughters (5 miles – 8km)

A leisurely walk, mainly on field paths and bridleways, with short stretches of road, and involving only one climb.

Although described as starting and finishing in Bourton-on-the-Water where there is plenty of car parking, walkers may prefer to base the walk on either of the Slaughter villages, where parking is, however, very limited.

The Georgian tower of St Lawrence's Church is a prominent landmark towards the northern end of Bourton's High Street and a tarmac path runs northwards from the churchyard, past Bourton Vale School into Station Road. Turn left and follow this to the Foss Way (A429). Turn right along this, and before reaching the Coach and Horses inn, cross the busy road and

Bourton-on-the-Water. The bridge was built in the late eighteenth century

take the surfaced field path leading to Lower Slaughter, entering the village alongside Slaughter Brook, soon joining the road through the village and following the stream.

Continue to the brick-built mill, with its chimney and waterwheel. Cross the stream and walk by it between the mill buildings, Collett's Bakery and the post office, through two kissing-gates, past the long mill-pond on the left with the fenced fields of Cotswold Stud on the right. Slanting up across ridge-and-furrow pasture, cross stiles and go through gates, entering woodland and joining the road into Upper Slaughter. Turn right, apparently away from the village, down to the river bridge, and immediately left along the 'No Through Road', past charming cottages to the ford, across the footbridge and up the short hill to the centre of the village near the church.

Turn right at the triangular 'square' and up the main street to the road junction, where a gate opposite leads into a narrow bridleway, climbing directly up a hillside towards woodland at its crest. Turn right at the top, through a gate, diagonally across a field to join a lane on the right of a farm. Where this joins the road turn sharp left, past the extensive range of buildings of Manor Farm, and follow this road for almost ½ mile (800m) until a signposted bridleway forking right indicates a delectable track that gradually descends southwards into Bourton Vale. Scenically, this is the most rewarding section of the walk.

Continue down the hill towards Aston Mill, but before reaching it, turn left, and for a short distance follow the trackbed of the former Banbury–Cheltenham railway through woodland thicket. Soon the footpath leaves this and follows the edge of fields to the riverside meadows of the Windrush before reaching the main road, A429 at Bourton Bridge. Cross the road and take the Lansdown Road into Bourton. Opposite Mill Cottage take the signposted footpath on the right along a pleasant riverside path past many attractive private gardens behind the village, joining the street leading back into Bourton, within sight of the dome of the church tower.

6. Hailes Abbey (About 4½ miles – 7km)
Allow 2½ hours for this walk, starting and finishing at Hailes Abbey car park. Good tracks, one climb, rewarding views.

Follow the road (signposted Cotswold Way) eastwards towards the foot of a wooded hillside, and where the Hailes Fruit Farm road goes right, keep ahead up the roughly cobbled bridleway which climbs at an easy gradient through beech woodland. Continue past the Cotswold Way sign on the left to the top, enjoying good open views over the valley on your right. In North Farmcote continue as far as the church (well worth a visit), before retracing steps a short distance to the first gate on the right, and, passing through this, ascend the brow of the hill to a wooden gate at its crest. Enjoy the expansive view westwards to the Malverns before following a good track due east, keeping a stone wall on the right and with arable on the left. At the third metal gate join Campden Lane, turn left and follow this ancient track northwards along the edge of woodland.

Beyond the wood the lane becomes a wide grassy drove between bushes and small trees to a disused quarry, now filled in, by a small plantation. Go through the gate, swinging slightly right. The bridleway continues north-eastwards, past dilapidated barns on the left, along a beech avenue, with the sound of traffic on B4077 ahead and a large quarry face beyond.

Join the road at Stumps Cross (appropriately named) and immediately climb a stile on to the footpath signposted 'Cotswold Way: Wood Stanway'. A splendid grassy path ahead starts to descend, diagonally right, in about 200yd (183m). Look for CW signs here and as free-standing posts, down the hillside, crossing a fence by a large ash tree beyond Lower Corscombe, and continuing downhill across old ridge-and-furrow, now sheep-pasture, to the hamlet of Wood Stanway in its sheltering trees.

At the foot of the hill cross a stile, go through a gate, and join the lane past Glebe Farm. Continue past more houses to join a surfaced road, and where this swings right at a small widening, with a single tree at the junction, turn left (signposted Footpath to Hailes), passing a gabled house on the right. Turn right, past more attractive cottages, and follow the waymark signs, along field paths, through gates and over stiles, and keeping a hedge or boundary fence on the right all the time. The church and village you see to the right is Didbrook, but the route gradually swings away from it, heading south-westwards towards Hailes whose church comes into view as Didbrook is left behind. After following the edge of a large arable field the track turns right and soon joins the road which leads back into Hailes.

7. Brimpsfield Circular (7 miles – 11.2km)
A delightful walk, much of it in deciduous woodland, particularly rewarding in spring, early summer, or autumn. Mainly fairly level but with two short, steep sections. Muddy sections in wet weather. Waymarked throughout. Limited car parking on grass verges near Brimpsfield, or at Caudle Green. Most space available at Gloucester Beeches layby on A417 (*958122*) opposite turning to Elkstone, but starting and finishing here adds a mile (1.6km) to the walk. Gloucester County Council leaflet *Cotswold Walks from Ermin Way* gives pictorial plan of walk on large scale. The following route is based on starting and finishing at Brimpsfield.

Take the 'No Through Road' heading westwards from halfway down village street. This soon becomes a field path running due west that passes the end of a short green lane and continues westwards along the edge of arable fields, crosses a metalled road at Longdole Barn and heads towards woodland in a valley. Entering this at the second of two wicket gates, the path descends gradually past wooded banks of bluebells, primroses and anemones. The track gradually swings southwards into more open valley below Climperwell Farm and crosses another road, soon passing springs below rocks on the right, followed by pools. Look for blue bridleway arrows on trees, and, keeping the stream always on right, follow good track down the valley.

After swinging round eastwards, go through two more gates (blue waymarks) and, still keeping the stream on the right, where the valley opens out past the new plantation 'Clement's Brae, 1979' (conifers and hawthorn), keep left where the track forks (*no* waymark) and climb for 275yd (250m) away from stream, turn left at the top towards a stone wall, then follow the side of this wall eastwards to a barn, soon joining the road into the charming hamlet of Caudle Green.

Before the telephone box turn left (north) off the road, passing a five-bay Georgian house on the left and aiming for yellow waymark ahead. Descend very steeply to the valley, cross the stream and turn sharply right (south-east) to some cottages. Keep left at the road, past cottage 'Fernhill', and walk uphill for 76yd (70m), branching right at yellow waymarks along a drive, past a house, through a gate and into the beautiful pastures of the upper Frome valley. Follow this valley northwards (yellow waymarks all the way), into Ostrich Wood and Poston Wood, eventually turning left (north-west) towards the house of Brimpsfield Park, along a good track.

Turn right after the first lake, cross wooden footbridges, up a grassy field, when Brimpsfield church comes into view. Follow waymarked path through more woods, gradually gaining height, before climbing steeply towards a cottage. Go along a private drive, join the road and climb the hill, curving southwards, and take the waymarked field path which passes west of the church, leading into Brimpsfield village.

8. Painswick Circular (6½ miles – 10km)
A pleasant walk embracing the lower Painswick valley, the Slad valley, woodland and field paths with some short road sections. One muddy part near the start, two steep climbs. Good views and sustained interest throughout. Most of the route is waymarked, yellow or blue (bridleways), though you need to keep your eyes alert for them. Car parking in Painswick village (Stamages Lane). Walks leaflet: walk No 3.

From the cross, NE of the church, go down Tibbiwell, right into Kemp's Lane, swinging left and across King's Mill Lane to Painswick Mill in the valley bottom. Follow a track behind the mill and, where the path forks, keep left into Ticklestone Lane, quite steep and invariably muddy between its enclosing hedges. Continue ahead through fields to the farm group at Greenhouse Court, across Yokehouse Lane, over stiles into Frith Wood, straight across and upwards (blue waymark on trees), to a five-way junction. Take the second on the left, immediately right towards a clearing, then left on to a good path and track (blue signs), descending towards Slad, behind houses and gardens, eventually turning sharp left to the main road opposite the war memorial.

Cross directly and continue downhill to Steanbridge, passing its graceful mill-pond on your left as you turn off and head south-eastwards up a field to the end of a copse, over a stile and into a meadow. Keeping the hedge on your left work generally southwards towards Furners Farm, noting yellow waymarks which clearly identify the path all the way along this eastern side of the charming Slad valley. The village looks far more attractive from this angle than from the main road through and it is easy to identify Laurie Lee's boyhood home, below the road and to the north-east of the church, a large T-shaped house.

Look for the waymarks beyond Furners Farm, which loop you across a small combe, across fields and stiles, contouring south-westwards to join a lane below Knapp Farm, dropping to cross the valley by some houses, before joining the main road, B4070. Turn right (north) and immediately after Woodside House, left up a very steep tarmac path, becoming a track, through a gate into a field. Continue climbing steeply, close to the wall on the right, along the edge of Worgan's Wood. At the top, a shorter way back to Painswick involves turning right, then left at the next junction on to the Juniper Hill track leading to Stepping Stone Lane with Painswick beckoning ahead. This reduces the distance by about 2 miles (3.2km).

For the main walk, turn left at the top of Worgan's Hill, then right in 300yd (270m), into a field at the end of which you join a lane, passing woodland on the right and then woodland on the left. Descend to and cross the Painswick Old Road to Hammond's Farm, and right over a stone slab-stile immediately before the farm. Follow the yellow-waymarked path along the edges of successive fields, generally NNE along the Painswick valley, across Pincot Lane, between the buildings at Sheephouse, to Skinner's Mill in Stepping Stone Lane, then left into Stamages Lane and the long steady climb to the car park.

9. Sapperton (5½ miles – 8.8km)
Broad-leaved woodlands, valley pastures, the towpath of a disused canal and associations with the early twentieth-century Arts and Crafts Revivalism provide sustained interest and charming landscapes throughout this walk in the Frome valley. Two short steep climbs and some muddy patches in wet weather. Rich woodland flora makes this walk particularly rewarding in spring (early May). Limited car parking space near Sapperton church.

Take narrow surfaced footpath immediately west of churchyard down to another village road, turn left along this and soon right, downhill, to a stile. A field path slants down across pasture, entering woodland at a stile, soon emerging above the western portal of the Sapperton Canal Tunnel. From here, for about a mile (1.6km), the route follows the former canal towpath and, surfaced with rough chippings, offers relatively clean, level walking. Cross the road below Daneway Inn which originated as a canal pub, and continue on the north bank (signposted Chalford) passing a 'Nature Reserve' sign of the Gloucestershire Trust for Nature Conservation.

Pass a succession of old locks, through woodland, cross a footbridge to the south side, and emerge at the brick-built Whitehall Bridge. Cross this and climb straight ahead into Siccaridge Wood (GTNC Nature Reserve) notice, following the yellow waymarks. Continue climbing, initially steeply, gradually easing. Eventually the track swings right, then left, to a clearing among birches. Ignoring any cross tracks, follow the broad track along Morley Ride through birch-hazel coppiced woodland, across a road into a valley pasture, descending slightly to the opposite corner by a house, where another road is crossed above Daneway House. A footpath sign points the way which climbs into Dorvel Wood. In 300yd (270m) fork left, climbing steadily, and in another 500yd (450m) take a prominent path turning up left towards the edge of the wood. Go through a broad gap in the stone wall and continue directly across an arable field where the line of the path has been trodden out. Cross a farm track, over a stile, and follow a field path, keeping wall and hawthorn hedge immediately on your right, through two fields.

At the next farm track by Gloucester Beeches and a polo field, turn right. Keep right of ruined buildings, then left into cleared woodland, descending through hawthorn scrub, looping northwards before turning south into the valley bottom, to cross the River Frome by a wooden footbridge adjoining a ford. Follow the bridleway steeply up the hill past Pinbury Park (house and associated buildings) on to a surfaced drive. Cross the grassy valley by a pond, swing right past a spring, go through a gate (yellow waymark), and contour along the eastern side of a lovely valley, below woodland, through a succession of gates, entering a short stretch of beechwood before emerging above Leasowes, the house that Ernest Gimson occupied earlier this century. Follow the path, now between wire fences, back to Sapperton, entering the village at the telephone box near the church.

10. Four Wold Villages (8 miles – 12.8km)
This links Notgrove, Hazleton, Turkdean and Cold Aston, mainly on good, little-used paths, bridleways and lanes, savouring the lonely atmosphere of the high wolds, with secretive valleys providing contrasts. Muddy sections in wet weather and no waymarking. Start and finish at any of the villages. The route described is taken anti-clockwise from near Notgrove. Grass-verge parking on Turkdean road, west of village.

Take the farm lane leading west from opposite the large, decorative, iron gates at manor drive. Beyond Kitehall Barn the path continues down a grassy field into the valley, ahead uphill along the edge of arable to wood, and along left (southern) edge of this. At the western end branch half left (south-west) diagonally across arable (trodden path) and at field boundaries continue ahead following line of small markers diagonally across next field, dropping gently to a steeper slope above Lumley Covert (wood). Turn right (west) along the northern edge of this, emerging by a cattle-grid and follow

High wold country above Turkdean. Note the lynchets in the middle distance

a good farm track left, uphill, right at the top along a good lane into Hazleton.

Take the road left immediately after the church, down and up, left at the T-junction, and where the road forks right, keep left, descending to and past an untidy group at Lower Barn, continuing on a good track, through gates, eastwards along the valley, following the track round, with small stream on right, through another gate, and at T-junction, turn right, still in the grassy valley. At the next gate turn left and climb, via a farm lane, through a farmyard, into Turkdean.

Go right on the road, then left at small triangular green, down the lane, heading north-eastwards, past woodland, on a well-defined and easy track for 2 miles (3.2km) to Cold Aston, crossing a delightful quiet valley on the way. Beyond Bangup Barn (the only group of buildings on this stretch), fork left by cottages, continuing ahead (northwards) to join a road west of Cold Aston village. At the cottages just mentioned, the right fork leads into the village, where the Plough Inn does morning coffee and lunches. The Notgrove road should then be taken.

A short way along the road turn off through a gate, taking a grassy path along a charming avenue of trees for ½ mile (800m). Go through a gate at the end, turn right on a track, and very soon through a gate on the left, descending across grassy pasture to a gate at the opposite corner, with the houses and farm buildings of Notgrove beckoning. Go through the gate, left along the road, across the small valley, up the hill, turning sharp right at the top, then left to a crossroads surrounded by walls and parkland. Go straight across (west), soon joining the road a few hundred yards north of your starting point.

Guided Walks

The Cotswold Warden Service is designed to harness the practical support and assistance of volunteers dedicated to the objectives of protecting the qualities of the Cotswold countryside and promoting its enjoyment to a wider public. Administered by Gloucestershire County Council's Planning Department, it now has 250–300 voluntary wardens. Their work includes tree-planting, litter clearance, footpath maintenance and waymarking, and implementing a programme of guided walks, which runs throughout the year but with the greatest number between April and October. Starting from different centres and of various lengths, the walks are led by experienced volunteer wardens and follow public rights-of-way. Detailed brochures are available at Tourist Information Centres.

GAZETTEER

Ablington A mile (1.6km) above Bibury the Coln glides past gracious gardens and the lacy tracery of willows. Ablington is a churchless village where high stone walls hide most of the houses, enhancing privacy and deterring curiosity. There is little to be seen of Ablington Manor (1599) which at the end of last century was the home of Arthur Gibbs, whose book *A Cotswold Village* became a classic. If you can find them, noble barn groups delight the eye.

Adlestrop Woods and parkland above the Evenlode valley separate the village from the Stow–Oxford road and the Worcester–Oxford railway. In the few short verses of his poem 'Adlestrop' Edward Thomas evoked the place and the period (World War I), experienced when his express made an unscheduled stop:

Yes: I remember Adlestrop –
The name, because one afternoon
Of heat the express-train drew up there
Unwontedly. It was late June

. . .

No one left and no one came
On the bare platform. What I saw
Was Adlestrop – only the name.

Little stirs now. The station has long gone, but its chocolate and cream sign adorns the bus shelter.

Jane Austen used to stay at the rectory with her uncle, who served there for forty years. Sanderson Miller rebuilt her mother's ancestral home, Adlestrop Park, in the Gothic style (1762), and Repton laid out the grounds a few years before her 1806 visit. Miller also rebuilt the church, since Victorianised, which completes an attractive group. Attractive stone cottages in the small village include a thatched cottage orné.

Aldsworth Typical village of southern wolds north of the Burford–Bibury road. Its hillside situation faces the morning sun, with the main part of the village separated from the church by a tiny tributary of River Leach. A lived-in place, with cottage gardens behind low walls – nothing too pretentious. A tree-shaded path climbs to the church which was a 'Peculiar' of Osney Abbey (Oxford) from 1130 to the Reformation. The north porch is full of interest, with a dated door (1636), niche and cresset stone for lights. The north aisle (c1500) is also well preserved.

Ampney St Mary Traffic roars along the A417, from which a field path leads to an isolated, village-less church with stone slab floors, a wagon roof, medieval wall-paintings, hat-pegs and candle-holders in the nave. All very atmospheric and peaceful in its meadow.

Ampney St Peter North of A417 but worth a small detour for this pleasant group of Cotswold-style houses around a small triangular green. The church has a Saxon nave and tower arch. A cottage by the main road was once The Old Packhorse inn.

Ascott-under-Wychwood Evenlode valley village on Cotswold fringe. Worcester–Oxford line provides commuter convenience to and from the village. Stone houses, some terraced, form a square around a large churchyard, where headstones lean in amusing disarray, scarcely a single one vertical. The church has a crudely rustic priest's door, and to the north a good avenue of limes gives stately grace to the scene.

Asthall Beautifully situated on south bank of the Windrush below Burford, a site favoured since Roman times. A gabled manor house overlooks a churchyard with seventeenth- and eighteenth-century tombstones. The church interior is also full of interest, architectural variety, furnishings and details with enough monuments and stained glass to satisfy the demands of a catalogue. The three-arched stone bridge across the river has a wartime graffito of a Lee-Enfield rifle.

Aston Subedge 2 miles (3.2km) from Chipping Campden, a small village with unassuming charm and good, modest houses. Seventeenth-century Manor Farm has gabled dormers, finials and mullioned windows. Charles I's ambassador, Endymion Porter, lived here (when he was not travelling for the king) and Prince Rupert stayed here with him for Dover's Games. Sheep and lambs graze the white-railed churchyard, and St Andrew's Church is homely and discreet – Gothic Revival, Greek-style, with west gallery, pulpit and furnishings to match.

Avening Modern houses of reconstituted stone sit uneasily in the steep valley-side setting a few miles from Nailsworth. Eighteenth-century cottages and larger houses were homes of weavers and clothiers, but the church above all commands attention: large, cruciform, early Norman and probably planned by the Conqueror's Queen, Matilda. Soon afterwards it was given to the Abbess of Holy Trinity, Caen, then to Syon Abbey. Its lavish details, fine masonry and good monuments are worthy of admiration.

Bagendon Memories of former importance rest lightly on this tiny village in a quiet, tributary valley of the Churn, north of Cirencester, which was once tribal capital of the Dobunni. A high earthwork bank borders the southern side of the drovers' road above Perrott's Brook. Today's village, to the north, is centred on the church, which is mainly early Norman, with gabled roof to tower and the chancel rebuilt in 1460 by the Weavers' Guild of Cirencester. The village has a memorable setting, backed by tall trees. Nearby, part of Trinity Mill has been incorporated into a house, whose garden path utilises the course of the old mill leat.

Barnsley Linear villages are not always visually appealing, but Barnsley is an exception, because cottages are in small varied groups, with colourful gardens, trees and woodland providing a gracious backdrop. The eighteenth-century turnpike, now the busy A433 from Cirencester to Burford, bends at each end of the village, closing the view and apparently limiting expansion. Formerly an estate village, with commercial and council development not permitted, it is now owned by a charitable trust and designated a conservation area, albeit inhabited by incomers rather than local farmworkers. Pub, village hall and church are conveniently sited near the centre. Grotesques grin from the church's tower and corbel-table. Barnsley Park lies to the north, an eighteenth-century baroque mansion; unfortunately it is not open to public and too distant for easy viewing, but Barnsley House, the former rectory, has gardens open all year round.

The Barringtons Twin villages on opposite sides of Windrush valley west of Burford. Great Barrington, on the north, is an estate village opposite the gates and high walls of Barrington Park. Slow dereliction of village houses reached its nadir about 1977, since when, through District Council action, some rehabilitation has occurred. It still has a ghostly, empty feel, however, and many stone houses seem empty. So does the church, almost in the mansion's pocket, built for Earl Talbot (1736–8), possibly by Kent. Excellent monuments to the Talbots and the Brays include a superb Nollekens. The churchyard contains an unusual long stone bench, probably thrown out of the chancel at 1880 restoration. Little Barrington is far more attractive, with cottage groups and rows along three sides of a large, triangular, sloping green, with a winter stream in the middle. Here is vernacular variety, with harmony of scale, texture and colour. The Norman church, standing away to the east, is simple and undisturbing, with tympanum, wall paintings and sculptures on the porch exterior.

Batsford Guy Dawber supervised the rebuilding of the mansion (1888–92) in Elizabethan style for Lord Redesdale. The park, originally landscaped in the middle of the last century, now houses the Batsford Arboretum, with over a thousand different trees and shrubs and a replica of a Chinese temple. Picnic area and scenic walks are open to the public from April to October.

Belas Knap On the high wolds 2 miles (3.2km) south of Winchcombe, reached by a steep climb on the Cotswold Way, this Neolithic chambered long barrow features enormous slabs of limestone for its burial chambers, but the thin ragstone dry-walling which forms the 'horns' of its false entrance commands greatest attention – Cotswold masonry which is four thousand years old!

Bibury William Morris thought this the most beautiful village in England, but did he view it as a whole, or merely concentrate on what is the 'honeypot' today – by the river, the eighteenth-century bridge, Arlington Row and Arlington Mill? The charms of these parts are undeniable, easiest appreciated on a winter's day, or glowing in the low sunlight of evening but the main village lies off the busy road, stone cottages grouped around a small square. The splendid church (Saxon in origin, but mainly twelfth to fifteenth century) is interesting and beautiful in spite of Scott's restoration of 1863. Alec Clifton-Taylor thought the churchyard the most enchanting in England – and he knew more than most. Spacious green sward, elegant Georgian tombstones with rococo motifs, mottled by lichen: the clothiers sleep quietly by the gently gliding Coln.

Birdlip Stone village high on the western escarpment, now bypassed by the endless traffic on A417 Cirencester–Gloucester road. The village grew to serve travellers on this old London–Fishguard road, turnpiked in 1698. Extra horses were needed for waggons and coaches struggling up Birdlip Hill's 1 in 6 gradient. There are marvellous views northwards from nearby Barrow Wake.

Bisley Hilltop village north of Golden Valley, near Stroud. The southern approach reveals an amphitheatre of gabled stone houses, grouped in uneven terraces on either side of High Street. From the north, it appears suddenly, almost formless. Different levels emphasise rhythm of roof-lines and gables, and rich variety of house styles and sizes creates liveliness and yields surprises, like Bear Inn at the top of George Street, formerly the court house, with detached seventeenth-century columns supporting upper floor. Church Hill climbs to All Saints, with its huge lychgate, and at the opposite end of the churchyard, a rare thirteenth-century 'Poor Soul's Light', with niches for candles used in outdoor mass. The church is mainly thirteenth century, restored in the nineteenth century when Thomas Keble (John's brother) was rector. He restored Bisley's seven wells in a gabled semi-circle below the church. Wells are dressed on Ascension Day; ducks favour them throughout the year. The lock-up (1824) in George Street has two doors. Outlying houses in widespread parish were homes of successful eighteenth-century clothiers, or professional people, and Nether Lypiatt Manor (1702–5) is a particularly outstanding example.

Bledington Attractive spacious village in Evenlode valley east of Stow-on-the-Wold. Stone cottages are casually grouped around a large irregular green with brook and ducks. Up-ended Cotswold slates are used in garden walls. The mainly Perpendicular church is full of light and delight with fine fifteenth-century glass and roofs. The Oxfordshire Way passes on the south side of the churchyard, but the church looks best in summer evening sunlight from the north.

Blockley Large village of northern Cotswolds, near Chipping Campden. Blockley Brook powered Domesday mills and, much later, silk mills, now flats. Other small factories and foundries contributed to its industrial history, but they are silent now. Cottages and houses spread around the hillside site, seventeenth, eighteenth and nineteenth century, all in golden stone, originally built for clothiers, merchants and artisans. Date-stones and details dignify their appearance and Regency terraces display elegant formality. The large church in the village centre has a Gothic tower (1725) and splendid monuments. Blockley is one of the most rewarding Cotswold villages to explore, not least because it is so obviously lived in, and the shops in the High Street are used.

Bourton-on-the-Hill Suffers from its situation on the A44 west of Moreton-in-Marsh. Traffic sweeps down Bourton's single street, largely ignoring speed restrictions, diminishing pedestrian pleasures of cottage-crawling. There is no car parking, except in the lay-by at the bottom or by the eighteenth-century Horse and Groom at the top, whose windows look down the hill to pleasantly varied houses on both sides of the road. The seventeenth- and eighteenth-century idiom prevails, even in the Old Bakery, which still retains its free-standing bakehouse with chimney. The church has much merit: splendid gargoyles on the north, a light interior and a rarity – a Standard Winchester Bushel and Peck measure, made of bell-metal, dated 1816. At the bottom of the hill Bourton House, early eighteenth century, prefers privacy, and seven-bay barn to the east is dated 1570.

Bourton-on-the-Water Criticised, often denigrated, because it is too popular and lives off its charms. People simply recognise a good thing when they see it. The River Windrush holds the secret, lively and lovely, rippling beneath low stone bridges. Tree-graced, broad grass verges keep the roads at bay. Of course there are cars, but a coach and car park beyond the village encourages most visitors to use their feet. Birdland, the model village, and a wide range of shops may not be subtle, but draw the crowds, who can scarcely fail to notice some of the many good buildings around, mainly seventeenth and eighteenth century, some bearing date-panels. Manor House, at the end of the green, originated about 1200 on the site of the Abbot of Evesham's house, rebuilt in the sixteenth century, again in 1890, and restored in 1919, but its delightful sixteenth-century dovecote survives. The beautiful nineteenth-century church has an unusual domed tower (1784) and a fourteenth-century chancel with painted roof of 1928.

Brimpsfield Only a mile (1.6km) from the A417 near Birdlip, yet it feels remote. Quiet lanes approach from all directions, respecting the curves and contours of high wolds landscape. The lonely Norman church lies isolated to the east, reached by a field path passing the tree-covered moat and earthworks of John Giffard's thirteenth-century castle. Good headstones and table-tombs, with the nave roof constructed from barrel-shaped timbers. Seventeenth-century Brimpsfield House dominates the village and has a medieval chimney decorating a gable.

Broadway The 'broad way', verged and lined with red chestnut trees, is on the main road between Oxford and Worcester, now the A44. The position of the old

Broadway Tower, built by the Earl of Coventry about 1800

church, St Eadburgha's, along the Snowshill road, suggests the original village was there and migrated (probably during the sixteenth or early seventeenth century) when Fish Hill became the main road down the escarpment. The honey-gold Guiting stone used for Broadway's houses, in their happy mixture of Tudor, Stuart and Georgian styles, ensures harmony and dignity. It *is* a show-place, deservedly so, but the incessant traffic displeases. Use the car parks and walk the length of Broadway's main street, up one side and back the other, to see each in context, each in detail. You will soon realise that the eastern end, beyond the Stratford road, is the quietest and most satisfying. Shop windows may make you pause, especially the many displaying antiques, but they do not show the essence of Cotswold. That is in the stone, its texture, shape and colour, and the care with which it has been used.

Broadway Tower Country Park Privately developed 35 acre (14ha) country park on the crest of the Cotswold escarpment above Broadway – open daily from end of March to early October (with admission charge). Wonderful views and dramatic central accent of Broadway Tower, built by Earl of Coventry in 1800 as a folly tower, with three round turrets and three canted sides. It looks appropriately lordly astride the 1,000ft (305m) contour. Waymarked walks, nature trails, a landscaped picnic area and a children's play area are popular. The Cotswold Way pays suitable homage before descending to Broadway if you are southbound, or contouring Fish Hill if you are walking north. Walkers pay no admission fees.

Broadwell North-east of Stow-on-the-Wold away from main roads, Broadwell gives the impression of being wooded, with stately trees. Houses keep their distance beyond a huge, manicured green, with evident signs of wealth and the desire for privacy. A few barns have not been converted and cottages add a homely touch, as does the ford. Excellent bale-tombs and table-tombs in the churchyard, west of village.

Buckland Small village in sheltered combe below the north-western edge, a mile (1.6km) from Broadway. Wooded hillsides, trees and humpy ground add to the enchantment, and the lane into the village ends beyond the church which is full of good things. William Morris restored the sixteenth-century glass; medieval English embroidery and small carved angels may have come from Hailes at the Dissolution; wainscotting with hat-pegs shows the quality of the Tudor oak; seventeenth-century gallery and seating also survives. So does the rare pre-Reformation rectory (occasionally open) with its fifteenth-century open timber roof and first-floor chamber. The north-west front is largely unaltered.

Burford See pp127–8.

Calcot Tiny village in Coln valley, with seventeenth-century gabled houses, cottages and great barns. There is no church and no through road, so leave your car at the top of the hill and walk down, or approach by footpath from across the river to appreciate the setting. An unassuming gem in a jewelled valley.

Chalford Bewildering, fascinating jumble of stone-walled lanes, alleys, stepped paths, clinging cottages, gables, chimneys and valley-bottom mills. The early nineteenth century saw the Golden Valley's heyday and much of Chalford dates from then. Many local streets are too steep and narrow for vehicles, and as virtually nothing is on the level, even a walkabout is demanding – but very rewarding. There are several nuclei, each centred on a mill, and though there are many late eighteenth-century mill-houses, it is a great pity that the Thames–Severn Canal is now in-filled. The former lengthman's Round House (c1790) is now in a landscaped setting and has been restored. Satellite weaving hamlets are scattered on hills above Chalford: Oakridge, France Lynch, Chalford Hill are also worth visiting. The 2sq miles (5km^2) of the Frome valley around Chalford is unique in the Cotswolds and should not be missed.

Chastleton Fine house, small church and tiny village in an appendix of Oxfordshire, east of Stow-on-the-Wold. Built c1603 by Walter Jones, a Witney wool merchant and little changed since then. Mellowed and modest, with stepped gables and pinnacles, south-facing to a gabled dovecote with cupola, across the road. The house contains original panelling, furniture and tapestries, and has a topiary garden of c1700. Open from Easter to end of September.

Chedworth Large scattered village along steep-sided tributary valley of upper Coln, best seen from the brow of the steep hill on the lane from Stowell and Yanworth. The nucleus of the place is around the church which is late Norman, sumptuous, with a light Perpendicular interior. Good houses and cottages in the village, some seventeenth, most eighteenth century. Cobbett noticed poverty and dilapidation in the 1820s: not now (apart from the long-dead railway line along the valley), for the place seems to be thriving.

Chedworth Roman Villa A mile (1.6km) north and not reached directly by road from Chedworth, but by a circuitous, signposted route, this is one of the best-preserved of all villa sites. Combe-sheltered below Chedworth Woods, the extensive surviving buildings reveal hypocausts and superb mosaic floors. Some walls stand up to 3ft (.91m); good plans of the layout, an excellent museum and shop are kept open by the NT throughout the year. Everything is protected under covered structures, with limited illumination.

Chipping Campden See pp128–32.

Chipping Norton See pp132–3.

Churchill Attractive village in Oxfordshire Cotswolds. Birthplace of geologist William Smith (1769) and Warren Hastings (1732). Georgian church (1826) has a slim-line Magdalen College tower and hammerbeam roof copied from Christ Church Hall, Oxford. There is a large cricket field nearby, with huge sycamores inside the boundary, and a splendidly ugly fountain (1870), a memorial to James Langston.

Cirencester See pp133–4.

The picturesque village of Chedworth

Clapton-on-the-Hill Remote village on high wolds south of Bourton-on-the-Water. Compact, unassuming, a working village with farms, barns, cottages and thirteenth-century church only six paces across and eight from door to altar. The rare Latin inscription on the chancel arch probably dates from 1239 when the rebuilt Evesham Abbey (which owned nearby Bourton and the Clapton chapelry), was dedicated. The interesting churchyard gate is made from horseshoes. Manor House and Church Farm are characteristic of Stuart times. Clapton's quiet charm is an antidote to Bourton's crowds and there are good views eastwards across the Windrush valley.

Coberley A mile (1.6km) south of busy Seven Springs road junction. Narrow, winding lanes lead to this scattered village, whose great mansion has vanished. The church is approached through private-looking barn doors, then by the churchyard wall with Renaissance openings. Berkeleys, Brydges, Chandos and Castlemaines were former owners of the estate, remembered in church monuments. One of these commemorates Sir Giles de Berkeley (1295), a 'heart burial', with the knight in chain mail holding a heart in his hands above a shield. Field paths around main part of village give rewarding views.

Colesbourne The Cotswold's most scenic main road, the A435, curves an enchanting route from Seven Springs down the Churn valley to Cirencester, passing gracious parklands, plantations, lakes and rare trees of Colesbourne. The early Victorian mansion was largely demolished, but rebuilt in the 1960s. The church is modest, but is brightened by the sun-splash altar frontal. The Colesbourne Inn is unusually constructed of quartz and tufa, but otherwise the place proves that Cotswold was the prevalent style in 1827. There is an insignificant hamlet above the road on the opposite side of the valley to the park.

Coln Rogers Tall trees shade houses secluded behind shrubberies and the church has to be sought down a quiet walled lane. Its Saxon nave and chancel survive almost intact, and north-west of the churchyard is a partly roofless ruin, probably of the medieval priest's house. For walkers there is a pleasant riverside path to Calcot a mile (1.6km) away.

Coln St Aldwyns Enclosed within a loop of the Coln, east of Bibury. Estate cottages proclaim themselves by style similarities and paintwork, their nineteenth-century idiom continuing that of the seventeenth-century cottages in the village, grouped around a small green at crossroads, with the over-restored church to the west. Almshouses (c1947) of stone and timber from Williamstrip House, commemorate Countess St Aldwyn (1851–1940); The vicarage and National School (1856) are appropriately Gothic. There is a pleasant riverside and woodland walk to Bibury from the lodge by the bridge.

Coln St Dennis Beeches and yews half hide a large Norman church; huge door to the north porch, good monuments, especially the one to Joan Burton (1631). A small stream runs along the churchyard wall and houses nearby are attractively grouped where three lanes meet.

Compton Abdale Expansive landscapes rise all round, with the A40 along the ridge to the north. A village of the high bare wolds, yet in a sheltered valley, so all approaches are downhill, past good farms and barns, and some new housing. Roof-patterns delight, and the path climbing to the church gives a fine view of the village. Puzzling pinnacles on the Perpendicular tower resemble heraldic beasts carrying staves. Below them, gargoyles grimace, corbel-carvings include a man blowing a horn and couchant animals adorn the buttresses. By the roadside in the village a spring gushes forth from the mouth of an eighteenth-century stone crocodile. The ancient White Way runs through the village, north to south, and the Salt Way is only a mile (1.6km) away.

Condicote Remote village on high wolds north-west of Stow, reached only by narrow lanes, where strings of David Nicholson's racehorses exercise. A medieval roadside cross, a huge stone-walled green with seventeenth- and eighteenth-century farms roughly at its four corners, a charming cottage group, and an over-restored small church, complete this unassuming, utterly charming, unspoilt village.

Cornwell Clough Williams-Ellis's essay in Cotswold Picturesque of the late 1930s, in a small, wooded valley west of Chipping Norton. The stone-built stone-roofed cottages, village hall (former school) and stone-walled green are all contrived, neo-Georgian and charming. Cobblestones and water-splash add variety. Cars are rightly discouraged; but there is a good roadside view of the manor house in its parkland setting.

Cotswold Way 100 mile (160km) long-distance footpath from Chipping Campden to Bath, essentially linking existing rights-of-way, and following as closely as possible the western escarpment, with resultant wide views and many descents to scarp-foot towns and villages. Selected sections are probably more rewarding than the continuous seven- to ten-day trek. Many prefer to tackle it south to north, with sun, prevailing wind (and rain) on the back.

Cowley Compact village at head of Churn valley, mainly of late nineteenth-century cottages of Sir James Horlick's estate. Manor House originally of 1674 was rebuilt from 1855–60 and is now a County Council conference centre, with park and woodland sloping down to an artificial lake. The church has a good fourteenth-century waggon roof, and an impressive table-tomb in the churchyard showing figures in contemporary clothing.

Cranham Small village in sheltered hollow beneath ancient beechwoods, burnished in autumn, a National Nature Reserve, with miles of woodland walks and bridlepaths. There are both old and new stone cottages; Old House in the village is gabled and has date-stones of 1687 and 1727. Cranham Common, opposite the woods, is humpy, rich in meadow-grass, and leads to the mainly fifteenth-century church, with sheep shears carved on a tower buttress, a fine screen c1500 and a contemporary waggon roof in the south aisle as well as a number of good monuments.

Cranham's annual feast and ox-roast held over the weekend nearest 6

August, includes a procession, open-air service and venison for commoners and the lord of the manor. The beechwoods' glory lasts throughout the year.

Crickley Hill Promontory on escarpment edge, at 875ft (267m) above A417 east of Gloucester, a country park of 148 acres (60ha) managed by Gloucestershire County Council and National Trust. Plenty of car parking, visitor facilities, information centre, and various waymarked trails of archaeological, geological, plant and woodland interest, none taking more than an hour. Neolithic and Iron Age settlements have been investigated annually during summer archaeological digs since 1969; over the rest of the year, interpretative displays try to shed some light on what lies buried and obscure. Geology is easier to understand and always visible: poor-quality limestone was quarried until 1963 and used mainly for constructional in-fill and roadstone, possibly some walling. Grassland is rich in plants. The woodland beeches were planted during the eighteenth century, and there is also evidence of hazel coppicing. The Cotswold Way threads through the country park along the route from Leckhampton to Birdlip. A splendid place for summer afternoons and evenings with glorious views of the escarpment.

Daglingworth Small village in Duntisbourne valley north-west of Cirencester, with attractive cottage clusters, many reached by tiny stone footbridges. There are a few modern houses but they tend to be sensibly placed. An impressive nucleus at Lower End around Manor Farm, features associated buildings and a circular medieval dovecote. There is fine Anglo-Saxon work in the church; a sundial above the doorway, crucifixion scene on the south wall and other sculptures inside. A magnificent fifteenth-century door in the porch is worth investigation, but the rest is drastic early Victorian restoration.

Didbrook Small scattered village at scarp-foot between Hailes and Stanway. The church was rebuilt by the Abbot of Hailes c1475, so is nicely unified, light and airy, with its west tower supported on arches within the nave. The wood-panelled Georgian chancel arch escaped Victorian restorers. Timber-framed and stone cottages in the village are the result of upland/vale dichotomy, but Nos 62 and 63 are not to be missed as here can be seen the rare survival of cruck-frame construction, possibly contemporary with the church.

Dowdeswell Fine cruciform church set on wooded hill slope above Cheltenham, with interesting secular buildings around, although not much can be seen of any. Privacy prevails.

Dumbleton At the northern foot of Dumbleton Hill, a Cotswold outlier north of Winchcombe. Laburnums line the lane from the B4078, leading to a corner by the entrance to the park and Hall (Repton, 1830). There is a proud church with weeping ashes, pansies and some huge headstones, beautifully lettered, in the churchyard. Some typically Cotswoldish estate housing can be seen as well as the dignified Old Rectory, which is part timber-framed with gables, with 1700 wing added and hipped roof. It is now divided into cottages.

Duntisbourne Villages Duntisbourne Brook links a sequence of village gems in the wooded, secretive valley north of Cirencester. From the south, approached via Daglingworth, Duntisbourne Rouse appears to have a tiny Saxon church and little else. The church is indeed all, memorable on its steep hillside, with crypt beneath the chancel. The midget tower, dated 1587, has a saddleback roof. Beautiful stones, shelly and textured, adorn the churchyard where flowers flourish, grasses sigh; a peaceful setting and a place to love.

Middle Duntisbourne has a farm and an 1811 stone footbridge. Duntisbourne Leer embraces the ford at the foot of the hill. The harmony of the stone in walls, gables, lintels, finials, roofs, troughs, dovecote, cottages, barns, is naturally set against sloping fields.

Duntisbourne Abbots perpetuates the name link with St Peter's Abbey, Gloucester. A tapsell gate leads into the churchyard in the village centre. From this hill-position there is a good view of the surrounding Cotswold roofs and gables.

Eastleach Villages Twin villages on opposite sides of the Leach, in the Cotswolds' south-eastern corner, linked by the road-bridge and stone clapper-bridge associated with the Keble family. John Keble, poet and reformer, was non-resident curate of the two churches following his ordination in 1815. St Martin's on the east bank is now in the care of The Redundant Churches Fund; calm, beautiful inside and out,with a fine stone barn beside the churchyard. Eastleach Turville is the larger village with streets at different levels. Cottages include nineteenth-century estate houses, together with an almshouse and the former school. St Andrew's church shows good Norman and thirteenth-century detail, and an attractive churchyard path of huge stone slabs. Unfortunately many tombstones have been cleared away. The villages and their river setting are full of glory in spring, with daffodils, willows and alders lining the broad clear stream.

Ebrington Near the northern edge of the Cotswolds above Chipping Campden. A working, lived-in village, with farms and modest cottages; rust-coloured stone, some thatched roofs, gardens of flowers, ferns, roses and vegetables. The church has contributions from all centuries since Norman times: texts, woodwork and monuments. Seats around the three oaks on the small green, with the Ebrington Arms adjoining, enhance the Cotswold cosiness of the village. A place for lingering and being at ease.

Edgeworth A few farms, barns and houses by a lane that dives down into the hanging beechwoods of the Frome valley. The church and manor ½ mile (800m) south can be approached by a narrow lane contouring the combe, with good views. Churchyard paths are lined with small headstones, mainly 1652–82, of simple pattern, with initials and date, this type being unique to the locality. Other good stones make the churchyard rather more rewarding than the church. The nearby manor house is of the Queen Anne period, altered c1900. An inviting path leads down to the valley bottom and a packhorse bridge.

Elkstone Bleak upland village off the A417, rather scattered, with a few older houses and some indifferent modern ones as well as farm buildings being converted. But here is the best Norman church in the Cotswolds. See it in spring, in its setting of tall traceried trees. Nothing displeases, even the gargoyles on the Perpendicular church tower and buttresses seem to laugh. Zodiac animals and birds adorn the corbel-table of the nave; and more strange faces fringe the Norman tympanum which depicts Christ in his conventional pose with lamb, angel and dove. The interior is memorable. Midday sun goldens the Norman carving, chancel arch, and tiny chancel; the rare groined roof glows with light reflected from the worn stone floor. Climb the spiral stair (26 steps) behind the pulpit and you will reach the columbarium with 43 holes for doves. The whole church is a prayer in stone: eight centuries of sanctity, beautiful and moving, set in a charming churchyard. If you were limited to seeing one small Cotswold church, this should be it.

Evenlode Near the head of the Evenlode valley 3 miles (4.8km) from Stow. The village straggles along lanes forming a small rectangle, with pleasant groups of cottages and a small triangular green. Rose Terrace is appropriately named, but its roofs of Welsh slate introduce a foreign element. The church has a stone elbowed sanctuary chair and a tiny Nine Men's Morris scratched on a south aisle window. The parish was a Worcestershire island until 1931 when it was transferred to Gloucestershire.

Fairford Nearby gravel-pits south of A417 confirm that the Cotswolds fade here into vale country and the River Coln soon joins the Thames. The narrow, winding London Road borders the south side of Fairford's large Market Place, where other sides are flanked with elegant eighteenth-century houses and hotels of Cotswold style and stone with some timber-framing. The Market Place narrows northwards into High Street with its houses and shops, opposite a large churchyard, with the former eighteenth-century school on the corner. Then the church, Fairford's glory: handsome, dignified, unified, almost wholly 1490–1530 and displaying the richest of late Perpendicular prosperity. Magnificent masonry, carved figures, armorial devices and a proud pinnacled tower complete its stunning appearance. The large windows by Barnard Flower, the greatest glazier of the early sixteenth century, are not all first class, but they form the only complete surviving set of medieval stained-glass windows in a British parish church, depicting the Bible story from Adam and Eve to Last Judgement. John Tame and his son Sir Edmund, wealthy Cotswold wool merchants, could afford the best masons, sculptors and glaziers, and the results of their privileged piety are unique and breathtaking. There are other furnishings and memorials to match: don't miss the woodwork, particularly the misericords in the chancel, illustrating the life and characters of Fairford c1500. There are more good memorials in the churchyard, including a table-tomb to Valentine Strong, (1662), great mason of Barrington and Taynton. There is also, near the south porch, a modern memorial to Tiddles, Church Cat.

Mill Lane, north of the church, leads to the river, from which there is a superb view of the church from a distance. Beyond, an interesting range of sheep or cattle-sheds can be seen, in good Cotswold style.

Farmcote Tiny remote hamlet on the hillside above Hailes Abbey. It has a small church, with a Norman nave, charming furnishings, Laudian communion rails and Elizabethan effigies. There is also an excellent view from the churchyard. Great Farmcote is very much seventeenth-century Cotswold in character, and the barn and farm buildings to the north may have been part of a monastic grange.

Farmington Six lanes converge here, that from the A40 east of Northleach, passing between gate-piers. The centre is a triangular green adorned with a huge sycamore and small octagonal pump-house (1874) restored by folk of its namesake, in Connecticut. The churchyard gate is made of horseshoes and the churchyard itself contains some interesting memorials. Church pews have elegant candle-holders and there is an unusual east window. Good quality Farmington stone has been quarried locally for centuries.

Filkins North of Lechlade and on the Cotswolds' eastern edge. A lane winds through this village of mainly modest houses and cottages, all stone-roofed, many with upright stone slabs as fences, but G. E. Street's mid-nineteenth-century church is out of key, with its pink tiled roof. Filkins Quarries reopened in 1981, producing fine roofing slates on a small scale. In the village, a large barley barn (1720) has been converted into an excellent art gallery and centre for local crafts: wool-weaving, rush-weaving, wood-turning, as well as other stable and woodcrafts, and stone work. Sir John Cripps and COSIRA deserve congratulations for this. Open all year, free admission.

Frampton Mansell Hillside village above Frome valley between Cirencester and Stroud. Many cottages were designed by Gimson and his associates, but residents created the productive gardens. The church is neo-Norman. A steep lane descends to the valley, past Manor Farm (late seventeenth century) with its gables, stone mullions, and charming stone trough opposite.

Guiting Power Compact village in upper Windrush valley, restored and revitalised through self-help village housing trust. Groups of cottages nestle around the triangular village green. Council houses have been sensitively built in Cotswold idiom and stone. The Farmers' Arms is appropriately named. A plaque by the green commemorates Sally Latimer Cochrane (1904–77), founder of Amersham Playhouse, 'who gave much to Guiting Power'. The church at the southern end of the village has good Norman doorways, but overall has rather a cold atmosphere.

Hailes 2 miles (3.2km) north-east of Winchcombe, meagre but hauntingly beautiful ruins of a late Cistercian monastery in a wooded setting below the edge (NT and EH). Graceful arcades, arches and stones in the ground bear silent witness to past sanctity. Autumn colours add special benediction. The tiny church across the road pre-dates the abbey and has its own tranquillity, with medieval wall-paintings and heraldic floor-tiles. There are pleasant walks all around, particularly monks' lane to the grange at Farmcote.

Hampnett Quiet, unassuming wold village near Northleach. The River Leach rises from springs on the sloping green, separating the two parts of the village. Modest cottages in friendly groups; sheep and lambs in spring; and the church in harmony with the scene. There is attractive Norman work inside the church, and the sanctuary's medieval-type decoration painted on the walls is by Clayton and Bell c1868.

Haresfield Beacon Famous viewpoint promontory on Cotswold edge 3 miles (4.8km) north-west of Stroud. A National Trust car park at the north end of Standish Wood allows convenient access to the Iron Age hill-fort and triangulation point which command an excellent view from a height of 700ft (213m).

Hatherop Model estate village in Coln valley north of Fairford, with good paired cottages, c1850–60, in late seventeenth-century style, but with Welsh slate roofs. Groups of terrace houses lie at angles to the road and here is a neat, gabled bus shelter. Lord de Mauley's 1850 castle is now a girls' private school. The Victorian church is French-Gothic, full of gloom and awful glass. Memorials suggest the marked immodesty of the de Mauleys. Too many footpath notices underline squirearchal attitude rather than generosity.

Hawling At 800ft (244m) one of the highest wold villages, lonely between Northleach and Winchcombe, its bleakness softened by the sheltering trees. There is a medieval church and an Elizabethan manor house alongside, both of which were remodelled in the mid-eighteenth century. The churchyard is rich in grasses, wild flowers, and splendid, lichened stones which glow golden in the summer sun. Houses and cottages are generally attractive, but derelict farm buildings at the western edge of the village detract, as do 'Private: Keep Out' notices at the manor gates.

Hazleton Remote upland village north-east of Northleach, in a dry landscape. The churchyard has some interesting memorials. Also worth seeing are the noble seventeenth-century stone barns, one with a dovecote in gable, one being converted, along with a few other farm buildings. Tall chestnut trees cast a deep shade. Unfortunately nearby quarrying disturbs the peace of the village.

Hetty Pegler's Tump On the edge of the Cotswolds between Uley and Nympsfield is one of the best Severn–Cotswold long barrows, with reconstructed east entrance. It is normally locked, but the key is obtainable from Crawley's Barn, ½ mile (800m) south. The archaeologically minded may think it worth a visit, but inside it is damp and dark (torch needed). Views from the Cotswold Way nearby are more rewarding.

Hidcote Near the Cotswolds' northern limit, north of Chipping Campden. Tiny twin hamlets, Hidcote Boyce and Hidcote Bartrim, with outstanding garden at Hidcote Manor (NT). 10 acres (4ha) of famous 'gardens within a garden' were created from hillside early this century by Major Lawrence Johnston. Avenues of lime, oak, pine, holly; long grassy walks, terraces, dells; rose garden, rock banks, spring slopes: a planned riotousness of seasonal colour, scent and shape which is unique and glorious. Open from spring to October.

Horsley Hill-top village on the B4058, above the steep-sided valley south of

Nailsworth. Modest Cotswold houses line a single street. Eighteenth-century clothiers are commemorated by monuments in the church. Groups of former weavers' cottages make up surrounding hamlets.

Horton Court 3 miles (4.8km) north-east of Chipping Sodbury, 1 mile (1.6km) west of A46. Cotswold manor house with Norman north wing (c1140), main house Renaissance, over-restored in 1937. Ambulatory (1527) in garden, modelled on Italian loggia. This and the Norman hall are open from April to October (NT).

Icomb On lower slopes of Icomb Hill, south-east of Stow, below the A424 which follows the ridge between Windrush and Evenlode valleys. This unspectacularly but delightfully Cotswold village features two short streets of houses and cottages, a village green, water pump and a church at the end of a lane opposite farm and cowsheds. The walker is spoilt for choice for good views from the surrounding hill-climbing lanes.

Idbury Tiny Oxfordshire village a few miles north of Burford, grouped around a church. Of particular interest is the fifteenth-century woodwork of the screen, pulpit and bench-ends, and some plain early nineteenth-century box-pews. There are some lovely headstones in the churchyard, whose grass is cut only three times a year, so flowers flourish, as did the Morris-tune of dance 'Idbury Hill' written down by Cecil Sharp (1923) when he heard it whistled by an old man.

Tall, gaunt, gabled Idbury Manor was the home of J. W. Robertson Scott from 1922, where *Countryman* magazine originated in 1927, and was produced for next twenty years before editorial offices moved to Burford. A roundel over the door bears the inscription:

> O more than happy Countryman
> If he but knew his good fortune.

Ilmington Below the northern tip of Cotswolds, and the idiom is diluted. Approach lanes from the south give rewarding views. Ilmington Downs, along Campden road, highest point in Warwickshire (793ft/242m). Pleasant village, splendid church, good churchyard.

Kingham Large village on Oxfordshire side of Evenlode valley, where Worcester–London trains stop at the station a mile (1.6km) south. Broad village green, trees, rust-tinged stone cottages, most with wooden lintels. Streets form a rough rectangle. Manor Cottages in West Street have a medieval chimney. Late seventeenth-century houses near church, include a very elegant rectory. The church is much more rewarding inside than out, as it was refurnished (1853) in Strawberry Hill Gothic, rare in the Cotswolds. The unusual stone bench-ends were executed by Jackson, the local mason. Two cast-iron stoves can also be seen, one with the trade-mark of Coalbrookdale Co Ltd, the other a genuine tortoise stove.

Lechlade See pp134–5.

Leckhampton Famous scarp-edge quarries yielded much of Cheltenham's building stone early last century and provided one of the Cotswolds' most distinctive landmarks, Devil's Chimney, a tall ragged pinnacle of rock. The Cotswold Way passes close, and many rewarding paths cross Charlton Kings Common nearby.

Longborough Named from the Neolithic long-barrow (mutilated) north of Stow. No frills, pleasantly attractive village with good seventeenth- and eighteenth-century farmhouses and cottages grouped informally around a sloping triangular green. Restoration work has been sensitively carried out. There are interesting features of twelfth- to fifteenth-century styles in the church with notable transepts and monuments.

Mickleton Large main-road (A46) village below edge, at the northern tip of the Cotswolds, with timbering and brick diluting the visual effect of Cotswold stone. Inns and hotels attract travellers: Medford House (1694) exemplifies transitional Cotswold architecture from late Tudor, gabled, to Queen Anne, classical. Manor House (now a school) has three-storey gables with oval windows and finials, mullioned, transomed windows and eighteenth-century wings. The church is worthy of the village with its two-storeyed porch, fine windows and good hatchments.

Minchinhampton Populous but widely spread parish on the plateau between Frome (Golden) valley and Nailsworth valley. A long narrow street of stone houses leads to the small, compact centre at market square, with pillared Market House (1698) and fine buildings around, especially in High Street. The twelfth-century church has a beautiful south transept, rebuilt in the early fourteenth century, with a superb Decorated window. The tower has a truncated spire, reduced in height in 1563.

Minchinhampton Common 570 acres (231ha) of splendid grassland (NT), crossed by many roads. Walking, riding and golf with wide views to the north and west. The Common is girdled by a number of small villages with former weavers' and clothiers' houses.

Minster Lovell Enchanting Windrush valley village between Burford and Witney. The Swan Inn and some cottages are partly timber-framed, and some are thatched, along a street which climbs gently eastwards to the church (which is better inside than out) and the ruins of Minster Lovell Hall (EH). The situation is memorable; trees, water-meadows and pastoral peace surrounding bitter-sweet memories of fifteenth-century greatness. Imagination is needed to flesh out the surviving walls, gables and foundations of Lovell's manor house, but its picturesque appeal is undeniable, although it is rather over-tidied.

Miserden Suspended above beechwoods of the upper Frome valley, with gracious parklands between the village and ancient castle mound. Here is the gabled Elizabethan mansion of the Sandys family, with additions by Lutyens, who also designed the war memorial (1920). The memorial is contemporary with village cottages by Sidney Barnsley, though these harmonise successfully with older ones around the small green. Their arrangement is unified, if slightly contrived. The churchyard is entered through a yew arch and has good memorials in shelly limestone, with copper plates. There is a nice epitaph to Samuel Horrell, a shepherd who died in 1807:

> From youth through life the sheep were all his care
> and harmless as the flock his manners were.

Elaborate, fine memorials in the church are dedicated to the Sandys, Kingston and Mills families.

Moreton-in-Marsh See pp135–6.

Nailsworth Busy workaday town near Stroud. Old mills now house new enterprises. The Cotswold style survives in weavers' cottages and clothiers' houses, especially on nearby hillsides.

Naunton Distinguished Cotswold village in upper Windrush valley, well seen in roadside view from the B4068, with broad-breasted wold rising to the north. The church lies to the west, with its good churchyard memorials, sundials on south and west walls of the tower and huge beech trees nearby. The village then spreads eastwards along the valley. Seventeenth- and eighteenth-century houses illustrate the flexibility of Cotswold style in smallest cottage, larger house, farm, barns, dovecote and modern in-fill. Only the degree and functions of the buildings change. Artisans' nineteenth-century cottages retain quiet dignity. Gables, gardens, cat's-breath elder in July and a sparkling stream behind the cottages with path alongside, require that Naunton be savoured slowly.

North Cerney The A435, 4 miles (6.4km) north of Cirencester splits the village, east of road, from the hillside church to the west. All Saints Church will delight in every respect: twelfth century, with Perpendicular nave roof and tower and its medieval chancel rebuilt c1730. Most of its present beauty and splendid condition are the result of benefactions since 1910, by William Croome. Full of exquisite details, outside and inside – especially the Norman doorway, stone pulpit, eighteenth-century gallery, stained glass, modern rood-loft, monuments, late-sixteenth-century manticore and the somewhat out-of-place leopard doodled by masons. The sheep-grazed churchyard is the setting for the fifteenth-century Old Church House, which enjoys a superb view up the valley. There is an interesting mix of seventeenth and eighteenth century as well as modern council houses in the village.

Northleach See pp136–8.

Notgrove Remote upland estate village north of Northleach, with honey-coloured houses loosely scattered above both sides of a steep hollow at the head of a quiet combe. Vegetable and flower gardens garland the informal green, and, grouped apart there is a dignified manor house (seventeenth century) farm and associated buildings. The small tree-shaded church has a curious little crucifixion carved on its outside east wall. Inside it is too dark to appreciate fully the furnishings and monuments to the local Whittington family and the modern tapestry on reredos worked by the Anderson family which depicts the village in June glory, bordered by trees and flowers. A long barrow by the main road is now a huge grassy mound.

Nympsfield Unspectacular small village near the edge of the plateau west of Nailsworth with some new housing. A gliding field nearby attracts enthusiasts who appreciate the thermals caused by the nearby edge. Nympsfield Long Barrow, by the road to the west, is uncovered, thus allowing easy viewing of what the interior was like, and where many skeletons were discovered in a double burial chamber.

Oddington Elongated village off the main road east of Stow above Evenlode valley. There is a variety of good buildings, including artisans' terraces and barn conversions. Green Farm has former turnpike gates from the main road. Old Stone House by the green is a 1900 remodelling of three late medieval cottages. The village has moved away from the old church which is now ½ mile (800m) away down an inviting lane. This is one for the connoisseur and not to be missed, for its wall paintings, sixteenth- to eighteenth-century woodwork, hatchments, monuments and an atmosphere of love.

Owlpen Unique and unforgettable, in a secret southern Cotswold valley, east of

North Cerney, near Cirencester

Uley. The manor house dates from the fifteenth to the eighteenth century but the styles coexist in happy harmony. Outbuildings, barn, corn mill, summer-house and church (1828–1912) also rise against a beechen backdrop. The house was uninhabited from c1850 until 1926, when Norman Jewson bought and lovingly restored it. It is occasionally open, but the setting can be appreciated from paths nearby.

Oxfordshire Way A 65 mile (105km) long-distance footpath between the Cotswolds and the Chilterns, from Bourton-on-the-Water to Henley-on-Thames. The Cotswold section uses quiet waymarked paths linking Bourton, Wyck Rissington, Bledington, Shipton-under-Wychwood and Ascott-under-Wychwood, totalling 11 miles (18km). The path takes walkers through the calm pastoral and arable landscapes of Windrush and Evenlode valleys to parts that roads cannot reach. There is a good guide leaflet available that provides practical details.

Ozleworth A high-hedged narrow lane south-west of Wotton-under-Edge leads, via Wortley, for 2 miles (3.2km) along the valley pastures of Ozleworth Bottom, with wooded hillsides closing in at the end. Ozleworth's Norman church has a rare central hexagonal tower and other unusual features, enclosed in a circular churchyard. In the adjacent parkland, there is a fine Georgian house with Regency additions.

Painswick See pp138–40.

Prinknash Abbey Completed 1972 in Guiting stone, Prinknash Abbey is starkly functional and modern set in a luscious landscape below the scarp near Gloucester. It bears an unfortunate resemblance to an office block. The mellowed manor house across the combe served the monks of the abbey for half a century and looks much more appropriate. Prinknash Pottery uses local clay.

Quenington In the meandering Coln valley 2 miles (3.2km) north of Fairford. The older part lies along the river, with sloping gardens, willows and mellow stone walls. St Swithin's churchyard is regrettably denuded of stones, but the church has elaborate Norman doorways on the south and north which are well worth a look. The high worn gatehouse of the former preceptory of the Knights Templar survives, up the road from the church.

Rendcomb Backed by beeches, high-perched on the eastern side of the Churn valley, Rendcomb's late-fifteenth-century church, built by Edmund Tame, of Fairford fame, now serves as a chapel for Rendcomb College housed in Hardwick's Italianate house (c1863). The church exterior exhibits fine masonry and there are matching glories inside – fragments of medieval glass, a superb Norman font, a sixteenth-century chancel screen and good monuments. Also of interest are the Victorian estate cottages in the village, the ornamental cast-iron bridge across the village road and a classical river-bridge down in the valley.

The Rissingtons Trio of villages along Evenlode's eastern valley side south of Stow. Wyck Rissington touches meadows and has widely spaced houses along the east side of the green, with trees and a pond. The southern end contracts into a compact huddle by the church where young Gustav Holst was organist 1892–3. The building looks good from any direction, especially east, showing the beautiful thirteenth-century chancel and tower built by the monks of Evesham Abbey.

Little Rissington, a mile (1.6km) south, climbs the hill, until the road from Wyck reaches the ridge at Wyck Beacon. A footpath through fields reaches Little Rissington's isolated church. There are many churchyard memorials to airmen from Little Rissington RAF base, which still stands massive, brooding, peopled, on the ridge. Village children lay posies at an annual service.

A bridleway provides a direct route to Great Rissington, a mile south, passing a prominent flight of lynchets. Motorists must take the high or low road to the village which has two greens, one triangular near the gabled Lamb Inn and one square to the north-west. The church is tucked away at the west end, grouped with the rectory, manor house and farm. New housing extends the village but does not greatly intrude – yet!

Rodborough Satellite settlement to Stroud, rising southwards up a steep hill, with scattered houses, groups, inns, and, at the top, 240 acres (97ha) of common land (NT). Access is free and from here there are fine views over Golden Valley. The name of the Woolpack Inn on Butterow road reminds one of former local trade. A good place for walkers.

Rodmarton Between Cirencester and Tetbury, this village merits inclusion because its Manor House represents the last perfect flowering of Cotswold style. Designed by Ernest Barnsley 1909–26 the building was his most important work, fitted and furnished by his friends and associates. He also designed some of the village cottages.

Rollright Stones On a lonely ridge of the Oxfordshire Cotswolds 6 miles (9.6km) east of Moreton-in-Marsh stands this stone circle, probably middle Bronze Age (c1500BC). Intriguing rather than impressive, the stones are corroded and pitted, and the fir-trees in the background destroy the sense of isolation. Nearby is the King's Stone, and the Whispering Knights ¼ mile (400m) distant are remnants of a burial chamber. Little Rollright, in a remote hollow to the south, has a small lonely church (1617) with fine tombs, a cottage-sized seventeenth-century rectory and a gabled manor farm.

Saintbury On the northern edge of the Cotswolds with houses and cottages straggling, often tucked away, along a hill-climbing road. The church stands above, reached by field-paths, with memorials and fittings from almost every one of its eight centuries' life. There are magnificent views across the Vale of Evesham, particularly in blossom-frothed spring.

Salperton A remote upland village north-west of Northleach, between A40 and A436, its name suggests the fact that it is sited on an old salt-trade track. A workaday, unassuming village, it has, to the south, a small Norman church adjacent to a large seventeenth- and early nineteenth-century house amid gracious wooded parkland.

Sapperton Above the Frome valley between Cirencester and Stroud. Individual and small groups of cottages, stone-walled and tiled, snug-gabled, are the older ones. Around the small village green are Arts-and-Crafts houses by Gimson, Barnsley and Jewson (c1900). Their memorials are in the churchyard, near a path which descends to a beautiful church almost wholly rebuilt by Sir Robert Atkyn, the Gloucestershire historian, in Queen Anne's reign, so the atmosphere is predominantly early eighteenth century. Splendid monuments, matched by those outside, many bearing copper plates, dated from 1687 onwards.

Daneway House, across valley, has fourteenth-century origins, with a high gabled section added in 1620, and was used by the Gimson group to store furniture. Nearby, an old towpath alongside the bed of the Thames–Severn Canal leads to Sapperton Tunnel, whose entrance is muddy and tip-like. The northern portal is disintegrating, but the southern one, 2 miles (3.2km) distant, has been restored and is well worth seeing. There is a good former canal pub nearby, and a splendid local history book has recently been published, by the head teacher and children of the village school.

Selsley Small roadside village south-west of Stroud. The tall saddleback tower of Bodley's French-style church dominates the landscape. Very interesting stained glass includes early work by Morris and Webb, (of which the west window is most outstanding) and the nativity window in the apse includes contributions by Morris, Burne-Jones, Rossetti and Ford Madox Brown. Above the church stretch 150 acres (60ha) of Selsley Common, with expansive views to the north and east.

Sezincote (pronounced 'Seez-in-Cote') A few miles west of Moreton-in-Marsh, in its large and lovely park, this late Georgian house is a beautiful example of classical Greek revival style, encased within an oriental skin, complete with onion dome and corner minarets. Repton designed the park, and Thomas Daniell designed the charming temple bridge. All is gloriously exotic and enchanting, and the garden is open throughout year (excluding December). The house is open during May, June, July and September on Thursday and Friday afternoons. There is no village.

Sheepscombe In a sheltered wooded combe at the head of a valley north of Painswick and Bisley. Narrow lanes thread each side of the combe, converging on a huddle of houses and cottages beneath the beechwoods. The Butchers' Arms provides a focus for the village, and the churchyard provides the best view.

Sherborne Elongated village on the south side of the valley of Sherborne Brook. A former Winchcombe Abbey property, the Renaissance-style mansion c1550 (rebuilt in the same style by Salvin c1840), is now converted into flats. The adjacent church has a cold atmosphere but does have good monuments. The 4,200 acres (1,700ha) of Sherborne Park encompass most of the village, now all owned by the NT. Cottages stand in pairs or terraces, mainly early nineteenth century, all with attractive cottagey gardens. No 88 at the eastern end of the village incorporates twelfth-century doorways and the tympanum from the original Norman church. Lodge Park, 2 miles (3.2km) south-west, was a seventeenth-century deer-coursing pavilion but was converted into a modest house towards the end of the last century (NT).

Shipton-under-Wychwood Main-road village (A361) north of Burford. Jacobean Shipton Court and its associated buildings are largely hidden behind high walls. The Shaven Crown Inn dates from the fifteenth century and may have belonged to Bruern Abbey. It overlooks the large village green and church.

Slad The B4070 from Birdlip sidles towards Stroud, descending from Bull's Cross through beechwoods, past the clinging cottages of Slad. Below the road, the T-shaped roof pattern of Rose Hill identifies the house where Laurie Lee lived his boyhood. His vivid recollections in *Cider with Rosie*, present a picture of life in this green valley during the 1920s, the end of the rural, pre-motor-age dream. The Woolpack Inn revives similar memories.

The Slaughters Dissimilar twins on the River Eye, tributary of River Windrush, south-west of Stow. Lower Slaughter is the pretty sister, with grassy banks bordering a stream: low bridges cross over the water to picture-book cottages, all Cotswold ingredients combining to create the inevitable tourist attraction. In the lower part of the village tall trees cast a deep shade and new housing at The Whitmores oozes affluence, but keeps the idiom. Manor House was built by Valentine Strong c1650 and is now a hotel. Modern council houses have traditional roofs, but the mill, at the head of the village, is early nineteenth-century brick, with waterwheel in situ. There is a pleasant walk to Upper Slaughter, though it can be reached more deviously by the hill-climbing road to the west.

The valley narrows at Upper Slaughter, and the village is less self-conscious than its sister. Cottage gardens have vegetables and flowers and the village centre is based on a Lutyens layout with housing grouped around a central triangular space. Worth a visit is the fine church, with its churchyard, to the west, approached along a sunken path. Good buildings abound, especially down the lane which descends towards the stream, with ford, footbridge and stately trees.

Snowshill 3 miles (4.8km) south of Broadway, below the edge of a plateau, Snowshill is apparently snugly placed with woods behind, but at almost 800ft (244m) and north-facing, suffers long-lasting snows in bad winters. Scenically the village is a gem, though the situation of its church is far more impressive than the actual Victorian building which is of poor proportions. Delightful clutches of cottages are grouped at different levels; Manor House dates from 1500, but is mainly seventeenth and eighteenth century, and its terraced gardens with ponds, shrubs and flowers are well worth a visit. Its hall, c1600, was the priest's house, and was occupied earlier this century by Charles Wade. His extraordinary collection of curios and bygones fills every room in the manor, from floor to ceiling. Claustrophobically breathtaking, wildly whimsical, hardly lovable, but quite unmissable. Open from May to October, Wednesday to Sunday afternoons.

Southrop In the lower south-eastern corner of the Cotswolds, on the west bank of the River Leach. A street-village of neat houses with tended gardens.

Lower Slaughter

Cottages at Snowshill, near Broadway

Ball-finials proliferate and an excellent barn-conversion retains a columbarium. The small green by the Swan Inn and road to Eastleach is chestnut-shaded, and the post office features an old-fashioned shop-window. At the east end of the village is Manor House, a great range of barns, and the church, associated with John Keble, who lived at Old Vicarage 1823–5. The interior features a famous Norman font depicting armoured virtuous women, trampling on a variety of vices.

Stanton Just off the A46 at the foot of the escarpment, Stanton exudes Cotswold perfection with apparent authenticity. Gabled, dormered cottages, with window-glass set directly into grooved stone, seem to be of the great period 1570–1640, but their present appearance owes much to rebuilding and restoration by skilled craftsmen 1906–37, under architect-squire Sir Philip Scott. Large barns at vale end were imported as reminders that Stanton's feet are in the vale. They are now converted into houses. The parish church, distinguished by modern furnishings and twentieth-century Comper glass, is almost too perfect – pictorially enchanting but rather inert. The council house estate to the north-west preserves Cotswold tradition in style and materials.

Stanway Stanton's very aristocratic neighbour 1½ miles (2.4km) south, arguably the Cotswolds' most gracious group of golden buildings with medieval church, late Tudor mansion and a memorably picturesque Jacobean gatehouse. For good measure, there is a fourteenth-century tithe barn around the corner to the north. The cricket field in the park has a thatched pavilion by Sir James Barrie, and the village war memorial is a fine bronze St George and Dragon, with Eric Gill lettering. A few homely cottages are gathered on the edge of the park.

Stow-on-the-Wold See pp140–2.

Stowell Great estate and park south-west of Northleach, approached by a drive marked 'Private' past wide views southwards. The cruciform church is famous for its Romanesque Doom wall-painting. The Elizabethan mansion, enlarged in 1890, is private: nearby stables house Lord Vestey's polo-ponies. Stowell park and estate is obviously managed with care and efficiency, but public rights-of-way are few.

The Swells Twin villages on the River Dickler, a tributary of the River Windrush, west of Stow. Upper Swell on B4077 looks inviting but is not: cars rush up the hill from the bridge, a dangerous bend makes parking impossible, and tall trees cast deep shade. Privacy prevails, affluence oozes, but the church is appealing for lots of money! It smells damp.

Lower Swell, a mile (1.6km) south by the narrow road or field-path near the river is larger and livelier, with a pub, shop, school and modest cottages in terraces, mostly well restored. The small green has a Lutyens war memorial, and the church has Victorian murals by Clayton and Bell.

Swinbrook 2 miles (3.2km) below Burford, on the north side of Windrush valley. Coiled and cornered by tiny, tall-tree'd green and ford, with seventeenth- and eighteenth-century houses and cottages, it looks very typical Cotswolds. The church looks down over the village and has splendid stones in the churchyard, including bale tombs and a modern memorial to Nancy Mitford. Unity Mitford is also commemorated here. The Lords Redesdale were squires from early last century up until 1958; their predecessors were the Fettiplaces, who are spectacularly remembered in the lovely church. Sixteenth- and seventeenth-century members of the family are stacked on shelves against the chancel's north wall. Earlier ancestors are commemorated in stone (1613) outside the altar rails, armoured, each stiffly reclining on an elbow. Their successors (1686) are carved in alabaster, slightly more comfortable with one knee bent. The Fettiplace mansion was demolished in 1805.

Taynton On Oxfordshire slopes above the Windrush valley north-west of Burford. An informal, unplanned, evolved euphony of Cotswold stone and masonry at its brilliant best. Four large farms, barn groups, steep roofs, gables, angles, mullions in houses, cottages and conversions – all is felicitous and functional. This is a quiet village, but a living one, whose quarries to the north, productive for nine centuries, are today only occasionally used. The glorious churchyard has fine stones, lichened and mellow, and the church is outstanding, famed for sculptured heads and stone portraits.

Teddington Situated below an outlier of Oxenton Hill, Teddington's church has a tower arch and west window brought from Hailes Abbey in 1567. Features include an enormous painted royal arms of William and Mary (1689) and sixteenth- and seventeenth-century furnishings add distinction.

Tetbury See pp142–4.

Toddington Small tree-shaded village north of Winchcombe with a magnificent church by G. E. Street (1873–9) on the edge of the park. Wildly un-Cotswold in character it features an orange-gold exterior with white stone inside. To the north is what appears to be a miniature Houses of Parliament – a great Gothic-Revival house (1820–35) by amateur architect Hanbury-Tracy. To the west of the church can be seen the ruins of a former Jacobean gatehouse to the manor. Also of interest is the restored station and short stretch of railway nearby.

Turkdean High wold village north of Northleach. The road climbs through a beech avenue to houses with colourful gardens. Woodland views unfold round corners and open views lie beyond.

Uley In the south-western Cotswolds where the road to Dursley descends from the Edge. A long street of houses, full of architectural distinction, reflects eighteenth-century clothiers' prosperity; there is a particularly elegant grouping around the small green. The post office occupies a Stuart house, and the King's Head and Old Crown inns coexist harmoniously with modern bus shelters. The church by Teulon is eccentric even for him. Uley Bury, an Iron Age hillfort above beechwoods to the north, commands magnificent views.

The Washbournes Hamlets in the vale between Winchcombe and Bredon Hill. Very rural, quiet and charming, with tiny churches, farms and a handful of cottages, some half-timbered. Great Washbourne church is simple, Norman, with good furnishings and a pleasant atmosphere. Little Washbourne church is similar, but untouched since Georgian times. Usually it is locked, but clear glass windows allow one to view inside.

Weston-sub-Edge Below the northern escarpment, with good seventeenth-century houses and farms around the square, and along the roadside up the hill. There is an elegant manor house and dovecote, and a welcoming pub, the Seagrave Arms.

Whittington Off the A40 a few miles east of Cheltenham this tiny one-street village of unspectacular, unostentatious Cotswold houses and cottages, dating from the sixteenth to nineteenth century, demonstrates no concessions to artiness or tartiness, but is quietly beautiful. Whittington Court is accessible by main road: late Tudor, gabled, Renaissance details, on the site of a Roman villa. The church is basically Norman with Tudor details and good monuments.

Widford Below Burford in the Windrush valley. There is no village but a tiny gem of a church, isolated in fields on the site of a Roman villa. It can be reached only by footpath, but justifies the ½ mile (800m) return walk with its clear glass, plaster, textures, wall-paintings, box-pews, and bits of Roman pavement in the floor.

Willersey Below the north-western escarpment north of Broadway, stretched beside a long green between two right-angled bends of the A46. The village, with its seventeenth- and eighteenth-century houses, looks homely and lived-in, with few concessions to tourists, who concentrate on Broadway. In Church Street, more good houses and cottages line the way to the church, which is dominated by a Perpendicular tower built by Evesham Abbey. The Bell Inn typifies the best of Cotswold character.

Winchcombe See pp144–5.

Windrush Pretty village on the south side of the river above valley meadows, west of Burford. Centred on triangular, lime-shaded green by church, with nice views northwards up the valley, its situation is more rewarding than its content, though interesting features surround the church: a mounting-block by the churchyard wall, sheep's heads on bale tombs, and chancel arch inside. There are also exuberant beak-head carvings on the Norman doorway. The famous oolite quarries are above the village to the south – now hidden, overgrown and silent.

Winson Quiet village along the winding lanes of the Coln valley above Bibury: farms, barns with new uses, well-restored cottages in attractive groups, and church presiding above. It is worth wandering behind the village, along the riverside path.

Winstone Rather bleak, scattered upland village beyond head of Duntisbourne

Nineteenth-century labourers' cottages at Withington. The wooden lintels denote the cheaper building materials that were used in their construction

valley, only a mile (1.6km) west of the A417, though it feels more remote. Interesting Saxon and Norman work in the church.

Withington Podded at the head of the Coln valley. Large village with deep roots, and six converging lanes. The untidy Neolithic long barrow in the woods and the site of a Roman villa nearby suggest long settlement here, confirmed by the intricate mesh of lanes, tracks and paths around. Upper Withington, west of the river, clusters round the proud, spacious, cruciform church, and is complete with rectory, manor, dovecote and mill – Mill Inn and Mill House now cater, successfully, for visitors' needs. For a gentle walk, take the inviting, flowery, shady path down below the church; or the equally inviting road opposite, past a group of cottages to Halewell Close. Lower Withington, to the east, has some newer housing, plus a village hall and playing-field. Village life thrives – this is not a tourist village, but an enticing one nevertheless. It is a pity the railway line has vanished, though.

Wormington Small compact village in the Ishbourne valley between Winchcombe and Evesham with attractive timber-framed or stone houses and a particularly charming little church (supposedly built by Abbot of Hailes, c1475). There are fine examples in its interior of a pre-Conquest crucifixion, medieval and Morris glass and good furnishings and woodwork.

Wotton-under-Edge See pp145–6.

Yanworth Remote, small linear village on wolds' edge above upper Coln, above Stowell Park. The Norman and twelfth-century church has fine masonry, a worn stone floor, good furnishings and fragments of medieval glass. Dignified farms and barns adorn the surrounding landscape.

BIBLIOGRAPHY

Atkyns, Sir Robert, *Ancient and Present State of Gloucestershire* (1712)

Baddeley, W. St C., *A Cotteswold Manor: the History of Painswick* (Reprinted by Alan Sutton, 1981)

Beresford, M. W. and Joseph, J. K. S. St, *Medieval England* (Cambridge University Press, 1979)

Bowden, P. J., *The Wool Trade in Tudor and Stuart England* (London, 1962)

Brill, E., *Cotswold Ways* (Hale, 1985)

Cotswold Crafts (Readers Union, 1977)

Life and Tradition in the Cotswolds (Dent, 1973)

Old Cotswold (David & Charles, 1968)

Clifton-Taylor, A., *The Pattern of English Building* (Faber, 1972)

Clifton-Taylor, A. and Ireson, A. S., *English Stone Building* (Gollancz, 1983)

Clifton-Taylor, A., Moriarty, D. (ed), *Buildings of Delight* (Gollancz, 1986)

Crosher, G. R., *Along the Cotswold Ways* (Cassell, 1976)

Derrick, F., *Cotswold Stone* (Chapman & Hall, 1948)

Dreghorn, W., *Geology Explained in the Severn Vale and Cotswolds* (David & Charles, 1967)

Dyer, C., *Lords and Peasants in a Changing Society* (Cambridge University Press, 1980)

Evans, H. A., *Highways and Byways in Oxfordshire and the Cotswolds* (Macmillan, 1905)

Finberg, H. P. R. (ed), *Gloucestershire Studies* (Leicester University Press, 1957)

Finberg, Josceline, *The Cotswolds* (Eyre Methuen, 1977)

Gibbs, J. Arthur, *A Cotswold Village* (Cape, 1929)

Greenoak, F., God's Acre (Orbis, 1985)

Hadfield, C. and A. M., *Introducing the Cotswolds* (David & Charles, 1976)

Hadfield, C. and A. M. (eds), *The Cotswolds, A New Study* (David & Charles, 1973)
Henriques, R., *The Cotswolds* (Paul Elek, 1950)
Hill, Susan, *The Spirit of the Cotswolds* (Michael Joseph, 1988)
Jewson, N., *By Chance did I Rove* (Private, 1952)
Lee, Laurie, *Cider with Rosie* (Hogarth, 1959)
Lindley, E. S., *Wotton-under-Edge* (Reprinted by Alan Sutton, 1977)
Maggs, C., *Railways of the Cotswolds* (Peter Nicholson, 1982)
Marshall, Wm, *Rural Economy of Gloucestershire* (1788)
Massingham, H. J., *Wold Without End* (London, 1932)
The Cotswold Country (Batsford, 1937)
Millward, R. and Robinson, A., *The West Midlands* (Macmillan, 1971)
Moore, John, *The Cotswolds* (Chapman & Hall, 1937)
Muir, R., *The Shell Guide to Reading the Landscape* (Michael Joseph, 1981)
Pinnell, P. M., *Village Heritage (Sapperton)* (Alan Sutton, 1986)
Playne, A. T., *History of Minchinhampton and Avening* (Reprinted by Alan Sutton, 1978)
Ponting, K. G., *The Woollen Industry of S. W. England* (Adams & Dart, 1971)
Power, Eileen, *The Wool Trade in English Medieval History* (Oxford University Press, 1941)
Rackham, O., *The History of the Countryside* (Dent, 1986)
Rudder, Samuel, *A New History of Gloucestershire* (1779)
Sale, R., *A Guide to the Cotswold Way* (Constable, 1980)
Smith, B., *The Cotswolds* (Batsford, 1976)
Sutton, A. and Hudson, J., *Cotswold Images* (Alan Sutton, 1988)
Tann, J., *Gloucestershire Woollen Mills* (David & Charles, 1977)
Thirsk, J. (ed), *The Agrarian History of England* (Vol IV) 1500–1640 (Cambridge University Press, 1967)
Verey, D., *Shell Guide to Gloucestershire* (Faber, 1970)
Cotswold Churches (Batsford, 1976)
Witts, Rev F. E., Verey, D. (ed), *The Diary of a Cotswold Parson* (Alan Sutton, 1978)

The appropriate volumes in the *Buildings of England* series have been constant companions on my Cotswold travels:

Pevsner, N., *Worcestershire* (Penguin, 1968)
Sherwood, J. and Pevsner, N., *Oxfordshire* (Penguin, 1974)
Verey, D., *Gloucestershire, The Cotswolds* (Penguin, 1970)

The AA/OS *Leisure Guide to the Cotswolds* has been particularly useful, and various booklets, leaflets and small local guides about towns, villages, walks, countryside features and historic houses have all been valuable sources of information. Other reference sources include articles in: *Transactions of the Bristol and Gloucestershire Archaeological Society; Cotswold Life; Gloucestershire County Council – County Structure Plan.*

INDEX

Page numbers in **bold** indicate illustrations